Deadly Focus

A Vega & Middleton Novel
By
Sue Hinkin

Literary Wanderlust | Denver, Colorado

Published in the United States of America by Literary Wanderlust, Denver, CO.

www.LiteraryWanderlust.com

ISBN print: 978-1-942856-22-1
ISBN digital: 978-1-942856-23-8

Cover Design by Ruth M'Gonigle

Acknowledgments

Many bemoan writing as a lonely, singular enterprise but I've found it to be incredibly collaborative. Any success I achieve could not have been accomplished without the love and support of many people. Sonja Massie, aka G.A. McKevett, author of the *Savannah Reid Mysteries,* was the mentor extraordinaire of my first writing group in Ventura, California. In this group, I felt the first inklings that maybe being a professional writer was something I could actually aspire to. Thank you valued friends, Holly Foster-Wells, Kathy Lyerla, and particularly Gaye Lucas and Sigrid Orlet who kept the flame burning and the hugs coming. Both live in Germany now and I miss them terribly.

A special thank you to Philip Spitzer, the literary agent who, eons ago, requested the full manuscript of the first iteration of what is now *Deadly Focus*. He didn't take the book, it was far from ready, but the fact that he read it and responded with dead-on feedback, helped me realize there was a spark of strength in the story worth pursuing.

As the years progressed, I moved to Denver via Los Angeles, Savannah and hometown, Chicago. In Colorado, I became involved with the Rocky Mountain Fiction Writers (RMFW). I can say from the bottom of my heart that without this organization, I'd still be trying to figure out POV and 'show don't tell.' My colleagues would attest to the fact that I'm actually still pretty erratic on that first one. My amazing Thursday night critique group at Tattered Cover in Littleton includes Mindy McIntyre, Michael Hope aka Michael Arches, Kevin Wolf, Mary Ann Kersten, Michele Winkler, Liesa Malick, Charles Senseman, Liz Funk, Wendy Arnold, Kathy Reynolds, Peter Meredith, Martha Husain and Charlie McNamara. All amazing writers, teachers and colleagues. Thanks also to Libby Murphy at Book Alchemy LLC, who I also connected with through RMFW, for her wise help in editing.

Sincere gratitude to Susie Brooks, publisher at Literary Wanderlust and long-time RMFW board member, who rescued me from a meltdown between sessions at the Colorado Gold Writers Conference registration desk last year, when I'd hit the wall with this book. Susie read the manuscript and decided to take a chance with a rookie author. It's a privilege to be part of this great indie team.

And last but definitely not least, thank you to my husband, Alan Klein, who's been patiently watching me disappear into reading and writing for years, and to my amazing beta reader and daughter, Lacey Klein. I love you both.

Dedication

To my parents, Lois Davis and Thomas Matthew Hinkin, the poet and the preacher, who gave me the gift of unconditional love and acceptance.

CHAPTER 1

At four in the morning on December twenty-first, the winter equinox, the graveyard shift was taking its toll. Lucy Vega, photographer for KLAK-TV News in Los Angeles and Ray Truckee, audio engineer and field producer, looked at each other with tired, bleary eyes. The pre-dawn gloom permeated the van with an unsettling pall. Lucy slipped her stiff fingers into an old pair of leather gloves. Truckee fired up the heater. After a night of sheer boredom, he couldn't stifle a yawn, several of them.

As they were about to head back to the station, audio feed from the police scanner crackled to life, reporting that a naked man had climbed onto the top floor ledge of the Hollywood Highlands Hotel. According to a witness at the scene, the man looked ready to jump.

Lucy shivered and her shoulder muscles tightened

with dread. She'd seen a person take the leap once before, from a bridge onto the freeway. It was not something she wanted to witness again.

Now there was garbled chatter about a robbery at a Seven-Eleven, an event too routine to raise an eyebrow of interest. She adjusted the volume on the scanner and drained what was left of her gas station coffee. "Let's roll on the jumper. If we're lucky, it's a crank call, or the cop's will have it under control before we get there."

"Hope you're right, Luce." Truckee sighed. "Don't need a splatter to finish the night."

A former USC linebacker with a bushy ginger beard and a neck like a redwood, he pulled a U-ie in the middle of Laurel Canyon Boulevard. Fish-tailing on the wet, slick street, he barely missed taking out a spindly palm tree that looked to be serving as poster central for garage sales, acting classes, and lost pets. Lucy gripped the door handle as they sped toward the Hollywood Freeway onramp. Even at this hour, the traffic on the 101 was a writhing snake of white lights slithering westward, and a blood red trail creeping east. Truckee merged into the traffic at full speed. He careened past vehicles like a pinball in a game, then exited at Highland.

Lucy and Truckee pulled up in front of the hotel--a faded *grande dame* once favored by the Tinseltown elite in the early years of the film industry. The LAPD hadn't arrived. Lucy immediately spotted the object of the alert. Teetering on a ledge high above Hollywood Boulevard, a young man in his late twenties waved his arms like a jerky cartoon character. His slim, well-muscled nude body was silvery white and reflected colors from nearby buildings and marquis like a human movie screen. She captured him in her telephoto lens and reeled him into close focus.

A jolt of adrenaline cut hot through her chest. "Shit," she blurted. "I don't believe it."

"What?"

"It's Gary fucking Mercer."

Truckee's jaw dropped. "No way." The Moon Pie he'd just opened dropped a shower of powdered sugar onto his lap. "Damn. You're working his shift tonight. Isn't he supposed to be at his grandmother's birthday party in Sacramento or something?"

Lucy scowled. "Yeah, that liar. Now that I think of it, he told me once his grandparents are dead."

Gary Mercer had been the Photo Department head for two years. Word was he only had the job because of his father's formidable connections. For a while he seemed to work well but in the last six months she'd seen him going downhill like an avalanche. The crew all knew he was an addict but it was easy to rationalize some of his craziness. This was, after all, Hollywood, a place where craziness was tolerated, even venerated--until it affected the pocketbook. Mercer's erratic behavior was causing the station to miss stories and thereby lose almighty ratings. Ratings were money. And their ratings were tenuous enough.

Lucy knew that their Executive News Producer, Maxwell Wedner, had given Gary an ultimatum the day before. *Shape up or clear out your locker—this time for good.*

She grabbed her camera and jumped out of the TV station's dented silver SUV. Truckce knocked the pastry dust off his lap and followed.

"Truck-man, you know how this baby works." Lucy passed the field producer her camera. "I'm always covering for Mercer, I've been a goddamn enabler. I keep thinking he'll get clean, but it never happens, never will. This is the last time I'll fall for his bullshit."

Lucy tightened her dark wavy ponytail, then bolted for the hotel. A vision of Mercer smeared across the sidewalk fueled her urgency. He was a mess of a human being, but there had to be an alternative to shoveling his remains into a coffin.

Shouts to Lucy from Truckee, about waiting for the police to show up, went unheeded.

A clot of hotel workers at the end of a long night slogged through the high-ceilinged foyer. Exquisite in its prime, it was now haggard and crumbling. Lucy shoved past a security guard and threw herself into an open elevator. With decades of profanity and love notes carved into its scuffed mahogany-paneled surfaces, the car smelled of mold and stale sweat. A discarded condom had been kicked to a corner. She pushed number sixteen, the top floor. The decrepit lift began to groan.

Cautiously, Lucy stepped out into a dim hallway. She took some deep breaths to calm herself. The ancient wallpaper was peeling and stained with brownish blotches. Lights flickered. A man who appeared to be a hotel administrator, wearing a black suit a few sizes too big, huddled with another security guard. They were surrounded by a half dozen young men Mercer's age and much, much younger in various stages of undress. Several were hysterical, screaming, blubbering—high, and out of control.

The guard, an arthritic, light-skinned black man in

at least his mid-seventies, was attempting to calm them down. "Boys, boys, it's gonna be aw'ight, now just chill, y'all," he said in a nasally voice.

Lucy rushed up to the panicked knot. "The guy on the ledge, I know him. I can talk him in," she said, heart hammering.

"Who are you?" the hotel executive stepped forward. His complexion was heavily pitted, with a thin film of sweat shining on his face. One eyebrow twitched. "And where the hell are the police?" His inflection offered a poor attempt at sounding British. The brow twitched again.

Another few minutes and Lucy feared he'd be joining in the hysteria.

"I dunno where the cops are but the guy out there, Gary Mercer—we work together at KLAK. Please, get me to him."

The manager folded his arms across his narrow chest. "I'll wait for the police." He stuck his lower lip out in an attempt at intimidation but looked more like he was going to start bawling. He was all of 5'5" and 130 pounds.

Lucy, flushed with frustration, grabbed him hard by the tie to get his attention. "If you wait and he jumps, the media, myself included, will be all over you and this sleazy shit-hole. And you can bet that'll be the last of your little pajama parties. If I talk to him, maybe we can avoid all that. Your choice."

"He's gonna juuuuump!" a shirtless Hispanic man shrieked. He was tall and well-built, fully tattooed, and his nipples were pierced with gold spikes. "He won't listen to anyone, and I'm so close to him. Sooooo cloooose!" He fanned himself furiously, red fingernails flashing. His voice reached a keening wail. Lucy winced and gritted her teeth.

Following his lead, all the men began to cry out and whimper.

"Shut the hell up," Lucy shouted. "Acting like a bunch of idiots is not going to help him."

She was shocked when the group actually quieted. She let go of the administrator's tie. He looked about to faint.

"What's Mercer on?" Lucy demanded.

Their eyes opened wide in a perfectly choreographed but failed attempt at innocence.

"What-is-he-on?" she repeated.

"X and coke," a red-headed man-child said. "And lots of the tiny white ones." His spindly legs dropped into glittery platform boots *à la* ABBA 1975.

"Nuh-uh," pierced nipples corrected. "He was smoking meth."

Lucy groaned. "Shit. Get me to him right now, before it's too late."

"Daddy Gary locked us out," a sallow-skinned boy said. His voice was still childlike, and his hair hung in angelic ringlets. ABBA boots put his arm around ringlet-boy's shoulders and comforted him.

"Where's your swipe card or master key?" Lucy asked the hotelier. His brass nameplate caught the light—Edward Rivera, Assistant Manager. "Mr. Rivera, I need access!"

The hotel exec looked like he'd lost his hearing. No response.

"Rivera! Open that goddamn door!" Lucy grabbed

his arm and shook it.

The hotel manager's eyes popped wide and he appeared to snap back into reality. With an embarrassed flush, he held up a big gold key and inserted it into the lock. Lucy stepped into the room. The partyers attempted to follow, but one look from her put them back into the hall where they peeped through the doorway, seeking to get a glimpse of the train wreck that was Gary Mercer.

She heard the elevator open down the hall and gritted her teeth.

"Okay, Rivera, give me five minutes without the police. Got it? Tell them I know this guy and I'll talk him down. Five minutes. Can you do that for me?"

He nodded like a bobble-head. If Rivera didn't immediately give up the key to the cops, she fully expected they'd kick the door down in minutes. The LAPD wasn't known for subtlety.

She shut the door behind her. All was dark; the only illumination came from the street. A broken lamp lay on the floor. Lucy could smell the remains of junk food and marijuana. The sheer curtains billowed, beckoning. Could she talk him in? Or would she watch him turn to bloody pulp on the sidewalk? What the hell was she going to say? She took a deep breath.

Lucy picked her way through the debris to the open window. The threadbare rug sucked at her shoes like the sticky floor of a bad movie theater. The Hollywood sign glowed in the distance. How appropriate that he would choose this hotel to try and end his life. Mercer's father was a major film producer; Gary had grown up on the periphery of his power and megalomania. This night said everything about the damage that had been done.

Lucy went to the raised window. The night air was cool and silky. Truckee stood on the sidewalk looking up at her through the telephoto. She nodded, took another deep breath and leaned out.

Mercer was plastered against the brick façade. His feet were high-arched, his long toes curled over the ledge. A rattlesnake tattoo wound down his arm to his gold watch-clad wrist and another rattler slithered up from his naked groin, winding provocatively across his hip.

"Gary, get the hell in here," Lucy said in her most no-nonsense, authoritarian voice. Mercer was never one to be coddled.

His head swiveled—the shock at seeing her nearly caused him to lose his balance.

Lucy's stomach lurched. Mercer clawed at the rough brick wall behind him, finding enough purchase to save himself. He looked over at Lucy, his pale green eyes were lined with dark kohl, his eyeballs flew around like electrons, and his pupils were pinpricks. He could have been a model in a tripped-out Helmut Newton photo spread.

"Get your ass in here, Gary. Right now! You've got to be at work in four hours. Enough fucking around—I'm not covering for you anymore."

"I wanna fly." His voice was a nail file on cement. His body began to slump and sway precariously. "I can fly like an eagle." He waved his arms in a spastic flapping motion.

She had to get to him, fast. "It's the drugs talking, Gary. You're high as a kite."

"Gonna fly like a dove," he whispered, gazing off

toward the Hollywood Hills.

"Don't listen to the drugs. You can't fly, not without a plane. I hear you got your pilot's license. That's great, really great. Something to look forward to. Come in off the ledge, man. You jump, you're gonna freaking die."

In her peripheral vision, Lucy could see patrol cars arriving. A fire department paramedic unit followed with a Channel 6 van on its tail.

"Gary, get in here before you're all over the news. You do *not* want to go out like this—buck naked, without dignity."

"Fuck you, Lucille. Not your business."

At least he recognized her. "Fuck you, Mercer, it *is* my business. If you bail, I'll have to pick up your sorry shifts for weeks." If he could just move from despair to anger, maybe there'd be a chance. Sweat trickled down between her breasts.

"Get the fuck away from me!" His body began to quiver.

"I'm staying 'til you come in. If you jump, I'll take embarrassing pictures of you that you'll regret."

Lucy knew that despite his wild, middle-finger-to-the-world attitude, he was a man who feared being humiliated more than anything else. That black hole of shame made him dangerous and unpredictable at work, and in personal relationships, big time. That was why so many steered clear of him. He was a bomb always ready to detonate.

"Gary, look at me," Lucy said.

He glanced at her then broke eye contact and stared down at the gathering crowd.

"You don't want to be a footnote on *Hollywood This*

Weekend. People shouldn't see you like this, Gary."

He was mute. "Gary! Look at me, goddamn you."

She could see a minute shift in his body language.

Lucy's heart bludgeoned her chest, and her palms sweat like garden hoses. If he slipped, she couldn't catch him. Could she catch herself?

"Come on, man, please, get in here. You're gonna be okay. There are people who can help you get past this shitty night." She gripped the window frame and reached her fingers toward him again, calling. Each time she leaned out farther. "You can do this, just a hand from a friend. Take it."

He grimaced. "You are not a friend."

He was right. They couldn't stand each other. "Neither is that shit you're on, I can guarantee you that."

Mercer froze, then tears began to stream down his face in oily, black streaks. His head whipped back and forth, as if aware of his surroundings for the first time. "They're recording me?"

"Not yet," Lucy said. At least she hoped not, but probably. Truckee was for sure.

Slowly, he edged a few inches toward Lucy.

"Careful now," she encouraged. "Come on, that's good. Small steps."

Mercer's foot slipped on a loose brick. His body convulsed as he struggled wildly against gravity. Lucy couldn't suppress a scream.

He managed to regain his balance against a rusted-out gutter. Feathery remnants of a pigeon's nest dislodged and floated through the air with a lightness the falling human body didn't possess.

His eyes flashed with terror.

Lucy struggled to control her ragged breathing. "Okay, you're all right." Her voice droned in a reassuring sing-song rhythm. "Concentrate now, Gary." She noticed firefighters trying to wrangle a safety net far below. It looked very small.

And then, in a fast, impulsive move with a feral snarl, Mercer grabbed her wrist and launched himself through the window. Landing on top of Lucy, he mowed her down, along with the draperies. A curtain rod banged onto her head.

Lucy found herself on the floor, pinned against a wall with him in her arms. His body was cold and greasy with perspiration.

"Okay, Gary, you're safe now." Lucy tried to extricate herself from his grasp. "It's okay, let me go." The curtains tangled around her ankles.

Mercer put his face up next to hers; his breath was a sewer. His cheeks were scratchy and wet. The little hairs on the back of Lucy's neck tingled and a pang of nausea rose in her throat. She just wanted to get up and shut the window, lock it, then get the hell out.

His agonized face turned stony. The tears stopped. "Daddy made us watch him shag the pretty blond girls, over and over. Mother dearest cried and cried, drowning in pills, booze." He pulled Lucy's face closer. She struggled but he held her tight. She wanted to call for help but knew that Mercer could still make a lunge to the window and soar.

His words flowed amid deep, animal-like growls and groans. "He told her she was a frigid cunt. She would crawl into bed with me and make me do things. I threw up, I always threw up. And then, one day I threw her down the stairs."

Lucy remembered that his mother had died in what they'd called an accident. The police reported that she fell down the stairs in her home while inebriated.

"I killed the fucking whore! I hated her! Hated her!" His wail became a high-pitched cry, then flipped like a light switch to manic, shrieky laughter. His bladder emptied.

Lucy could feel the warm liquid soak her jeans. She gagged at the smell of sour urine. "The cops're almost here, let me go!" She squirmed and kicked to escape him, to no avail. His grip was a pipe wrench locked onto her arms. Mercer pressed his weight against her, his penis hard on her stomach.

"I killed the bitch! I threw her down, and when she didn't die, I smashed her head on a step! Crushed it, again and again, and again and again. Cracked it like a fucking egg."

"Jesus, Gary . . ."

Loud pounding started on the hotel room door. Somebody called her name. Lucy couldn't move. She tried to scream but could only manage a gasp. Mercer was oblivious.

Then, as if prodded by a taser, his hands flew around her neck, clasped tightly, and he began to beat her head against the wall.

Lucy's vision grew dim. Sucked into the maw of panic, she clawed toward the light.

He was going to kill her!

The door flew open. Cops. Truckee.

She came to in the hotel hallway next to one of the paramedics while the police tried to control Mercer.

He kicked a cop in the balls—the guy screamed and crumpled. The cuffs he was trying to close on Mercer's wrists flew away and wedged in an ancient floor heating vent.

"He's on meth," she choked to the paramedic.

"No, shit," he said. "Who's got the tranquilizer darts?"

Mercer lunged toward Lucy. She yelped and scrabbled from him. He shoved the man attending her out of the way and dove, trying to strangle her again.

"You tell no one about mommy dearest," he hissed in Lucy's ear. Two officers grabbed his arms and yanked him to his feet. He bucked and spit. "Or I will crack you like an egg, too, Lu-cille."

Lucy's vision blurred, crimson with fury. She shouted, "don't threaten me, you shit. I'm not your God damned priest, you murderer. I'm telling everyone. You killed your own mother!"

Mercer was finally secured and dragged into the elevator. The boy-men and the hotel manager were herded in his wake.

With one of L.A.'s most notorious homicide attorneys at his side, Gary Mercer later denied to the police that he had any role in his mother's unfortunate death.

Lucy knew he'd never forgive her for that night. She had seen him, the deep, dark corners of him, and he hated her for it.

CHAPTER 2

A Year Later

General Luis Alvarez lay naked in the sunlight. He stretched atop a teak chaise like a sleek harbor seal basking on a warm rock. Tanned and fit at fifty-something, his dark goatee was trimmed to perfection. On the penthouse terrace high above Wilshire Boulevard in Westwood, palm trees in huge ceramic pots swayed in the breeze and an infinity swimming pool shimmered. From this aerie, Alvarez could see everything he planned to possess—from the beaches of Malibu to Century City, Beverly Hills, downtown, and over to the Hollywood sign. Especially the Hollywood sign. California was the world's seventh largest economy, and he would get his luscious piece of it. Someday soon he would gorge on it like a lion eating its bleeding prey.

Alvarez's bedroom suite opened onto the deck through a huge sliding glass wall. Two young girls, barely pubescent, lounged amid tangled white silk sheets atop his big round bed. One was a flaxen-haired blonde; the other was dark with curly black waves that fell around slim, brown shoulders. Like little birds on a line, they watched the predator with wary eyes.

"*Ven aquí,*" he called to the girls.

They leaped from the bed, ready for service, tails wagging submissively. The little tag team knew exactly what to do to make the man happy.

Alvarez responded beneath their young, skilled ministrations. Once he was satisfied, he waved them away with a flick of his hand. They disappeared like sylphs vanishing in the air.

His cell phone sounded. He checked caller ID—few had this number. It was building security. He had a visitor.

"*Señor* Mercer is here? *Bueno.* Send him right up."

Mercer arrived in minutes wearing baggy black basketball trunks and a snug *Copa Americana* soccer playoffs T-shirt. His wavy bleached blond hair was wind-blown and stuck to his forehead as if he'd just taken a run along the beach. Reflective Ray-Bans were perched on his head. The men embraced each other for a warm but wary instant.

"I see you're fucking with baby *putas* again," Mercer said.

"*Sí, sí.* I can't help it, I have to have them. Sorry I don't have your kind of candy today."

Mercer shrugged. "Hey, I'm open to anything, but those bitches are too young for my taste. Been there, it was fucked up. They end up wanting you to be their daddy."

"Ah, merely *Different Strokes, sí?* I loved that '80s TV show with Gary Coleman—strange little dude." Alvarez slid on aviator-style sunglasses. "You like these?" He preened. "Bought myself an early Christmas gift. Paid a fortune. They're the actual glasses Tom Cruise wore in *Top Gun.*"

"Very nice. Maverick's shades. Congratulations. Everyone wants to own a piece of Hollywood, don't they?"

Alvarez grinned. He wadded up a towel, dried himself, and then tossed it onto the deck. "Please, sit, be comfortable." He took a pair of white silk shorts that had been placed on the table near his phone and slipped them on.

"Still love the white silk?"

"Light as a whisper and sensual as tiny, high breasts and tight, round bottoms, eh? He snapped the elastic waistband. "How does it feel to be back in L.A., *amigo,* after what, nine months as an expat in my country? Add that little venture in Florida, too, hey?"

"Feels like about fuckin' time." Mercer gazed out toward the UCLA campus.

A house-man, mid-twenties with long, coppery dreadlocks, brought Alvarez a large glass of water, a green smoothie, and a bowl of fresh fruit. He placed the tray next to the chaise on a table inlaid with Mexican ceramic tiles. Threw a quick and admiring look Mercer's way.

"Your breakfast, sir."

"*Gracias,* Brody. Anything for you?" he asked

Mercer.

"No, I'm good, thank you."

Brody gave a little bow, then left Alvarez and Mercer alone.

"So, you said you have a job for me." Gary Mercer sat down on a lounge chair next to Alvarez. In the distance over the ocean, thick gray clouds began to form on the horizon, moving toward the city like a wide band of zeppelins.

"They say a storm will come tomorrow night," Alvarez said. He adjusted his Tom Cruise glasses. "We're in production down in Long Beach on a movie I invested in. It's the big car chase scene. If it rains, it'll have to be postponed. *El Niño* will cost us big time."

Mercer sighed and stretched his neck. His vertebrae popped like muffled gunshots. "That's the film biz. Always some shit going down to suck up the money. Get used to it, man."

"Yes, yes, your father is a big producer, I'm sure you have much insight into the industry. Many stories to tell, *sí?*"

"My father *was* a big producer. He's dead."

"Of course, I'm so sorry. We were acquaintances for many years but I never knew him well. I'm a big fan of his work, I always told him that. You ever in one of his movies?" Alvarez's face lit up. He was as hooked on the Tinseltown dream as a junkie on meth.

"Yeah, a couple. *Stone Hammer* was my first. Was no big deal. I was somebody who got murdered in the background. Had one line. It got me a SAG card."

"I loved *Stone Hammer*. When Flynn was tortured, oh my God. What a scene. Better than the horse head in

The Godfather."

Mercer sat up and swung his feet onto the ground. "*Señor General,* forgive me if I am rude, but about the job?"

"*Sí, sí,* my impatient *amigo,* of course." He took a long gulp of smoothie then grimaced. "You've heard of Henry Vega? I think you are an acquaintance of his niece."

Mercer nodded, eyes dark.

Alvarez paused, waiting for more, but Mercer offered nothing.

"Henry Vega, her uncle, needs to be stopped before he becomes a big problem to me, to our organization," Alvarez said. "He is representing the State of California in economic talks in Mexico City and is distressingly convincing. Also supports the governor in refusing extradition to my brother, Carlos. Vega needs to be neutralized. And if you do well with that assignment, I have something really special for Governor Scanlon that I'd like your help with."

Alvarez finished the smoothie with a long, noisy slurp. He grimaced again. "I hate kale."

"You want Henry Vega eliminated? I was about to propose this to you myself," Mercer said.

Alvarez smiled and stroked his smooth, waxed chest. He rose from his recliner and began to pace. "You'll have to go back to Mexico City for a few days, find him, and follow him."

"Yes, of course," Mercer said, a new animation to his demeanor.

"And if removing Vega isn't enough to soften the governor's position on extradition, then we won't go after another powerful individual, we'll go after something bigger, something that will undermine the state's economy and the governor's political credibility." A faint smile flickered on his lips as thin clouds began to filter the sunlight. "I hope you'll find my thoughts on this very interesting," Alvarez said.

"I'm sure I will, and I have a few ideas of my own you may like as well." Mercer peeled off his clothes and gazed, naked, across the cityscape to the slash of ocean in the distance. "It's good to be home," he said and plunged into the aquamarine pool.

CHAPTER 3

The precipitation was light but persistent and cold. Lucy tugged up the hood of her khaki parka. Her umbrella had disappeared years ago and she'd failed to replace it. Why bother—it never rained. But when it did, it was killer. She jumped out of the Jeep, clicked the lock sensor and clutched her purse to her chest, preparing to make a dash toward the restaurant where Beatrice waited.

And then, there he was.

The air seemed to drain from Lucy's lungs. She gasped and stepped back. Gary Mercer's eyes hammered into her like silver nails, his nostrils flared as if a disagreeable smell wafted for an instant through the air. Then he turned away, slipping on a pair of reflective sunglasses despite the dismal rainy afternoon. He jumped into his tricked-out Chevy Kodiak, fired up the black monster, and pulled onto Ventura Boulevard toward Laurel Canyon. Mercer glanced back at Lucy and smirked. She felt it like a blow. Then he was gone.

Lucy hurried into Du-Par's Restaurant in Studio City and quickly found Bea ensconced in a back booth. Her whole body shook as she took off her coat and slid in across from her friend.

"Girl, look at you. What's the matter?" Bea asked. Her big brown eyes were filled with concern.

Lucy couldn't answer immediately. She struggled to calm down and shredded her paper napkin in the process. She looked across at Bea, grateful for her friendship and support. The two women had been close friends since they first worked together as colleagues in San Antonio. It was Lucy's first news job after graduating UCLA, and Bea's second. On the surface, they were an unlikely pair—Lucy was yoga and L.L. Bean; Bea was pole dancing and Prada. Beneath the surface though, they were swimmers in the same rugged ocean.

Lucy finally spoke. "Gary Mercer's back in town."

Bea's mouth dropped open. Her eyes narrowed. "Shit. If he comes near the station, I'm calling the cops. We'll get a restraining order."

"They're always so effective."

Bea shook her head and shrugged.

Lucy glanced across the dining room of the legendary restaurant to distract herself. She felt like she was watching the scene in a theater. A step above Denny's down the street, the place had a whole lot more character and was an entertainment industry fixture. A trio of Universal Studio's security guards slid into the booth behind Bea and Lucy. At a few minutes after

3:00 P.M., grips from a nearby studio were having a late lunch break. A rumpled screenwriter-type at the counter hunched over his laptop dipping toast into runny eggs. A group of high school girls wearing muddy soccer uniforms slurped down nutritionally incorrect ice cream sodas and bantered at their table.

"I haven't seen Gary Mercer since that night," Lucy said.

"About a year ago, right?" Bea chewed at her mauve thumbnail.

"Thirteen months, but who's counting? I think he was in rehab somewhere in Florida. Truckee heard he was doing some freelance work in Orlando or Miami."

"Great choice of town for a recovering junkie," Bea said. Her eyes scanned for a server.

"Gary was never one for good decisions. I wonder if he's back permanently." Lucy drummed her fingers on the table and glanced again at the customers, feeling like a furtive animal ready to bolt.

"Maybe he's home visiting family for the holidays." Bea snickered. "There must be a relative somewhere around here he hasn't murdered."

"He's up to something," Lucy said. "Seeing him gives me the creeps. His eyes are like, wow, like there's nothing in there."

A platinum blonde septuagenarian who ran the hostess station like a cop shop interrupted their conversation. She approached their table and shined up the Formica surface, almost taking out Bea's contact lens with an edge of the flying towel. "What'll you have, girls?"

"Herb tea," Lucy said.

"No herb tea. Lipton's—black or green."

"Make it black." Lucy smiled up at the sassy broad. She was like the soup Nazi on the old Seinfeld show.

"Coffee for me, and pancakes all around," Bea added.

"Atta girl." Old blondie turned and proceeded into the kitchen.

"Wish I could run my life like she runs this place," Lucy said. "No shit. Take it as it is, or leave it."

"Yeah, me too. Never quite works like that, especially with two teens in the house."

Her cell phone buzzed. She dug into her designer bag and after rooting around pulled out a leopard print phone case.

"Hello, Dexter," she said. "I'm in Studio City with Lucy and we're waiting for our pancakes. Late lunch. Yeah, you can stay until 5:30 and I'll pick you up then. Okay, baby. Love you too."

"Great kid," Lucy said.

Bea nodded. "When he's not pushing me to the limit of my sanity."

The food server, a clone of the hostess, except with red-orange hair and a few more pounds, slid plates full of pancakes across the table to Bea and Lucy. She plunked down a handful of plastic butter containers and a sticky pitcher of faux maple syrup.

"Eat up, ladies."

"Will do," Bea said, then turned to Lucy. "Glad I can talk you into this once in a while. Girls like me, born and bred in the South, can't exist too long without a hit of something carbolicious!"

Lucy laughed. "I figured that if I keep up these late pancakes breakfasts with you, I'm going to turn into the brunette version of a Du-Par's diva real fast."

"Count me in as the African-American version. This staff could use some color." Bea buttered up the crisp, golden goodies.

As they dug in, the rain intensified. Lucy glanced out the window. The intersection had turned into a vision of dripping lights and dark shadows against the glass.

"I've got to be in at six tomorrow morning to cover the news conference at City Hall on the storm drains," Bea said. "Are you on that one?"

"Huh-uh, I'm not scheduled until later. I'll be working with the new camera guy, giving him an orientation."

Bea sniffed. "He needs more than an orientation. He's an idiot."

She signaled for more coffee. The red-head slowly lumbered her way, a pot in each hand, caf and decaf.

"Give him a chance. He's nervous. You make him nervous," Lucy said.

"Yeah, I tend to do that. Anyhow, are you staying up at your uncle's tonight in Malibu? Another really bad storm is supposed to kick in for a few days."

"I heard. Looks like it's already starting." Lucy motioned to the window with her fork. "Auntie Elsa, God love her, is just getting too old to look after the house and the animals too. We've got to figure something out to help her. Uncle Henry's supposed to be home tomorrow night. I hope he can make it in," Lucy said.

"He's in Mexico City, right? Something for the governor?"

"Yeah, he's representing the State of California on this alternative economy program. The state provides grants, some of them very big, to groups in Mexico who choose to do something besides produce drugs. So much shit coming across the border right now, it's getting crazy and more violent than ever."

"I know, just last week they arrested that Mexican mob cartel guy."

Lucy nodded, then took a wonderful, maple syrup-soaked bite of pancake and swooned with pleasure.

Bea's phone rang again. She took a quick look at the caller ID. "It's Ernie. Gotta grab this. Hey, Ern, what's up?" Bea listened for a while, face grim, then signed off.

"What?" Lucy dabbed her mouth with a thin paper napkin.

"After storm drains, I have to meet him at LAPD headquarters for a news conference. Several pre-teen girls have been murdered over the last month, strangled. One more found last night. They're thinking serial killer."

"Sweet Jesus. So many kids run away," Lucy said. "Why do they think it might be a serial?"

"They were all wearing white silk shifts."

"A baby bride kind of fetish?"

"Who knows. Makes me sick. My daughter's that age," Bea said.

Lucy nodded and gazed out at the rain-drenched Boulevard. "Gotta take good care of our precious loved ones."

Bea took a last, long slug of coffee, crunched up her napkin and gazed longingly at her unfinished pancakes. Unbidden, old Blondie was there with a to-go container. Bea grinned, thanked her and turned toward Lucy. "I think you'd better get on the road ASAP, missy. Going through that canyon is downright scary in this kind of weather."

"I know. Remember when Kanan Road just fell off the cliff there by PCH? I was so glad when they finally got it fixed. Had to take these narrow back routes to the ranch through the mountains. I never knew what was going to be just around the next bend—a dead coyote, a motorcyclist down, a rock slide.

"Scary and unpredictable—like Mercer." Bea stood up and began putting on her coat.

"Yeah, like Mercer," Lucy repeated. "I hope he's on a return trip to the other side of the world soon."

"From your lips to God's ears," Bea said. "Gotta go." She gathered up the rest of her belongings, put down some cash, and hugged Lucy goodbye.

CHAPTER 4

The downpour clattered like buckshot on the roof of Henry Vega's Lexus. A handsome man in his sixties, he scrubbed his fingers through a full head of dark hair silvered at the temples. The weather was worrisome. Even with the windshield wipers on ultra-fast mode, he still drove practically blind. *El Niño,* a climactic effect named for the coming of the Christ Child in December, sent Southern California torrential rains north from the tropics. Electricity went out, roads washed away, Manolo Blahniks were ruined, waterproof mascara failed, and spin classes were canceled. Southern California blurred for a few rare moments.

The effect also brought flash floods and rock slides that carried mountains of mud into suburban living rooms and swallowed houses whole like chum down a shark's gullet.

On this tumultuous night, *El Niño* was having one hell of a tantrum.

The airport's silvery LAX sign loomed ahead then disappeared into the darkness as Henry pulled onto Century Boulevard with a quick jog onto Sepulveda. He reflected on his luck in being able to grab that last seat tonight on the final plane out of *Cuidad de México*. While watching the departures screen at the Mexico City air terminal, the midnight flight he'd previously booked turned from *On Time* to *Canceled* due to weather.

He shook his head and recalled the tall, slender gringo wearing an expensive black leather bomber jacket, bullying the gate agent and demanding that she magically conjure up an extra seat. He even flashed a hefty handful of American dollars. Had he seen this fellow somewhere before? The guy was hell-bent on getting to L.A., but Vega needed to get ahead of another kind of storm brewing up from the south-—this one potentially much more lethal.

Now, finally, in Los Angeles, the hour was late. Through Westchester, Venice, and Santa Monica to Pacific Coast Highway, commonly known as PCH, Henry Vega scrolled through voicemails hearing issues with a shopping center he was renovating in Pasadena, board meetings coming up for the hospice and for *La Raza* Hispanic Business Association.

Glancing into the rearview mirror, he was almost the sole traveler on the road. Big Rock Canyon flew by on one side, the dense inkiness of the ocean on the other. Vega couldn't see the water but he could smell its salty tang and feel the rumble of the surf crashing onto the rocky shores. Those who lived along this precarious strip of asphalt between the ocean and the crumbling Santa Monica Mountains were tucked away in their equally precarious homes. The twinkling of holiday decorations on ocean-side bungalows dripped down his windshield in wet smears of light.

Then a message came in from his niece, Lucy, who he had raised since she was a tot. He loved her with all his heart.

Unc, we'll see you tomorrow night. I'm staying at the ranch this weekend so we'll do your fave fish tacos and Modelo. Mucho muah! Safe travels.

He chuckled. She had no idea he'd be in a whole day early.

The tension that had burned in his intestines since boarding the plane from Mexico City began to dissipate. The death grip he'd had on the steering wheel loosened. Turning on the radio to a seasonal music station, he sang along to "I'll be Home for Christmas."

Finally, the last voicemail. It was Governor Scanlon with a two-word message: *call me*. He punched in the governor's cell phone number. Henry's intestinal reflux flared as he turned inland onto Kanan Dume Road through the rugged canyon toward his ranch.

"George Scanlon." The governor's voice was deep and coarse. He had given up smoking ten years earlier but the previous thirty, at four packs a day, had taken a permanent toll.

"George, sorry to bother you so late but I just got in. Took an early flight to try and beat the storm. Called as soon as I got your message. Quite a flight. Bumpy as hell."

"Weather's definitely shit," the governor said, "but

thank you for getting back to me tonight. There's an issue we need to discuss. Can we meet in person tomorrow? Better than over the phone."

"I'm at your disposal, sir. What does your morning look like?" As Vega approached the first of three tunnels through the Santa Monica Mountains pass, a heavy-duty pickup truck materialized, rooftop halogens glaring. The rain intensified as he swerved to avoid a minor rock slide. The truck followed, blasted through it, spraying mud and gravel—following even closer now. Who was this asshole?

The governor had a brief coughing spell. Vega waited impatiently for it to end. He was even more irritated when the pickup practically crawled up his bumper. He decelerated further. *Pass me, you idiot.* The truck receded into the darkness.

Noisily clearing his phlegmy throat, the governor continued, "Okay. Let's see here, I'm in a pop-up fund-raising breakfast until eleven—one of those spontaneous, last-minute affairs. Then there's a press conference about that drug kingpin we tangled with lasted week."

"Luis Alvarez?" Vega rummaged for some Tums in the glove box.

"We're refusing to extradite his younger brother, Carlos. Luis is going crazy. Threatened me, personally. Where the hell does he think he is? Goddamned Juarez? My family is under intensive twenty-four-hour surveillance. I mean we always have security, but this is taking it to a whole new level. I can't take a piss without two agents holding my dick."

"Hot dudes?"

"Ugly as shit."

Vega finally found some shabby-looking antacids in his briefcase, grimaced at the chalky taste as he chewed them. He glanced into the rearview mirror. The damned fool in his gas-guzzler was bearing down on him once again.

"Okay, Henry, how about noon? We can have lunch at the Santa Monica Airport before I fly back to Sacramento. At the Typhoon, upstairs in the sushi bar."

Vega was distracted again. Behind him, the truck's headlights bounced and gleamed annoyingly. The rack of rooftop spotlights had been extinguished. Something felt off, very off.

"Idiot tailgater," Henry cursed as he approached the dim sulfurous illumination of the second tunnel through the most treacherous portion of the pass. As he entered this dark artery through the Malibu Canyon the rain halted, replaced by big, gray drips from overhead. About a quarter-mile long, the tunnel was dank and narrow. He was relieved when the pickup at last pulled out to go around him.

Instead of passing, the truck veered hard into the Lexus.

The violent impact forced Vega's car against the wall. The sound of metal grating against concrete screamed. Sparks flew. The brutal hit sent the car flying out the far end of the tunnel. Rain rolled over the windshield like crashing surf.

"Holy shit." Vega gasped, disbelief squeezing his throat as if he was drowning.

The truck emerged from the darkness and swerved into him again with enough power and intent to send his heavy sedan careening into the metal guardrail, the only barrier between the road and the deep chasm over the swollen, rocky creek below. Tonight, the usually meandering waterway was like the Colorado River rushing through the Grand Canyon.

The pickup dropped back half a car length, then pounced forward beside his car; its headlights off now. The truck struck him again. The heavy driver's side door of the Lexus buckled against Vega's shoulder. His cell phone flew away as airbags exploded like bombs. Searing pain cut through his body, the taste of blood filled his mouth. Vega inhaled a burning gunpowder scent and heard his rear bumper scraping against the asphalt.

"Henry, talk to me!" Scanlon shouted. "I'm losing you!" His voice was far off, coming from somewhere below the front seat.

Just before the car flew into the darkness, the dim glow from a pole light illuminated the driver's face through the deeply tinted window. It was at that moment Henry Vega understood what was happening—the man in Mexico City and bribe money for a last-minute plane ticket to L.A. He'd seen this piece of shit before after all—with Luis Alvarez.

Lucy, find him. Make him pay.

For a long moment, the Lexus hung in the air.

Then it was over.

CHAPTER 5

Brent Lucas, a rangy, blond USC broadcast journalism student, sat alone in the KLAK newsroom working on his economics term paper while finishing up the last slice of pepperoni pizza with extra cheese. As the news production intern, he monitored the station's police scanner after the eleven o'clock news until six in the morning, two graveyard shifts a week. He would type a summary of each evening's events and email the file to the A.M. news director and his minions.

Tonight, the usual late night reporter hadn't shown up.

Word in the office was that the guy was a drunk going through a bad patch and was about to be canned. In lieu of a reporter, if something significant was streaming, Brent had been instructed to contact the on-call producer at home, at any hour. The chatter coming in over the scanner could be something.

Brent wiped his hands on a crumpled napkin, slugged down a big gulp of Dr. Pepper and reached for the phone. It rang about ten times on the other end.

Instead of voicemail, a groggy response came through. "Vargas."

"Hey, Ernie. It's Brent in the newsroom."

"Who?"

"Brent," he sighed, "the intern."

"Oh, Brent. Yeah." Ernie yawned. "Sorry, I'm so out of it. The baby's got colic. Finally fell asleep. Infant hell." He yawned again. "So, what's up?"

"Something just came through on the State Police emergency band. A car went off Kanan Dume Road down past Pepperdine. I think the driver is some friend of the governor. They said Scanlon himself called 9–1–1. The name of the victim wasn't mentioned but it might be worth checking out for the early edition."

Vargas didn't respond. Brent could sense that the exhausted new father would do just about anything not to have to go out tonight. And the weather, well, Southern California didn't have much weather, but when it happened, it was bad, and the mountain canyons were treacherous.

"Okay, Brent. Could be newsworthy," he finally said.

The baby began to wail again in the background. Brett could hear Ernie's wife weeping. This was obviously the part of new parenting that wasn't featured on the Family Life Network.

"Honey, I'll be right there," Vargas called, desperation edging his voice. Then he whispered to Brent, "Listen, kid—there's no way I can leave my family right now without losing my marriage. Lucy Vega's up in Malibu house-sitting for her uncle. Give her a call. Number's on the board. She can run out and see what's going on, grab some set-up shots and a sound bite. Got it?"

"Yes, sir. Sorry to bother you. Good luck with the baby."

Brent hung up the phone and silently vowed that the Boston terrier mix pup he had rescued from the shelter was as close as he'd ever get to child rearing. Then he hit a few buttons and brought up Lucy's contact info.

✳

It was two in the morning when her cell phone rang out with a dreamy Celtic tune—a soothing sound to wake up to, usually. Lucy rolled over toward the charger on the nightstand. Her eighty pound yellow Lab mix, Maddie, snorted, stretched, and oozed across the warm space Lucy had just vacated on the bed.

She pushed her long tangled dark locks behind her ears; the old St. Olaf College T-shirt Lucy wore clung to her slim body. Who the hell was trying to get her at this hour? She groped for the phone. Although she wasn't on call, the ID identified the newsroom. She hit *call back*.

The line picked up immediately.

"This had better be good," she said, rubbing her eyes.

The contrite intern explained it all quickly.

"Yeah, Brent, okay, uh-huh. You're right, no point in Vargas coming out here, it's only about fifteen minutes down Kanan. Okay. I'm on my way." She clicked off the phone, turned on her bedside lamp and sipped the last inch of day-old Diet Coke from a dented can. Yuck. She'd grab a hot cup of coffee and some oatmeal at the

Paradise Cove Beach Café after she finished with the accident assignment.

Throwing off the flannel sheets, Lucy headed for the bathroom. She took a one-minute shower, threw on jeans, a sweatshirt, rain boots, a waterproof jacket with the station logo, and jogged across the stormy yard to the garage. Maddie at her heels beelined it to the dog door at the Spanish rancho style main house and disappeared inside. The pup knew the drill. The plastic flap *thwacked* shut behind her.

As Lucy pulled out, the door to the house opened. Eighty-year-old Elsa Christianson, her father's cousin from Norway who was both Uncle Henry's housekeeper and Lucy's quasi-grandma, waved her down.

"Everything okay, sweetheart?" She wrapped a pink chenille robe tightly around her small, petite form. Skinny legs rose from tan UGGs. Her beagle, Bugle, poked his head out the door and sniffed. Maddie's face appeared above his. A doggie totem pole. They playfully snapped at each other and disappeared into the house.

"Go back to bed, Elsa. Just a routine on-call thing."

"Okay. But be careful honey. We've got to work on that special dinner tonight for Henry. Gotta whip up those Mexican-Norwegian tortillas. But no lutefisk this year. Salmon or sea bass, I promise."

Lucy laughed as she recalled that disastrous culinary experiment from many years ago. Pickled Norwegian whitefish was something that did not have wide appeal, even smothered in salsa. "I'll be back soon. Love you."

"You too." The old woman closed the door and waved through the window. The pups' heads appeared next to her for a moment then they all disappeared, probably heading toward the kitchen and treats. The motion-sensor porch lights extinguished.

Lucy couldn't shake the sense of discomfort that had been niggling at her since she got the call from the intern. It was a rough night, but it felt like something beyond the weather threatened. Water and hillside would be flowing down the mountain along with boulders that could wipe a semi off the road. Another crazy *El Niño* storm. But this was all part of her job. She pushed the lever that engaged her Jeep's 4-wheel drive.

In the deep-gray light of a rainy pre-dawn, a murder of black crows circled overhead before descending *en masse* into a stand of sycamore trees along the bloated, churning expanse of Medea Creek. Several of the big inky birds fought over a bloody morsel that screamed and struggled, then quieted. Finally, one of the winged creatures managed to secure the dying prey in its beak and disappear into the low, leaden sky.

Pulling into a turnout just north of the third tunnel, Lucy eased to a stop between a Los Angeles County fire rescue vehicle and a Malibu cop car—both empty. No other news folks had arrived but it wouldn't be long. She hopped out, grabbed her gear and headed for the fire road that scaled the edge of the canyon and led down to the water. The loose, decomposing granite scree and slick adobe mud created an added struggle to the trek.

Lucy zipped the video camera into the front of her jacket in hopes of keeping it dry and secure. Despite its nylon cover, the lens was getting wet and she hated those blurry, rain-pocked weather shots the other camera operators cranked out. She knew her cinematic tastes were classic in the midst of a period where halting, unfocused, and blurry were supposed to the give the viewer a sense of raw "reality." Reality was way overrated. She'd learned that early.

As Lucy made her way down to the scene, the L.A. County Fire Department backhoe tractor began pulling a wrecked silver Lexus sedan out of the creek. Her uncle had one just like it. Lucy looked forward to his coming home tomorrow, which was now, happily, today. She and Elsa would make those tacos with their delicious dill, mayonnaise, red onion, and cabbage salsa. The salmon would be wild caught from Alaska. Pricey, but worth it.

As she cautiously hiked her way down to the edge of the creek, one of the firefighters she'd befriended on other stories gave her a quick wave. Taut chains screeched in protest as the backhoe shivered and the car struggled to emerge. The windows were rolled up. The car's interior resembled an untended aquarium, full of greenish water slowly draining. The windshield hadn't shattered. The passenger side door and the pleated rear end appeared to have taken most of the hit.

A body floated against the glass. Lucy swallowed hard and held down a pang of nausea. Anxiety built in her diaphragm and the roar of the ocean rose in her ears. This was too close, too close to home. To the brutal loss of her family in a similar catastrophe.

I'm okay, I'm okay, she told herself. *Focus on the story, on the work. The work saves you, always has.*

Lucy clambered up the bank a bit to get a better angle on the accident, careful not to slip on the sharp rocks. She took a wide shot of the roiling water surging toward the Pacific a mile away.

Documenting the dangerous, hard work of the first responders, she grabbed a close-up of the whitewater moving an empty surfboard along the shore then shifted focus to her friend the fire department rescue worker in a bright yellow rain suit.

As the car finally cleared the shore and settled on a sandy berm, he tried to open the car doors with some kind of slim-jim tool but they wouldn't oblige. One of their colleagues appeared with the Jaws of Life but after a quick consult, he grabbed an ax and smashed in the windshield.

Water gushed forth like murky vomit. The floating body slid into view atop the Lexus' silver hood. A shoeless foot tangled against the steering wheel.

Lucy screamed, shook her head and stumbled backward. Surely, she was hallucinating. This couldn't be real.

Her camera dropped to the ground. For a moment, she was paralyzed.

She swallowed a sob then rushed toward the ruined car. Oblivious of the hands reaching to restrain her, Lucy threw herself into her uncle's cold, dead arms.

CHAPTER 6

From the rim of the canyon, the door to a mud-splashed, white KLAK-TV news van slammed shut like the crack of a shotgun.

"Lucy!" Ernie Vargas shouted. He came running toward her, slipping and sliding down the fire road to the banks of the creek, overcoat flying, his eyeglasses fogged.

"Luce! We didn't know," he said, panting for breath. He was not known for working out or for his interest in health foods. "The ID just came in on the police band about twenty minutes ago. I should have been here. I should have come." Ernie pulled her close. "Dammit, Lucy, I am so, so sorry."

Lucy buried her face against his shoulder. For a moment the smell of the scratchy wet wool of his coat held a flicker of comfort. Then she pulled away and wiped her nose on her sleeve.

"Ernie, stop with the guilt trip. Your baby's sick and I was right in Malibu." Tears and rain streamed down her cheeks. "It should have been a slam dunk."

"Let's get you out of here." He grabbed the camera and they trudged up the fire road toward the rim of the canyon. She moved like a dim shadow alongside him.

About a hundred yards down from the gaping rip in the guardrail along Kanan Road, Ernie and Lucy sat down together atop a low, flat boulder. He held a black golf umbrella over them. His fingers were turning white as he gripped the cold plastic handle. Gusts of wind threatened to rip it away.

Pale and drawn, Lucy wrapped her arms around her body and rocked. Back and forth, back and forth, like a heartbeat.

"Lucy, please let me take you home now," Ernie said. Gently, he placed his hand on her arm.

"No! Don't touch me!" She edged away. Her vision flashed with dark patches of blindness.

Ernie pulled his hand back as if he had reached into a fire.

"I'm sorry. I'm having a, a p—panic attack, she said, teeth chattering, legs rubbery. "Like I'm in, in the m—middle of a h—heart attack and g—going insane at the same time. Can't be touched. Not p—personal." *I can get through this. It's been ten years and tons of therapy since this last happened.*

"What can I do to help?" Ernie asked, looking at Lucy like he might start hyperventilating, too. "Let's get you somewhere warm. You're shaking!"

"I can't get into the car yet. I get this thing, this

phobia. My parents, brother, now my uncle—all killed in car accidents."

She tried to slow her rapid, shallow breathing. She put a hand on her chest and the other below her ribs to try and contain the panic.

"I'm with you," Ernie said. He fidgeted helplessly, pulled out a tissue, and wiped his eyes. His glasses still wouldn't un-fog and his shoes were soaking wet. The big umbrella turned inside out as the wind kicked up and the rain slashed horizontally. He finally gave up and fought it closed—they were both soaked anyway.

"Go to the van," Lucy said. "Turn on the heat and warm up. I'm okay. It's gonna be okay." She stood and began to pace. *Back and forth, back and forth, thump-thump, thump-thump.*

At the bottom of the fire road, a tow truck hauled the Lexus away, but her uncle remained in a body bag beneath a tarp at the edge of the creek. Lucy ran her hands frenetically through her dark wavy hair and tried to still her brain. "How could this have happened? Again?"

Ernie made no move toward the van and its heater. He reached out to reassure her, then quickly withdrew his hand. He struggled again to wipe his glasses, this time on his shirt tail until one of the lenses popped out and bounced over the cliff.

"Oh, damn." His shoulders drooped.

Lucy frowned and watched the lens disappear. Then her eye caught something else. "Ernie, look!" She pointed to a path heading down the hill where several men slipped their way toward the creek. "Lt. Pete Anthony, L.A. County Homicide. What the hell?" Anthony had fading Hollywood good looks with the requisite dark stubble beard. He was arrogant as hell but Lucy rated him as equally smart and effective.

Ernie squinted. "That's weird—they don't usually send a homicide deet to an accident site. Especially the head honcho. They're probably here 'cause your uncle's high profile. After all, I heard that the governor actually called in the 9–1–1. Maybe it's just a courtesy thing or a CYA."

"Maybe. But look, the other guy, McNeill, he's counterterrorism," Lucy said. Her panic attack began to morph into a chorus of desperate questions.

McNeill was a fiftyish former Marine intelligence officer with a jarhead haircut and a nose flattened like a lumpy donut against his face.

"Here comes Sheriff Mortenson too. He's joining Anthony and McNeill. The county sheriff being at the scene makes sense, but homicide and counter-fucking-terrorism? What the hell is going on, Ernie?"

Lucy struggled to pull herself together as best she could. She pressed her chest. "I'll be okay, I'll be fine."

Before Ernie could protest, Lucy grabbed her camera with shaking hands. She pulled a microphone from her pocket and pushed it toward him. He didn't take it.

"Sheriff Mortenson doesn't talk to anyone," he said. "Anthony and McNeill won't get near us."

"Well, the sheriff's going to talk to me. Let's go. I'm okay. He owes me this." She thrust the mic decisively into Ernie's hands and then lurched unsteadily down the hill. He hustled behind her, rubbing at his eyes and squinting.

Lucy and Ernie approached from above and behind

the investigators and the sheriff. Birch Mortenson was a tall, angular man whose physique resembled a suit hung on a wire hanger. She knew they all saw her coming and no doubt hoped they wouldn't have to deal with her, but no way in hell would she disappear.

"Sheriff Mortenson, I ID'd my uncle's body for your people and they promised you'd give me an interview." The interview part wasn't true but it sounded convincing. Lucy and Ernie trudged up to Mortenson. The soles of their boots were coated in several inches of heavy, plastic-like adobe mud. Every step sounded like a loud suck. Lucy struggled to control her emotions and appear calm. She tried to envision a quiet, peaceful moment of *savasana,* the still, meditative pose at the end of her yoga class. The pose of the dead body.

Wearing his one-lensed glasses, Ernie stepped forward with the microphone.

Mortenson glanced at his colleagues then shrugged. The scowls on the investigators' faces indicated that they were not happy campers.

"Thank you for the identification, Ms. Vega. I know it was difficult. So sorry about your loss." He pressed his narrow lips together, then gave in. "All right. I don't have much time."

"Thank you, sir." Her throat began to seize up. She breathed deeply and slowly let out the air.

Birch Mortenson was a Norwegian-American in his late fifties. Originally from Minneapolis, he still had the "Fargo" accent, even though he'd been with the Los Angeles County Sheriff's Department for more than two decades. Ernie and Lucy had done business with him many times. Although short on interpersonal skills, he was a straight shooter and they both respected him.

"You rolling?" Ernie asked.

Lucy nodded and planted her feet firmly in the mud. Her heart banged mercilessly loud. *Breathe. Focus. The work saves you.*

"So, Henry Vega's death was an accident?" Ernie didn't ask the usual who-what-when-why. He went for the big one.

Lucy saw the sheriff hesitate. Through her viewfinder, she looked directly into his icy blue eyes. Her skin itched in some ancient, visceral way.

"We have every reason to believe it was." Mortenson's words were gruff.

"Any evidence to suggest otherwise?" Ernie asked.

"The fire department just pulled the car out so we haven't been able to go over it yet. But we're confident that this was an accident. As you well know, it's a treacherous road, especially in the rain."

"You said confident, but not positive?" Ernie moved closer to Mortenson. The sheriff shot a quick look toward Anthony and McNeill.

Lucy heard herself ask a little too loudly, "What the hell is homicide doing out here? And counterterrorism?"

Until moments ago, it had not entered her mind that the death of her uncle could have been anything other than a horrible wintry accident, like so many sad, pointless others that had occurred in the years when Southern Californians faced the rains and mudslides of *El Niño*. It was just the brutal, heartless randomness of life. Or was it?

"This is routine with someone high profile like your uncle, Ms Vega," Mortenson said.

The sheriff's no-nonsense demeanor rippled just a touch, like a raindrop falling into a still pool. The disruption would be almost imperceptible to a lesser-trained eye than Lucy's.

"Of course, we can never say we're one hundred percent positive of anything until we study all the evidence," he added. "Would be irresponsible to act otherwise."

Lucy turned off the camera. "Sheriff Mortenson, what is it? I'm his niece, his next of kin. Off the record, what aren't you telling us? Please, I deserve to know."

He glanced uncomfortably over his shoulder again. His colleagues were restive.

"Off the record," Ernie confirmed. He killed the mic.

"All I can say is that evidence points to an accident. We'll check thoroughly to confirm that." Mortenson dug his hands deep into the pockets of his dark charcoal trench coat. "I don't think we'll find anything concerning." He looked like a bat ready to fly.

"We're not letting this go, sir." Lucy held the camera against her chest like a shield. After a brief respite, the rain had begun to fall again.

Mortenson's lips pressed into a thread-thin line; his jaw clenched and unclenched. "I'll let you know if we find anything newsworthy, ma'am. But right now, I have work to attend to."

He turned and joined the others. In their dark attire, the trio looked like an unction of undertakers. The men excused themselves and trudged back up the fire road. At the canyon rim parking turnout, they ducked into the sheriff's Crown Vic. Soon the vehicle disappeared over the rise toward Agoura Hills and the 101 Freeway.

"This is bullshit," Lucy said, her eyes narrowed against the growing wind. Then she sighed and rubbed her temples. "But then again, I'm probably not thinking straight right now. Am I crazy for even considering that this accident could be some kind of terrorist plot? Nuts, huh?"

"You know anyone who might want to harm your uncle?" Ernie's nose was running and his ears were gray with cold. He pulled out the soggy tissue again to clear his single lens.

Lucy shook her head. "Anybody in business makes enemies now and then but I can't think of a soul who'd have been pissed off enough to kill him. He was a kind man, did good every day. He was a sweetheart; you knew him." Her voice caught in her throat as she fought back an overwhelming sense of loss and despair.

Other news crews began to descend on the scene.

"I've got to get out of here," Lucy said.

Ernie nodded. "Come on, I'll take you home."

"Thank you, dear friend, but my Jeep's here." Fresh tears streamed down her face and dripped from her chin. "I have to go tell Elsa he's gone. Then I'm coming back to the station, Ernie. I'm going to edit this one myself."

CHAPTER 7

The rail yards of San Bernardino and the Inland Empire just east of Los Angeles were considered a major point of passage for goods and materials coming in and out of Southern California. A mix of industrial and agricultural products rode the rails in this part of the country. Bud Martinez oversaw much of it.

He sat inside the main office at an old wooden desk the size of a kitchen table. A balding man in his early sixties, his paunch strained the acrylic fibers of a hand-knitted tan sweater. The eagle on the front was nicely done by someone who'd known what they were doing.

Martinez tossed a pile of recently finished paperwork into an out-basket and stubbed his cigarette into a ceramic rainbow trout ashtray piled high with moldering butts. A loud flushing noise reverberated in the hallway. He shook his head and crossed himself piously, *¡Madre* *del Dios!* Hell, Lumpy," Martinez called, "you got it now, too? Food poisoning from those fish burritos, hey? Maybe the trainmaster sent them over to kill us. Real nice." He grimaced as another loud retch emanated from the bathroom. "Holy shitski, sounds like you need to go home, too, *hermano*. Now the whole regular crew's down but me. Gut of steel."

He chuckled and proudly patted his beer belly.

Lumpy Fargas, a replica of Martinez, only twenty years younger and twenty pounds lighter, staggered into the office. A wad of moist paper towel was pressed to his mouth. His eyes were glassy and his face greenish.

"You talk to the replacements?" Martinez asked. He lit up another cigarette with his Mexican flag-striped Zippo.

Lumpy nodded. "Told the boys to set it for three tons, point the loader, and let 'er rip. And I told them to mix in four bags of Dyna-Feed per ton. Pretty straightforward." He mopped his forehead with the remains of the paper towel.

"Okay, good. They catchin' on fast?"

"Seem to be. By the way, a couple of the big lights're burned out by the loading dock. Dark as pitch. And raining again, almost feels like sleet. This is Southern fucking California, not Chicago. What's with this weather?"

"I hear 'ya, Lump," Martinez said. "Thanks for letting me know about them lights. OSHA wouldn't be happy 'bout that. I'll call maintenance."

"We just put new bulbs in about a month ago." He belched, then belched again. *Eau de* rotting fish and stomach acid wafted in the air.

Martinez wrinkled his nose. "Shame. They cost a flamin' fortune. Usually, last a long time." Martinez peered out of the office window into the darkness. The glass was so dirty it was barely transparent. He walked over to the coffee machine and poured himself a cup from a pot that was as dingy as the window. "Cuppa joe?"

Lumpy's eyes rolled back in his head and he squeezed his knees together. "Uh, no. Gotta run, Bud. Maybe I'll see 'ya tomorrow. Maybe not."

"Okey dokey, Lump. We'll be fine here. Don't worry about nothin.' I'll keep an eye on the temp workers. Light rail traffic right now so how bad can they really fuck up, huh? Take care, *amigo*."

"*Adiós*." Lumpy gagged.

Martinez sniggered and took a long pull on his cigarette. It was turning out to be a very good night.

※

Outside, farther down the tracks beyond the grain silos was the loading dock. Slender and bearded, Sergio Nogales wore a dark knit cap pulled low on his forehead as he surveyed the scene. The wooden clapboard World War II vintage train depot was in dire need of renovation. Grime from the railroad, smog, and acid rain had turned the place into a peeling relic. Graffiti metastasized everywhere.

He watched the replacement crew at work. The men had been pulled from various points around the metropolitan area for some nice overtime. They appeared and disappeared into the darkness, hauling fifty-pound bags. The contents were emptied into the loader where various feed grains and supplements were being mixed and funneled into freight cars with Dyna-Feed logos emblazoned across the sides. The mile-long train would carry this livestock food to suppliers for farms up and down the San Joaquin Valley, the agribusiness hub of the country.

The workers looked like ghostly apparitions as the train hissed clouds of steam and the frigid mist pressed in from the low sky. A semi-trailer truck lumbered up toward the dock. Nogales, tonight's temp crew supervisor, guided the driver with a flashlight as the truck backed up. With so many overhead lights burned out, it was difficult to see much.

That was the plan.

He called to several of the workers, directing them to assist in unloading additional bags from the semi. Dyna-Feed bags filled the first two rows. Then, the label changed. In almost identical packaging, Dyna-Cide, a powerful organophosphate pesticide, was soon being mixed into the livestock feed. The men were wet, cold, and wanted to finish up as quickly as they could. The details of labeling were lost in the darkness.

At the end of the job, the bags were collected and hauled off to be incinerated. The workers hurried back to the station to warm up, grab a snack, and hear that they could go home early.

Nogales smiled to himself. It had gone perfectly, just as they had planned. He didn't join the others in the station but instead went directly to his new SUV parked behind the loading bay. The wintry, damp mist had become so thick that he could see only the faintest outline of his silver Ford Explorer. He squeezed the sensor on his keychain. The parking lights flashed and the muffled clunking of opening locks sounded.

Climbing into the vehicle, Nogales slammed the door shut and pulled off his wet cap. The leather seats were freezing, even through his quilted jumpsuit. Esmeralda had been right; he should have got cloth interior. "Who cares about looking classy? I just want to keep my sweet ass warm," she had said. And it was a hell of a sweet ass. Nogales heated up at the thought.

As he punched the ignition button, a match flared from behind him.

Nogales froze. Slowly, he turned around, eyes wide. *What the hell?* His heart threatened to stop. "*Señor* Alvarez, you, uh—I didn't expect you here."

Luis Alvarez wore a black overcoat which looked like cashmere, with a white silk scarf and a broad-rimmed black felt hat. He looked like a 1920s gangster, maybe Al Capone. Gossip was that if Alvarez had any weakness, it was for fine clothing, Hollywood memorabilia, and young girls. Very young. His aristocratic face with its meticulously trimmed beard was barely illuminated by the ember of what smelled like a Cuban cigar.

With a faint flick of a finger, Alvarez indicated to Nogales to turn back around. No problem. Nogales hated looking at the guy. He was a freak. If only he didn't pay so well.

"You take care of my business, Sergio?" His deep, smooth voice was chilling.

"*Sí, señor* Alvarez. Is done. All went very *perfecto*." His gut twisted.

"I wanted to see this for myself." Alvarez took a long pull on the cigar. The SUV filled with its pungent smell. "Governor Scanlon will regret the day he decided to go up against me. We're talking damages in the billions. And more importantly, he'll carry the blame. His political career will turn into *mierda de vaca*—a big fat cow pie."

Alvarez actually giggled like a child.

Sergio shuddered. A freak for sure. He looked out across the desolate parking lot. There was no place to run. For an eternity, Alvarez sat quietly in the back seat. Sergio sensed slight, rhythmical movements. Was the man jerking off? This situation was getting way, way too crazy.

When Nogales finally ventured a glance into the rearview mirror he saw the thick barrel of a silencer pointed at his head. Cold steel kissed his ear, then exploded.

Suicide is so tragic.

✳

A silver Town Car pulled up next to Nogales' SUV. The driver jumped out and rushed to open doors for Alvarez. Calmly, he slid into the back seat next to Cero, a large mound of a man wearing a Rams football parka and a matching flat top baseball cap.

"Tonight's business in *el Norte*'s finished, Lieutenant Cero. Now back to Guerrero, and we'll watch what begins to unfold up here."

The car melted into the mist.

✳

Bud Martinez checked his watch and thanked the temps for their help. At almost 1:00 A.M. they lined up to clock out. A melting pot of blue-collar Angelinos, all were seemingly anxious to be on their way across the vast metro area to places as scattered as a shotgun blast.

As the last workers slogged across the parking lot toward their cars and trucks, Martinez slipped on a khaki camo parka and grabbed his cigs. He was really burning through them tonight. He wandered outside to the rail platform as the heavily burdened train strained to pull out of the station and lumber toward the San Joaquin Valley. Taking a deep drag and holding the smoke in his lungs for a long moment, Martinez ambled past the loading dock toward the silver SUV that he couldn't see, but knew was there. He wouldn't get too close, just close enough to make out the slumped figure in the front seat and the splash of something dark on the driver's side window. He checked his watch again, then dialed 9–1–1.

Thanks to his cousin, Cero, it had been a $2,500 night, just to look the other way. If he played his cards right, maybe his daughter could afford to go to USC after all. And maybe there could be an ultra high-def curved screen TV in his family room to boot.

CHAPTER 8

Lucy tossed and turned. Sleep was a slippery fish that she couldn't hang on to. Back in her Santa Monica condo, a few blocks from the Main Street business district and steps to the sand, she stared at night shadows that played across the high ceiling. Her breath came fast and beads of sweat dampened her face. Caught in the grip of an old and tenacious nightmare, she thrashed helplessly. Lucy tried to will her dreams to fine days riding horses through the chaparral with the dogs yapping ahead on the trail but the other recollection was too strong.

Her father loved that lipstick red car. It flew over back roads, a blur of unnatural color against the amber landscape.

"Daddy, you're going too fast!" Lucy called out. Her hair raged around her head, lashing her face.

"Lucia's already a back-seat driver," he said,

laughing. A pro soccer player and the son of a Norwegian diplomat, Nordic blue eyes flashed at her in the rearview mirror. Those eyes were hers, too.

The old Mustang convertible was a great automobile but the shocks were a little on the rough side. It shuddered over a patch of cracks and potholes. Lucy felt uncomfortably vulnerable riding in an open car without being strapped in. In school, she learned that you should always wear your seatbelt. But her father had restored the vehicle to historically accurate, pristine 1967 condition, which didn't include seat belts.

Daddy cranked up the radio, vintage Beach Boys blasting, as the family began their ascent from along the cool, dappled creek into the bright, burned hills of a Southern California August. Riding in the back of that shiny vintage machine, the scent of dry grass, sweet sycamore, and creek willow filled Lucy's head. Warm air, interspersed with feathery rivulets of coolness, whispered across her sunburned skin. Her face was a sunflower turning toward the light.

Through the oak-dotted countryside just north of Santa Barbara, they zoomed down the two-lane highway on their way to their home in the Santa Ynez valley. It was the golden hour between daylight and dusk in horse and wine country. Red-tailed hawks rode lazy thermals as the sun dropped toward the horizon. Even before Lucy had ever picked up a camera, this light inspired her.

She glanced over at her brother Jon Erik Vega Arnesen, called JonJon by the family. Just six years old, he nursed a blueberry-blue Slurpee and hummed along off-key to the classic "Little Deuce Coupe." For a change, his freckle-nosed face reflected sweetness and serenity, not his usual pain-in-the-butt mischief.

Their father had one hand on the steering wheel and the other tight around their mother's smooth, tanned shoulders. They laughed, leaned into each other and whispered like teenagers. Father gazed at their mother with such naked adoration that it sometimes made Lucy uneasy. She couldn't imagine having someone look at her like that. It was wonderful and frightening and fascinating.

Her mother stuck her tongue in daddy's ear and laughed teasingly. Sometimes, even at the tender age of eight-and-a-half, Lucy felt so much older than either of her parents.

JonJon rolled his eyes and said, "So gross," then took a noisy sip of his drink through the jumbo straw.

"Beyond gross," Lucy added, grimacing.

When "California Girls" began to play, Lucy's mother, Theresa Maria de la Vega Arnesen, stood up in the front seat of the car and sang along at the top of her lungs. Her face radiated pure joy, her head back, dark wavy hair flying wildly, her arms outstretched to seize every inch of life. It was in moments like these that Lucy understood why no one could stay irritated at her for long.

Her dad looked up at her mother, grinning, pushing the accelerator. A bug splattered across the windshield. The Slurpee flew out of her brother's hands. He screamed. The gravel truck pulled out from the side road.

Lucy remembered her mother rising into the golden sky. She lifted heavenward, sandals falling away, her brown toes with red-polished nails pointed like a ballet dancer, and her pale yellow skirt billowed, gauzy as a parachute. Into the air Theresa rose, like an angel, and Lucy followed—Wendy trailing Peter Pan.

Lucy began having this dream soon after the firemen had found her, fifty feet down the road from the accident site up in an oak tree, impaled on a branch. They almost didn't see her but finally heard her whimper. Afraid that pulling her off the branch would release the pressure that kept her from bleeding out, the firefighters cut off the limb and loaded her into the ambulance with the branch still sticking out of her stomach.

Her brother was on the side of the road. They covered him with a blue sheet the color of the sky. Her father had been run over by the gravel truck. He was unrecognizable. Her mother lay crumpled on the yellow line that split the road. Lucy saw it all. A sheet snapped then settled over her body like a cloud.

Damn, she didn't want to be plagued by these constant debilitating thoughts again. For years she had struggled to contain her anxiety. At about fifteen years old she became violently phobic, terrified of riding in a car or flying in an airplane. Therapy, the hardest work she'd ever done, had helped her cope. Months in a treatment center helped her turn the corner. She was diagnosed with post-traumatic stress disorder dating back to the accident that wiped out her whole family and left her in that tree, skewered like a marshmallow on a stick, waiting for the turkey vultures, watching the ants come and go across the leathery green oak leaves.

Lucy sunk deeper into the covers, willing herself to calm down, to let the anxiety roll away like the dark wave that it was. She wouldn't let it drown her again. She had beaten the riptide before. She'd damn well do it again. Just a little anxiety pill was all she needed. She glanced at the clock. Three hours and she'd be at work. Exhausted, she fell into an uneasy sleep with shards of images piercing the blackness.

CHAPTER 9

A long caravan of cars, SUVs, pickups, tractors, and news vans filed slowly along Interstate 5 into the San Joaquin Valley. Blowing rain with intermittent pockets of hail pelted their vehicles. Their windshield wipers beat out an erratic mix of cadences. Lucy reached into her pocket for a couple Advil.

The Weather Channel had reported record-setting low temperatures. Snow was piling up in the mountains surrounding the highway. Come spring that would be a good thing for the chronically drought-ridden southwest. Today, however, it sucked.

From the KLAK-TV news van, Lucy looked out across the muddy gray landscape toward the site of the morning's assignment. Dawn had broken an hour ago, yet the sky only managed to brighten about an f-stop. That wasn't much.

"The details on the story we're supposed to cover seem kind of sketchy," Lucy said.

Ray Truckee sat clutching the steering wheel, muttering about how badly Southern Californians drove in the rain. He rocked to a tune on his iPod and stroked his abundant beard.

Riding shotgun, Beatrice pulled her long black Donna Karan winter coat tight around her legs. "All we know," she said, "is something came across the wire late last night about cattle having been poisoned with some kind of neurotoxin-type pesticide. Thousands, maybe tens of thousands, have been contaminated."

"Oh my God, that's horrible," Lucy said, eyes squinting painfully at the picture in her head. "How'd it happen?"

"Got nothing on that yet. Guess we'll find out soon," Bea said.

Ernie had fallen asleep next to Lucy and was listing seriously in her direction. She rescued a stainless steel commuter coffee cup from his hand.

Truckee shouted at the decibel people wearing earphones, or are half-deaf, think is reasonable. "Rumor has it the governor's going to put in an appearance."

"The governor?" Lucy chewed on her lip. What a stroke of good fortune. It would save her a trip to Sacramento and maybe weeks of trying to wrangle a few minutes of his precious time. She wanted to see Governor Scanlon's eyes when she talked to him. It had been almost two weeks since her uncle's death and Sheriff Mortenson still wouldn't return her calls.

Lucy put Ernie's coffee cup in a holder. He was snoring against her shoulder and smelled vaguely of talcum powder and spit-up.

Bea looked back at Ernie and chuckled. "If he thinks babyhood is hard, try having one in high school and one in middle school who thinks she's ready for college. And Truckee has four of these creatures!"

Truckee nodded. "Dazed and confused is my parenting style—that's when I'm having a good day." The van slid sideways on the slick road. Truckee mumbled a string of curses then went back to humming along with whatever played on his iTunes.

Bea turned intently toward Lucy. "I don't know why you insist on being here, Miss Lucy." She offered up a seriously concerned overbearing-mother look. "People need a few weeks just to be able to function after a loved one's death."

"I'm okay, I'm functioning fine—so stop worrying."

"You're putting on a great show but in the last week you covered the homicides of those girls, then an accidental drowning, and now this. Could be that those sweet-eyed cows are going to be exterminated this morning. Ain't gonna be pretty, girlfriend. Could even be hideous. You love animals. Lobbying for the worst assignment isn't going to help you cope."

Lucy fidgeted in her seat. She pulled Ernie's cold coffee out of the cup holder, took a swig and grimaced.

"Take some time off," Bea continued. "Go to Hawaii, or, I hear Tahiti's awesome. Meet a wind-surfing instructor and make sure he looks like that former football player with the big hair—Troy Polamalu. Remember him? Maybe he has a brother. Island Air has some awesome rates."

Lucy slumped in her seat. She didn't want to hear it.

She was not the type to be cured by a vacation.

Bea continued. "You have nothing to prove to anybody. You finished paying your dues a long time ago."

"I couldn't agree more," Truckee said. He pulled out his ear buds. "Devil with the Blue Dress On" leaked through.

"Hey, enough, you two," Lucy replied. "What doesn't kill you, makes you stronger, right? I'll be fine. Staying home or being alone on a remote island sounds depressing as hell."

Lucy saw Bea slide a skeptical look toward Truckee then she returned to sitting studiously in the front seat, making last-minute notes to herself.

Lucy ran her fingers over the sleek, high-tech camera at her feet and tried to focus on the work ahead. Struggling to move her thoughts away from the rock-heavy sadness that weighed her down, she pressed her warm hand against the cold window glass and watched the water vapor form an outline. Then she wiped it away. If only she could erase the image of her uncle in the car full of water as easily.

Ernie snorted and woke with a violent start. "Oh! Uh, sorry, I must have dozed for a minute." He scrubbed his hands across his stubbled whiskers.

"Try forty-five. Chainsaw snoring in my ear all the way," Lucy said. She handed him the cup of cold coffee she had rescued earlier.

Ernie chugged it down then poured himself another hit from a thermos.

"Want some, anybody?" he asked, to negative responses.

At last, they arrived at the site. Truckee pulled the van into a mucky parking area delineated by faded orange traffic cones. The crackle of plowed corn stalks sounded beneath the wheels.

"Okay. I'm out of here," Bea said as they eased to a stop. "Let's get this fast before we freeze to death. Fast, Vargas—that means you. You're supposed to be the leader of this charge. You awake now, little daddy?"

"I was just resting my eyes." They were red and watery as he put his contacts in. The broken, single-lensed eyeglasses were nowhere in sight.

"Yeah, uh-huh." Bea pulled her black beret on tight, then jumped from the van and slammed the door closed behind her.

A blast of damp frosty air invaded the warm cab. Ernie lingered in his seat, sucking up the tepid coffee. His nose was running and the tissue he wiped it with was disintegrating from overuse.

"Ready, Lucerino?" Truckee asked.

"Yep, ready to rock and roll." They made a dynamite team, Lucy on camera and Truckee on sound, Vargas field-producing, and Bea reporting. She wished they could work together as a unit more often.

Truckee pulled back the side door to the van and the full force of wind-driven sleet stung Lucy's face. She tucked her head down and crawled out after Ernie, hauling her cold aluminum tripod, a gear bag, and the camera.

Truckee grabbed his digital recorder and a couple of microphones. "Come on, Vega," he said, giving her a gentle nudge. "We have work to do, baby cakes."

A half dozen olive-drab National Guard trucks

pulled alongside the fenced-in livestock. Clutching high-powered automatic weapons in their hands, guardsmen and women jumped from the back of their vehicles, their faces blank. Boots crunched across the ground.

To the west of the parking area, thousands of head of cattle were packed tight into makeshift stockyards. The animals groaned nervously and struggled to move. As their breath steamed in the wintry air, the scent of fear and excrement was pervasive. A panicked heifer with dirty icicles dangling from her chin tried to break away and clamber across the backs of the others. The commotion was wild but momentary until she fell down into the herd amid the masses again.

The animals sensed danger. The desperation their eyes conjured the feeling of dread Lucy had been trying to suppress since Uncle Henry's accident. Maybe Bea was right, maybe she had compulsively covered one too many tragedies. Maybe she did need a vacation in some warm pastel place with a Samoan linebacker.

The soldiers loaded their ammo and Lucy braced for another horrific day.

CHAPTER 10

Bea stood with a farm couple near an aging Ford truck. Lucy and Truckee hustled to join them and prep for the interview. Other news teams were beginning to pull onto the scene so competition for coverage would be ramping up. Weather conditions were getting tougher by the minute. The wind slashed and the animals bleated— the sound was plaintive and disconcerting.

"Mr. and Mrs. Davis, this is our crew, Ray Truckee, and Lucy Vega," Bea said.

"Pleasure, ma'am," Truckee said.

Lucy nodded.

Claudia Davis, in her early forties, was a fragile-looking woman with lank hair and pale eyes. She peered out from the hood of a long, dark raincoat, its hem splashed with mud. Her husband, Ned, wore an Allis-Chalmers baseball cap with blue earmuffs, coveralls, and a down vest. Holding hands, they struggled not to look over at the cattle.

Bea directed Lucy and Truckee to prep for the interview next to one of the National Guard vehicles. She flashed a warning shake of the head at a San Diego reporter who had begun to circle their set-up like a shark ready for dinner. Truckee huddled protectively over his recorder while he put a new windscreen on his mic. Lucy secured her camera to the tripod.

In seconds, all were ready to go. "Rolling, Lucy? Truck?" Bea asked.

"Rolling."

Ernie pointed a finger at Bea, signaling for her to begin.

"Mr. Davis, you said that none of the State regulatory agencies ever contacted you to tell you that the Dyna-Feed, your livestock's food supplement, had been contaminated with a highly toxic, carcinogenic pesticide. Is that true?" Bea's voice was strong and dispassionate.

"They contacted us," Ned Davis replied, "but not for more than a week and a half. It was too late by then."

"What do you mean—too late?" Bea asked.

His face darkened. "Almost two-thirds of us Central California farmers give our stock Dyna-Feed. Now, almost everybody in the state's been drinking poisoned milk and eating contaminated burgers. God only knows what the long-term health effects will be."

"Jesus," Lucy said under her breath, thinking of all the lattes she had consumed in the last few weeks. This was looking to be bigger than any of them had figured. No wonder Governor

Scanlon was on his way. This thing was going to blow

up. By noon, livestock poisoning in California would be the biggest story in the nation.

"And Governor Scanlon knew about it and didn't do anything—just sat on it!" Mrs. Davis added in a voice stronger than her diminutive frame would indicate.

"How many head of cattle do you stand to lose?" Bea continued.

"Everything," Mr. Davis said stoically. "We have over fifteen-hundred head. We were one of the last family-owned, non-corporate dairies in the area. Everything we have is invested in those animals. Including our herd and all our neighbors'—must be thousands and thousands out there. I hear we're going to lose ten times that across the state. What a waste."

Mrs. Davis shifted nervously from foot to foot. Increasingly agitated, she pulled away from her husband and stepped toward Bea. She suddenly began screaming at Beatrice who managed to keep herself calm. Lucy kept the camera rolling; she glanced at Truckee who nodded agreement.

"I want some answers and I don't hear you people asking the questions! What I don't understand is how this could have happened! I mean how does this poison, this Parathion insecticide, get mixed into feed supplied to the whole damn state? How? There are supposed to be regulatory commissions, inspectors."

She shuddered and she began to sob.

"Claudia," Ned Davis pleaded, "the situation's not this lady's fault." He put his arm around her narrow shoulders.

Shaking off her husband, Mrs. Davis wiped her wan face and moved almost nose to nose with Bea. "The governor sits up there in Sacramento telling us we got to kill our animals . . . well then, who's gonna pay to feed my family and keep us from going bankrupt this winter? Who's gonna put my kids through college now? The compensation the insurance company offered us is a goddamned joke and it'll probably take years before this is settled and we see a dime. All the governor says is 'he's sorry, it was a tragic accident.' Well, it's our life he's talking about!"

Big tears rolled down her face again. She wiped them away with the sleeve of her coat.

"Lucy, Truckee, I need you right now," Ernie Vargas shouted. He came hustling toward them, the pages of his notebook flapping in the wind. "Hate to interrupt, so sorry, but I need you in that chopper. Pronto." He pointed to a helicopter coming in fast beneath low clouds.

Lucy's stomach lurched; she was not prepared for a flight. No anti-anxiety meds, no time to psyche herself up. She could feel her skin begin to dampen.

The county fire department's Huey loomed larger, a splotch of red and yellow above a gray, monochrome landscape. It began to circle, preparing for landing nearby on a muddy patch of what might have been a field of tomatoes.

Visibly infuriated by the interruption of her interview, Bea gritted her teeth before turning to the Davises and apologizing for having to cut it short. Mr. Davis followed his wife as she stormed away toward their pickup truck. The San Diego reporter jogged after them.

Bea stomped over to Ernie, her microphone aimed at him like a gun. "How could you do this? I was getting some great stuff!"

"Listen, Bea—that bird'll be going up and down fast. The governor's inside. We gotta move," he replied. "Immediately—tech crews only."

Bea lowered the mic and adjusted her hat. "It really was great stuff."

"Scanlon's here? Now?" Lucy asked. She quickly unlatched her camera from the tripod. This was the opportunity she had been waiting for. No panic attack or phobia was getting in the way of finding out what the governor knew about her uncle's murder.

CHAPTER 11

"The weather's getting worse. Gonna be crazy up there." Vargas danced around, hugging himself to keep his jacket tight. At least he had found an old, stained KLAK stocking cap to cover his balding head.

"Calm down, Vargas, you've had too much caffeine." Lucy took off after Truckee who loped toward the oncoming helicopter. Bea ran up beside her.

"Okay. Now, girlfriend, the governor's here. He's going up with you." Bea pulled her knit beret down over her ears.

"I'm well aware of that," Lucy said.

"I know, I know, but you tell that man we want to talk to him as soon as you're down."

"Okay, okay. Now move out of my way or I'm gonna miss the bus." She pushed past Bea and jogged toward their ride, camera tight against her chest.

"Get 'em first! By the balls, if you have to! Don't let those hick upstate crews elbow us out. And the secretary of agriculture just arrived. Get him too. All right?"

Lucy flashed a thumbs-up but didn't look back.

Fleeing the storm of swirling, stinging rain propelled by the incoming chopper's rotor blades, Bea joined Vargas who was mooching a donut and, hopefully, something decaffeinated from a group of National Guard officers.

Lucy, Truckee, and other news teams waited as the yellow and red Huey, a well-maintained veteran from the Vietnam War era, began to descend. Word was, the governor's brother had been a chopper pilot in 'Nam and these birds were known as the best transpo around for nasty conditions. Equipped with a big, aluminum water tank for firefighting attached to its belly, it had been upgraded to accommodate extra-heavy loads. She'd been in this one once before and recalled that it had ten available seats plus two on the floor at the open door. Would be like the running of the bulls to grab the best spots.

The chopper lightly bounced to a landing on its skids. The rotors slowed to a dull, whomping idle. The sound and motion triggered a feeling of nausea in Lucy's gut. She breathed slowly to keep her anxiety in check.

A co-pilot disembarked. He scurried beneath the downdraft, shoulders hunched. "Give us a minute, folks," he shouted and motioned the waiting news crews back away from the craft. They moved in even closer. Rain and debris from the fields stung eyes and faces.

In a khaki LACFD jumpsuit, the co-pilot jogged over shake hands with a fortyish, sandy-haired man who had just arrived on the scene in a silver Ford Explorer with an Enterprise car rental license plate holder. Scruffy beard and mustache, the guy looked ruggedly handsome in a shearling coat and worn cowboy boots. He was the star of some gritty Western stuck in with a bunch of newsies in bulky raingear and politicians in gray overcoats. Where did she know this cowboy from? The flier escorted him to the chopper so he was obviously some big deal.

As Truckee passed her an extra camera battery to stuff into her pocket, Lucy recognized the man. The beard initially disguised him. Michael Burleson was probably one of the most successful news correspondents on the job. He had worked for CNN for years, and now was directing his own documentaries. Word on the street was that he was thrown out of CNN for undisclosed "personal issues." That was usually shorthand for addiction problems or other forms of self-destructive behavior that could impact ratings.

"Isn't that Michael Burleson?" Truckee asked in a stage whisper. "I think his picture was in Newsweek a couple months ago. I saw one of his pieces on PBS about child soldiers in West Africa. Was good."

"I wonder what he's doing here."

"The facial hair doesn't do much for him." Truckee plucked at his own full, red beard. "Isn't he usually in Iraq, or Syria, or one of those war zones?"

Lucy bounced impatiently on her toes as more National Guard trucks pulled into the area. "Starting to look a hell of a lot like a war zone right here." She hugged her camera closer.

Truckee was the first to make a break for the chopper

and jump in, Lucy at his side. She stumbled in the slick mud. Her hood fell back and her wavy dark hair flew everywhere, obscuring her vision. From somewhere above, a hand reached and pulled her out of the hammering downwash from the rotor blades. She gave Truckee a grateful nod and then retied her ponytail.

The helicopter was loading up fast. Lucy's glance immediately moved to Governor Scanlon and the rotund secretary of agriculture seated next to him. She took a deep breath and slid in across from the governor. His slim, pasty-faced aide gave her a disapproving look which she returned with an equally disapproving look. This was not the best place for a private discussion, but it could be her only chance in lieu of waiting days for an appointment, only to have it canceled or rescheduled.

"Governor Scanlon, how are you?" Lucy said, conversationally. She wanted him to feel open, not defensive.

"I've been better, Ms. Vega. How are you, my dear? I am so sorry about your uncle. He was a dear friend, one of the finest." He patted her arm—it felt like a dismissal. She would not be dismissed.

Lucy leaned in close. Scanlon squirmed in his seat.

"Thank you, sir, for your kind words at the funeral." The rotor blades pounded louder. "And I'm doing all right, most of the time, thanks for asking."

"Glad to hear it. And how's the rest of the KLAK crew this morning?" he said, shifting focus to the hulking sound man fitting a telescoping pole together on the floor.

"Freezing my butt off," Truckee grumbled, barely audible. "And where the hell are the earphones?"

Lucy bulldozed over Scanlon's attempt to divert her. "Governor, we'd like to talk to you right after this ride," she said, voice insistent. "Bea Middleton'll kill me if you say no, and you and I both realize that I've got to survive here. After all, I'm the only one who doesn't back-light your bald spot."

The governor ran his hand through his thinning hair. "A favor for which I shall always be in your debt, Ms. Vega. And I join you in wanting to keep Ms. Middleton happy."

"Thank you, sir," Lucy said, a smile flickered on her lips. "Secretary Freund, it would be an honor to speak with you, too."

"My pleasure," he said, with rote congeniality.

Lucy leaned into Governor Scanlon again, just inches from his droopy pink ear. He shifted in his seat, she pressed closer. "Sir, I also need to talk with you about a personal matter, regarding my uncle's death. I think you were the last one to talk to him before he died . . . or maybe as he died. And sir, I think he may have been murdered."

The governor's eyes widened. "Oh?" he said, beginning to cough. "No, no." He patted her arm again. "Henry said he was skidding. Then I heard a crash. That's all, Lucy. I'm sorry. So sorry."

"That's all?" She didn't believe him and his face said he knew it.

"Yes, my dear. That's all. Then I dialed 9–1–1. It was awful."

Lucy felt a stab of deep disappointment and anger. So much for openness. What had she been hoping for? Maybe the truth. She wasn't going to discover it here.

Her eyes searched Scanlon's and he looked away.

"Then why was L.A. County Homicide and the head of the regional counterterrorism task force at the scene of my uncle's death?"

The governor didn't offer an answer.

"I will find out what happened, you know," Lucy said, now shouting above the whine of the engines. She patted the governor's arm in return. "You can bet on it."

Lucy turned to take the primo place Truckee had saved for her in the chopper's open doorway. Burleson slid into where she had just been sitting, across from the governor.

The rotors accelerated as the bird powered up, preparing to rise. Earphones were finally handed out to all passengers and the camera was back on her shoulder. Lucy compartmentalized her pain and shut the door on it. For now.

CHAPTER 12

Truckee squeezed his bulk into the spot next to her. "Strap in, Lucy," he insisted with the nod of his head.

She sighed. "Listen, as much as I hate going up, I've been in these things so many times—the belt makes me feel, kind of, trapped." *Very trapped.*

She could hear the other crews chatting on the same channel.

"Lucy, trapped or not, strap in. This'll be a rough ride. I don't want to lose you. A good jolt and that flimsy little so-called safety rope across the door won't do much for you."

Truckee gave her a determined look that precluded argument. She sighed and awkwardly strapped a belt from the floor across her lap. Her legs dangled in thin air. She flashed on her mother flying up into space and of the white sheet covering her body on the roadside.

She tightened the belt and chastised herself for ignoring common safety. Anxiety squeezed her chest. Lucy rummaged in her pocket and found the meds that she'd begun to take again. She twisted off the plastic cap and popped two into her mouth. The taste was bitter but she choked them down.

The helicopter lifted off. After hovering above the ground for several seconds, it dropped back down with a springy rebound and paused as a small Cessna airplane, wings rocking like a teeter-totter, made an insane landing on the road the crews had just driven in on. It braked to a stop, fishtailing dangerously close to the chopper. Lucy could hear the Huey's pilot cursing, even with her earphones on.

"That's one stupid asshole of a pilot," Truckee said.

A man carrying a camera ran from the Cessna, motioning wildly.

Lucy and Truckee looked at each other in disgust.

"Oh, shit," was all Lucy could say.

"We should've known what fool would be flying a plane like that," Truckee said. "Never could figure out how he could afford that thing on a cameraman's salary."

An athletic man in his late thirties, Gary Mercer jumped into the chopper and immediately began pushing for an advantageous spot among the already tightly packed passengers. Lucy felt a hot pang of anger. She swallowed hard.

Dark-haired and handsome in a vacant sort of way, he wore tight, stylishly torn blue jeans and a black leather bomber jacket. Jamming himself in behind Lucy, he swung his mini-cam recklessly onto his shoulder. Truckee eyed him with disdain. Lucy didn't bother to acknowledge him, despite that fact that the crowded quarters had him pressing against her. His touch made her skin crawl. He reeked of marijuana.

"Well, what fucking luck," Mercer growled. "Lucy Vega has managed to get in front of me . . . again."

"I'm surprised you managed to crawl out of your drug-induced stupor to even show up here so early in the morning," Lucy shot back. She refused to look at him.

The Huey lurched and bounced, struggling with turbulence. Lucy's stomach tightened as they finally took flight.

"So sorry to hear about your uncle," Mercer said. "Shouldn't have been out during that nasty weather. Accidents are bound to happen to careless people."

The comment felt ominous. Lucy could feel heat rising in her face and Mercer's breath hot on the back of her neck. He hunkered in tight. She tried to push him away. Haunting scenes from the night he was on the ledge strobed through her mind.

"Get anybody else fired lately, Lucille? Fucked anyone else's career?"

Lucy sizzled. "You never could take responsibility for anything—blame everybody but yourself. Grow the hell up, Gary."

"Okay, you two, chill. Right now." Truckee warned. "And back the fuck off, Mercer."

The helicopter began its slow, bumpy circle over the stockyards. Temporary chain link fences surrounded black pits that gaped like open wounds. The gale continued to buffet the chopper. Lucy struggled to keep her anxiety from spinning as high as the rotor blades. She despised flying but she despised Gary Mercer more, and that said a lot.

What did he mean about Uncle Henry being careless? Mercer knew the inference would drive her crazy. It was just a stupid, innocuous comment. Fuck Mercer. A master manipulator, he lived to cause havoc. This time she wouldn't play.

Lucy looked toward the governor—he was in deep conversation with Burleson, evidently on another frequency. What were they up to? The cowboy war reporter glanced over his shoulder. His look was hard and arrogant.

Shifting her attention back to the assignment at hand, Lucy steadied the camera on her shoulder. She opened her lens wide then drew in closer. The scene below was surreal. Automatic gunshots rang out, barely audible against the pounding rumble of the helicopter. Rows of cows began to fall and drop into the ditches. Moving wildly away from the front lines, the animals' mouths wrenched open in anguished bleats. Red explosions splattered across their light hides.

"Jesus Christ," Lucy whispered. Taking a deep, shaky breath, she went on recording the extermination. Bea had been right, it was hideous.

Lucy tried to capture it all, all of the horror and the struggle. It was one of those times when her brain became the camera, flowing out into the pits, feeling the warm bodies turning cold. As she focused on the confused face of a Holstein calf, its eyes suddenly erupted and became unrecognizable holes oozing thick, reddish-black tears.

All across the field below, wranglers with cattle prods forced the wailing livestock to the crest of the trenches. National Guard troopers sprayed round after round of automatic gunfire into the herds as they staggered over the edge into their mass graves. Farmers and farm families stood together on the outskirts of the stockyards, sickened by what they were witnessing. Many openly wept. How could this have happened?

The helicopter continued to be tossed unnervingly. One of the news crew members from the San Luis Obispo station vomited loudly out the door into the wind. Everybody flinched, bracing to have the contents of the man's stomach blown back into the cabin. Lucy covered her lens. Mercifully, the puke was sucked upward.

Then, what felt like a gun blast cracked into Lucy's skull.

Falling forward, her first thought was that she'd been caught by a stray bullet. Her second thought was that if Truckee hadn't insisted on the safety strap, she would have been out of the chopper. Lucy's eyes blurred. She struggled to hang onto her camera and not pass out.

Truckee grabbed Lucy with one hand, and Mercer by the neck with the other. "You sonofabitch," he practically spat. "You hit her!"

"It was an accident!"

"Bullshit! You just can't get over the fact that you were canned and she's head photog now, can you?"

"She'd been sucking up to that asshole producer, Max Wedner, for months, and probably even—"

"Shut up, Mercer!" Lucy shouted, furious. The effort sent knives through her skull. "You're the only one who's fucked anybody around here. Now get away from me!" The outburst made her head vibrate like a gong.

"I see you anywhere near her again, I'll kill you. Understand me?" Roughly, Truckee shoved Mercer away. Barely managing to avoid landing on the laps of the governor and his aides, he glared at the big man with hatred.

Turning to Lucy, Truckee put his hand on her shoulder. "You all right? He got you in the back of the head with his lens shade."

"Yeah, I'm okay," Lucy answered weakly. She hoisted the camera back on her shoulder and kept it rolling even though her vision wouldn't focus. "For a second there I thought I got nailed by a bullet."

"Shit, girl, that might've scored you a raise!"

Lucy groaned and weakly whacked Truckee.

Finally, the chopper began to descend. Lucy's stomach lurched. The passengers held on tight as the bird made a rocky landing. Breathing a great collective sigh of relief to be safely down, the news crews disembarked in record time. Mercer pushed by everyone and jogged toward his Cessna. A crowd immediately gathered around the governor and the secretary but Bea was there, guiding them firmly over to where she wanted her interview.

Slowly collecting her gear, Lucy struggled for balance, her vision still unclear. When she didn't follow right away, Truckee called back to her.

"You sure you're okay? Want some help?"

"No. I'll be right there. Need some space for a just quick sec, that's all."

Truckee hesitated but then turned away and proceeded toward the killing grounds where Bea was organizing the interview. Backhoes were beginning to rev up to push dirt into trenches filling up with cattle.

CHAPTER 13

The extermination continued. The air was pink and smelled of blood. Lucy could taste it on her tongue. Crawling out of the Huey, she attempted to follow Truckee. Ten steps and she began to weave. Staggering, she caught herself. She managed a few more steps and went down. Something was very wrong.

Michael Burleson dashed over from the helicopter. As Lucy struggled to sit up, her hood fell back. Rubbing her aching head, she came away with a glove covered in blood.

"I'm going to call an ambulance," he insisted. "I saw what happened up there. You're probably concussed."

"No!" Lucy held out her arms as if she was trying to stop herself from falling off a cliff. "First I have an interview to do. They're waiting for me."

"But you're in no shape—"

"You've never worked hurt?" Lucy struggled to focus on his face but it was only a blur. "This is the San Joaquin Valley, not Aleppo, but I'm still a professional, Mr. Burleson, just like you."

"I didn't mean to imply you weren't," he said.

"I'm fine."

Burleson offered her a hand up. She hesitated but accepted it because she couldn't manage to stand otherwise. When he tried to take the camera, Lucy clutched it protectively. Seized by a blinding stab of pain that took her breath away, she fell against him for a moment until she could steady herself. He grabbed her gear bag and tripod. She didn't protest.

Turning toward her colleagues gathered with the governor, she drove herself forward. "Come on, faster. You're holding up this whole thing," Lucy said.

Burleson stopped, appearing ready to toss the equipment into the cornfield but when she staggered again, he grabbed her arm and kept her from falling.

Lucy caught Burleson's concerned glance toward her crew. He knew they were unaware of what was going on with her. Sighing and shrugging his shoulders, he left her gear on a tarp next to Truckee's sound recorder.

"Hey, big sound guy," he shouted to Truckee. "Take care of your wounded."

Lucy heard him curse under his breath as he walked away. A group of reporters spotted him and began a barrage of questions.

She made it to the edge of the pits. The sound of automatic gunfire and death screams of the sickened cattle drilled into her head like an ice pick. Bea, Ernie, the governor, and Secretary Freund stood huddled together in the bitter wind.

"Okay. Are we ready?" Bea asked, voice impatient.

Lucy tightened the camera onto the tripod. *Damn edge's sharp as a knife*

"Truck, how're your sound levels?" Ernie asked.

"It's as good as it's gonna get. Let's go," he answered.

"Luce? You with us?"

"Rolling," she said.

Bea jumped right in. "Governor, you've been accused of risking the health of the population of an entire state by acting slowly and indecisively under pressure from the dairy and beef council lobbies. Why didn't we hear about this poisoning a week ago? Why are contaminated products just being taken off supermarket shelves now?"

"Well, Ms. Middleton," the governor shifted uncomfortably, "first of all, I deny that the agricultural industry in any way called for inaction on this matter. But before we could take the kind of drastic steps we're taking today, we had to make absolutely certain that the scope of the contamination warranted destroying tens of thousands of animals around the state, and the livelihoods of our already hurting farm families."

"I've been notified that the Republican leadership is asking for you to step down—"

"Governor, we're running behind schedule" an aide insisted. He darted around like a persistent gnat.

"We're all victims here, myself and my family members included, Ms. Middleton. I have done everything possible to protect our citizens and I will . . ."

Rocked by a wave of nausea, Lucy stepped away from her camera as it continued to record. The governor's voice faded into the wind. The secretary's words whirled around and blew away as well.

Stunned and disoriented, she gazed across the pit filling with dead and dying cattle, then forced herself back to the viewfinder. Lucy's camera was no longer on the governor and Bea. She was looking into the bloody eye of that brown-and-white Holstein calf. Blood was now streaming into Lucy's eyes as well. The sound of Mercer's plane taking off faintly registered.

Slowly, her lens slid into an extreme close-up of the cow's syrupy, weeping socket. The eye became Uncle Henry's eye, staring up at her out of the murky green water. He called to her above riffs of gunfire. His screaming split her head like a hatchet. Then it was all quiet and blackness, just the echoing thud of something hitting the ground and shouting from somewhere far away.

CHAPTER 14

It was late morning when the chopper made its way in from the farming communities in the Central Valley and set down on a monstrous yellow X at the edge of the Santa Monica Airport. The Pacific Ocean glimmered less than a mile away as the sun broke free from the clouds. The temperature in the San Joaquin Valley had been thirty-five degrees as the rain changed to sleet. Santa Monica was a sunny seventy. The striped blades of the Huey finally beat to a halt but continued to pound in the heads of its sound-thrashed passengers.

Security personnel quickly ushered the governor and his colleagues off the craft toward a waiting lineup of limousines. Tearing across the tarmac with lights flashing, an ambulance screeched to a halt next to the helicopter. Scanlon turned to watch a semi-conscious Lucy Vega moved onto a gurney. Bea Middleton was at her side, directing the paramedics, to their obvious irritation. He would have his secretary check on her later in the day, the day that had already been a bloody horror.

A navy blue Caprice bearing an emblem identifying the occupants as agents of the federal government pulled up to the limo the governor had just climbed into. George Scanlon was immediately joined in the back seat by Mac McNeill, long-time friend, advisor, and CIA counterterrorism consultant. A short, stocky man, he had the high-strung, terrier-like bearing of a Marine drill sergeant. What remained of his yellowish hair was worn in a military-style buzz cut.

"George, I hear you've had quite a time." The two men usually thumped each other on the shoulders when they met, but not today. Scanlon drew back coolly, his eyes intense, the handshake perfunctory.

"I didn't expect to see you here quite so early, Mac."

"Got in from D.C. about a half hour ago. Figured I'd just wait for you and we could ride over to your field office together. Give us some extra time to talk."

The governor pulled off his fine cashmere gloves and twisted them into a ball. He pushed a button and the limousine privacy window rose between the driver and passengers.

"I'm being destroyed here, Mac! Alvarez and his terrorists are getting away with murder, and I'm fucking looking like the bad guy. Why? Why aren't you and your people jumping on this?"

"Because this methyl-parathion contamination looks like the perfect accident."

The governor's fists clenched. "Henry Vega is dead.

Now we have two perfect accidents?"

McNeill shrugged. "If there was any hard proof, anything at all . . ."

The governor's motorcade left the Santa Monica Airport tarmac and pulled onto Bundy Drive with a right onto Ocean Park.

"My friend and colleague has been murdered. And now my state's been poisoned. It's called terrorism, McNeill. That's what you're supposed to investigate, right? People will die from this contamination. Maybe not today, but next year, or in twenty years when the cancer starts. Just because the motherfuckers didn't blow up a bottle of anthrax in a subway doesn't mean it isn't every bit as bloody horrific. You should be all over this. And I'm being set up big time. Isn't that obvious?"

"I wish it were." McNeill loosened his red, white, and blue striped tie. "These bastards are good George, very good."

"But you heard the tape of my phone conversation with Vega. You saw the notes they fished out of his briefcase. Alvarez threatened me and *my people*. That includes my family, my friends, staff, and the citizens of this state. He's made it bloody personal," Scanlon said. "What's he going to try next? Big Hollywood-style fireworks in L.A. or the Bay Area *à la* Bin Laden at the World Trade Center? Then we'd see some scrambling, wouldn't we!"

"George, right now it's your word and inconclusive evidence. Wait—inconclusive is not the right word— there's *no* evidence. Zero, zilch, *nada*. But I believe you, and that's why I'm here. I'm really putting my butt on the line."

"That's your goddamned job! You're not doing me any favors." They had him by the goddamned short hairs. The governor punched the car door, then winced at the pain he caused himself.

McNeill shrugged his shoulders again and sighed. "The president will be coming out at the end of the week to view the damage and give the farmers a pep talk."

"Pep talk? That asshole. This isn't the damn Rose Bowl." Scanlon glanced briefly at the huge gold and ruby University of Alabama class ring on McNeill's stubby finger. He hated the SEC.

The limo driver slammed on the breaks and laid on the horn as a bearded guy in a Prius gave him the finger and slowly changed lanes.

"All right, George, bad choice of words. POTUS will qualify your farmers for disaster relief, low-interest loans, the whole ball o'wax. But, quite frankly, he thinks you're being paranoid and attention-grabbing because this is an election year."

"Attention-grabbing because my state has been devastated and my friend killed, with more deaths likely to come year after year, like a ticking clock? I'm telling you, Mac, Luis Alvarez is behind this. He runs the Guerrero heroin trade. The stuff moves faster than an In & Out drive-through around here. Only Afghanistan and Pakistan produce more of the shit worldwide."

"You may be right, George, but POTUS thinks you're going off the deep end, trying to blame it on some phantom Mexican terrorists who got the *cojones* to take on the State of California. Does sound a little bizarre, don't you agree?"

"Life *is* bizarre, bizarre as hell," the governor said.

"He's just scared shitless I'm going to run against him. He'd love to see me go down in flames."

"Yeah, he would. That's why you've got to cool it and stay quiet about Alvarez until we have something substantive to link him with Vega's death and this poisoning shit. *Capiche*, my man?"

The governor took off his glasses and wiped his eyes. They wouldn't stop watering. He was getting too old for this crap. His wife was right. He should hang it up after this term and move to Napa Valley. And on top of everything else, he was dying for a cigarette. "All right. So tell me what else you and your boys have found out about Alvarez besides his cartel connections. Henry was calling out his name when he got pushed off Kanan Road."

Scanlon's psychic vibes for a smoke must have been desperate, because, at that moment, McNeill pulled a pack of Winstons out of his pocket. He looked at George, glanced wistfully down at the cigarettes, and pushed them back into his pocket.

"Sorry, I forgot you'd quit."

"Gimme one or I'm going to throw you out of this goddamned limo," the governor snarled. His fingers curled and uncurled in anticipation as the CIA agent held open the pack and dug a lighter out of his coat pocket. The two toked up in the back seat like a couple of college kids surreptitiously smoking weed. Scanlon took a long, ecstatic drag and slowly exhaled. McNeill cracked the window for ventilation. Savoring the nicotine effect, Scanlon's hands stopped shaking and he began to settle down.

"Luis Alvarez was once a small-time Mexican official

with minor drug connections," MacNeill said. "Made the right friends, scared some important people and managed to bring disparate groups together into one cartel. Now he's made himself kind of an El Chapo meets Al Capone. Used to be about twenty indie black tar heroin providers in Guerrero. Alvarez took over all but five, so we think he controls production and distribution of that shit to half the U.S. That's billions of dollars."

"I think this is what Henry Vega was going to share details about just before he got killed," Scanlon said.

The agent nodded. "Alvarez wants it all, and he wants to tie up California more than anything."

"Shit." The governor gritted his teeth then filled his lungs with nicotine again. "Fucking drugs, including these cigs."

McNeill gave a thin smile and shrugged. "So the asshole was going about his business quietly until this vendetta started because you won't extradite his brother, Carlos."

"You're damn right I won't. Carlos Alvarez is gonna to deal with his crimes here, in our courts, in our prisons. If I'd sent him back to Tijuana, he'd be a free man. I can't live with that. So, what else do you have on Alvarez?"

"He's connected everywhere, but his core group is small. We don't know who they are, yet, but we do know an American is involved." McNeill rummaged through his briefcase and pulled out a thin file folder which he handed to the governor.

"Any idea who?"

The agent shook his head. "Still unclear on that."

Scanlon opened the folder, studied the contents, then quickly closed it again. "That's it? With all your resources, that is it?" He pinched the bridge of his nose and sighed. Took a final drag of his cigarette before dropping it into a paper cup of cold gas station coffee. It extinguished with a sizzle.

"So far, as I said, we don't have much. He's been very low profile."

"Mac, the guy's a fucking iceberg. Gotta be a lot more underneath the surface on him. I guarantee it," Scanlon said, his spirits lifted only slightly by the nicotine. He had expected more of a buzz.

"We're digging deep. We have people down there now but it's tough getting anywhere close to the man. That's why we need Burleson involved. We've got it all set up. And it's got to look squeaky clean."

"I've known Michael since he was in diapers. His older brother is still my closest friend. Lived across the street in Burbank. So whatever you got set up, you'd better take good care of him. He needs this job. He's in a rough patch, so don't fuck him over. Have you filled him in on everything?"

"The less he has to know, the safer he'll be," McNeill said. "He's going down there, supposedly under the auspices of public television to do a profile on his old friend, Father Juan Jesus de Anza, a Catholic priest who has some kind of social justice, alternative economy thing doing on."

"Yep, in Guerrero—same area Alvarez operates out of." Governor Scanlon gazed out the window as his gaggle of shiny vehicles crawled toward the 101.

McNeill continued. "Word is Alvarez is HQ'd somewhere in the southern foothills. Burleson'll feed back any information he might hear on Alvarez. It's very informal, low-key. He would reject the whole thing if he thought he'd be working for the CIA. But we'll have operatives down there keeping an eye on him every minute."

"Why don't I trust that?" Scanlon took a deep breath and pressed on his aching chest. If he made it through the day without having a full-blown coronary, he'd be lucky. "So, it's all off the record. I guess you and I aren't having this conversation," he finally said.

"Exactly. We're completely safe on this one, the press doesn't have a clue."

"Because there aren't clues? What bull. There's always shit out there floating around." The governor felt another twinge in his chest. Did the press know more than he thought they did? He wasn't at all comfortable with the fact that Lucy Vega discovered he'd been on the phone with her uncle seconds before he plunged into that Malibu creek. The 9–1–1 call was supposed to be classified. She was smart, tenacious, and clearly adored her uncle. They would have to watch her.

"As I've indicated, we've got to handle this carefully and unofficially for now," McNeill said.

"Yeah, I see where you're going, but I don't like it," the governor said.

"Claiming publicly that Mexican terrorists are responsible for the poisoning is only going to give the assholes everything they want. It would make your credibility look even more suspect than it already is. Plus, half of your constituents are of Hispanic descent. They don't want you trash-talking Mexico. They only want to hear you bashing the Russians or the Syrians right now. This just won't be good for you any way you look at it."

As the governor's motorcade turned the corner toward his Westwood offices, Scanlon looked through the dark, tinted window and rubbed the hand he'd punched into the car door. These assholes had him, for now. He could offer the people of California nothing but humiliating condolences. The poisoning chipped away at his psyche. He loved this state, yet he had unwittingly brought on such a tragedy. It had started with the Carlos Alvarez drug arrest.

Had he only guessed the enormity of their vengeance and the skill of their execution, would he have insisted on putting Luis Alvarez's little brother away for good?

CHAPTER 15

Michael Burleson had just arrived at the Bel Air Hotel. After the red-eye from Atlanta and the miserable morning in the Central Valley, he luxuriated in the balmy December evening in Los Angeles.

After finishing dinner in his fresh tan and white suite, compliments of the governor's office, he turned on the television to catch the late network news and was hit by the images of the early morning. Involuntarily, he winced at the memory. The gentle tap of a Mexican fan palm against his windowpane was replaced by the kinetic blast of automatic weapons.

"Residents of the state of California are facing a gruesome task this week." The reporter was the pretty, no-nonsense black woman from KLAK. "A highly carcinogenic pesticide called Parathion was accidentally mixed into food supplements used by farmers to feed their livestock in over seventy percent of the state's agricultural communities. Officially banned by the EPA a decade ago, significant traces of this chemical have already been found in supermarket dairy and beef products, all of which are being pulled from the shelves as I speak."

Michael stood, toppling a pile of magazines and correspondence he had placed precariously next to his armchair. He rummaged for the remote, turned off the sound, and continued to watch the broadcast images while pacing back and forth across the floor. Tractors shoveled dirt over the bodies of the dead and still-twitching cattle.

He thought of the woman photographer falling away from her camera into the pit among the animals. Her face was as white as a Holstein's and her coat was splattered with blood. He and the big sound man with the red beard had pulled her out and called an ambulance. The local EMT stabilized her enough to so she could make the trip via copter to Santa Monica where she lived.

"Michael, why did you turn the sound off? I wanted to hear it."

A stunning blonde, half his age, and a journalism student from Atlanta who was studying at USC, lay stretched across the sand-colored duvet. She wore a low-cut, purple sundress which she was slowly slipping out of. She rose and sat back on her heels, her pale pink nipples thrust seductively in Michael's direction.

The sight made him stop and catch his breath. He looked back at the TV set, feeling both aroused and irritated.

At that moment he became aware that his shoes,

socks, and pants were covered with mud and dried blood. Quickly, he removed his clothing and threw everything in a garbage basket next to the desk. The girl uttered a little wail of pleasure, thinking the demonstration was for her.

Fucking his brains out would put the images out of his mind. Lifting up the blonde, he threw her over his shoulder and spun her around. She screamed and laughed. She weighed about the same as the woman photographer. The governor said her name was Lucy Vega. With her dark hair, porcelain skin and perfect mouth, Lucy'd looked like goddamned Snow White lying amid the cattle. Steam rose from their mutilated bodies in the cold air.

The blonde wrapped her legs around Michael's hips and threw back her head. He drew down on her soft neck like a vampire. She moaned with pleasure as he pushed her up against the wall and entered her. He'd kill any almost fifty-year-old man who did anything like this to his twenty-year-old daughter. He was such a goddamn hypocrite. He hated being a user, and here he was again. For just a moment he'd feel like a kid himself—brand new and a million miles away from death, degeneration, and too many sound bites from the front lines of an insane world. Young girls didn't carry all the emotional baggage of past relationships gone bad or the failure with kids you hadn't been there for.

Later, Michael lay in bed, feeling utterly alone despite the young woman sleeping peacefully next to him. He knew he had to stop doing this, stop grasping for anything that would dull the pain, because it always came back, and worse. George Scanlon had offered him another chance, a chance to do a good story, to get launched back into the field he loved.

He couldn't blow it, not this time.

CHAPTER 16

Lucy's bed was on the window side of a double room in the newly refurbished Santa Monica Community Hospital. She sat impatiently and looked out across the city. Like a polished knife, a thin split of ocean gleamed a half a mile away. A darkening shroud of cumulous clouds roiled on the horizon.

Buildings here were low-rise. The maximum height was, thankfully, mandated to retain a human scale. Neighborhoods ran from ghetto to castle, and even the castle-dwellers agreed that the cost of living in Santa Monica was ridiculous. Some people called the town the Republic of Santa Monica, disparaging its leftist politics and supposedly anti-business leanings. Lucy and Bea both called it home.

A toilet flushed, slippers scuffed, and Lucy's hospital roommate, Sylvia, a feisty, white-haired former public school teacher who was minutes away from being hauled down to the OR for a gall bladder operation, poked her head around their shared curtain.

"Good luck, Lucy. It's been a pleasure watching HGTV and chatting. You are so nice," she slurred.

Lucy smiled. "Right back at 'ya, Syl. We'll have drinks and watch House Hunters International as soon as you recover."

The woman's kind-faced husband, along with a nurse sporting big loopy gold earrings and shoulders the size of an Escalade bumper, charged into the room, gurney in tow.

The nurse pulled the curtain open between their beds like she was ripping off a Band-Aid. "There you are, Mrs. Gelber! We were in a panic—you took out your IV and wandered off. You're supposed to *stay* in the bed and relax before surgery, baby doll." The nurse scolded in a low, raspy voice.

"Nurse Georgie, you're such a nice gal," Sylvia said as she was helped back onto the gurney and strapped in this time. "Come for drinks with Lucy and me soon, won't you, dear?"

"Wouldn't miss it, girlfriend," the nurse said. "Now stop kicking your legs around so we can cover you up and get you all cozy."

Sylvia's husband, stoop-shouldered with leathery, sun-damaged skin, cooed reassuring endearments to his wife as they trundled down the hall.

More than ready to get the hell out of the hospital, Lucy sat dressed and ready to go in jeans, a blue cotton sweater, and a pair of orange flip-flops. She felt almost energetic and human. But where was Beatrice? Probably stopped for "just a sec" at a sale she couldn't resist. Would it be shoes or purses? The woman was a clothes horse.

The phone rang on Lucy's bed stand and she stretched to pick it up.

"Bea, you running late?" There was a brief silence when she realized that it wasn't Bea. "I'm sorry, who is this?"

"One guess, my long-lost friend," said the caller.

Lucy recognized the voice immediately. "Oh, Carly! It's so great to hear from you. It's been way too long." Lucy stood up and went to the window like a cat seeking a sunny sill. "How're you doing? How's everything? Keith, the kids?"

"All is good with the fam, but the question should be—how are you, Lucy? Your uncle passed away, and now your head injury."

"I still can't believe he's gone. I'll never recover from that. Thank you so much for coming to the funeral. I'm sorry there was no time to catch up. But the noggin situation—I'm fine, fine, just a bump. Ready to get back into action."

"If there's anything at all I can do . . ."

Lucy took a deep breath. "Actually, I think there is something. I have a favor to ask. I saw on LinkedIn that you're working for Dynamic Chemical in San Bernardino now. What a schlep, huh?"

"Yeah, it's a killer commute, but *c'est la vie* in L.A., right? So, yeah, I've been at Dynamic Chemical for a year and a half."

"Head of HR?"

"No, assistant director. The current head is retiring

this spring, so maybe I'll have a chance to move up. Not sure I want to, though. I mean my passion was always alternative energy and now I'm working for a chemical company. How did that happen? And then this Dyna-Cide fiasco."

"Carly, the favor relates to that."

"Ah, sounds intriguing. I'm up for anything, but only if you promise to have dinner with us Saturday night. The twins are practically in college—you're missing everything!"

"Carly, they're only one-and-a-half."

She laughed. "Yeah, but we shouldn't lose touch like this. We ran the high school paper together for two years; we ruled the world!"

"We did, indeed. But now I need your investigative help again."

Lucy rose from the windowsill and peeped out into the empty hallway. The hum of the hospital HVAC and distant voices was all she could hear. She closed the door, then lowered her voice.

Lucy chewed at her fingernail. She could confide in Carly, trusted her with her life. "This will sound nuts, but I think my uncle was murdered. I have this gut feeling that there could be some connection between his death and your company." The line went quiet. "Carly, you still there?"

"Yeah, I'm here, just shocked. Insanely shocked." The line went quiet again. "Okay. Luce, what can I do to help? You know I adored Henry. Whatever it takes, I'm with you."

The response brought tears to Lucy's eyes. "Thank you, Carly. Can I meet you for coffee—don't want to do this over the phone."

"Absolutely—how about that Starbucks we used to hang at in Woodland Hills? It's about halfway between us both."

"Sounds perfect. I'll text you to confirm."

"I'm here!" Bea exclaimed just as Lucy clicked off the phone.

Looking way too fit in sleek black leggings and a pink cashmere hoodie, Bea grinned, hands on her hips like she was posing for a photo shoot. "So, what was that little discussion all about? Sounded very serious."

"A chat with a dear friend from high school, Beebs. Thanks for coming to rescue me!"

Bea gave Lucy a warm hug. "I'm always up for a rescue. They say you're required to go down to the main lobby in a wheelchair, by the way. Liability issues or something. I talked to the orderly. He'll be here any minute. Truckee's picking us up in his van and we're going to the Third Street Promenade for lunch with the kids. Sound okay?"

"Totally good. I can't stand any more yellow Jello with fruit cocktail."

"Sounds vaguely hallucinogenic."

"It was, and not in a good way. Forget the wheelchair." Lucy grabbed her bag and was out the door on her way to the elevator before Bea could say Neiman Marcus.

CHAPTER 17

Truckee drove a dark blue Navigator. He claimed it was the only thing he could comfortably fit his whole family into. Lucy kissed him on the cheek through the rolled-down window then pulled back the door and crawled into the back seat. She stretched out amid what looked and smelled like unwashed athletic uniforms and the remains of a major fast-food frenzy.

"Had half the basketball team in here last night," he said apologetically. "We beat the crap out of Westlake in the pre-holiday tourney, by the way."

"All right, go Oak Park Eagles!" Lucy declared. Then she grimaced and pushed basketball socks and food wrappers to the floor with two fingers.

Truckee glanced over his shoulder at Lucy and smiled. "You look good, darlin'. Happy to see those big blues focusing again." He flicked a switch and the sunroof began to slide open.

"Thanks, Truck. Was only a couple days, but I feel like I've been incarcerated for months, abused in ways I hadn't thought possible."

"Okay, friends," Bea announced, "I've got a reservation at Panetta to celebrate Lucy's escape. After that I know Truckee has to head out—somebody has to work today. Then I'm meeting my kids in front of Banana Republic, they're doing some Christmas shopping."

"So, school's out for the holidays?" Lucy asked. She could hardly believe it was almost Christmas. She was not ready for it, not on any level.

Bea's phone buzzed. "Probably my baby girl running out of money already." She checked the caller ID then let it go to voicemail. It wasn't her daughter. She listened to the message then turned to Lucy, face serious.

"What is it?" Lucy asked.

"It's Burleson. He wants to talk to us."

"About what?"

"About your uncle." Bea dropped her phone back into her purse.

A pang of dizziness reminded Lucy that her brain was still concussed. She chewed on her lip. "He sure was all cozied up to the governor at the extermination site. Something's going on. Why is he interested in Uncle Henry, unless there's some tie-in?"

"I don't know, hon. Should I tell him we'll meet, like early next week? The station holiday party is Tuesday—like tomorrow. He suggests *Chez Mimi* in the Palisades."

"Sure, let's find out what he's up to," Lucy said. Maybe he'd be another way to tap into the governor."

❈

Traffic was light as Truckee drove down Wilshire Boulevard toward the ocean. The farmers' market was a few blocks away. It was that picture-perfect postcard kind of a day that made Southern California winters the envy of the rest of the planet.

"So," Lucy said, "aside from whatever Burleson is up to, anything new on the story?"

"Maybe. There was an interesting discovery at the rail yards outside of San Bernardino." Bea looked over her shoulder at Lucy. "They located the guy who was the loading dock supervisor on duty the night the pesticide got mixed in with the livestock feed. They found him in the depot parking lot with his brains blown all over the inside of his SUV. The cops are saying he shot himself when he realized what he'd accidentaly done."

"Sounds like they arrived at that conclusion a little too fast," Truckee said. He cruised around the block for the second time.

Bea nodded agreement. "Ernie and I talked to the cops down in San Berdoo yesterday and they're calling it an open-and-closed case of suicide. A deet named Berkowitz's the lead."

"Sure would be interesting to see their forensics report," Lucy said.

"Get this," Bea said, "they didn't do one."

"Are you kidding me?" Lucy was astounded.

Horns honked behind them. Truckee had slowed to about two miles an hour trolling for an on-street parking spot.

"Heaven forbid you'd use the public parking structure," Bea said and sighed. "Wait! There's one! There's one!" She stuck her hand out the window to warn off another vehicle approaching the same spot.

Horns blared again. Curses were shouted. Truckee nosed ahead.

"The guy who killed himself—he didn't call anyone to try and stop the shipment?" Lucy asked. "Or leave a note?"

"No note. No call. Who knows what motivates people, especially when they're distraught," Bea said. "But one thing I do know for sure is that the San Bernardino cops are stonewalling."

"Everybody's got a cork up their asses," Truckee said, watching his vehicle's backup camera as he squeezed the Navigator into a parking spot marked *Compact Cars Only*. "Everybody wants the easy answers. Especially this time of year, nobody wants to work."

"The dead guy's girlfriend says he was totally *not* suicidal. His friends say he was crazy about her; he had just proposed and she said yes. Supposedly he never owned a weapon. But the gun was registered in his name. Was purchased a few days weeks earlier at a gun show in Pomona," Bea continued.

"The whole thing sounds off," Lucy said, almost to herself.

"Not according to the cops. As far as they're concerned, it's a done deal. But they may have more information than we're privy to, as usual," said Bea.

"Yeah," Lucy said, shoulders drooping, "information like why there was a homicide detective at the scene of my uncle's accident and why the accident report was sealed. I want to see his car."

"I know somebody who might be able to make that happen," Bea said.

"You have a contact at impound?"

"I do," Truckee said. "I'll email the info to 'ya both."

"That's great," Lucy said, carefully fingering the thirty stitches in her head. They really screwed up a hairstyle.

"There are Bea's little monsters." Truckee pointed to Dexter and Alyssa who stood on a curb outside of the Apple Store. "They appear to be pretending not to know each other."

"So what else is new?" Bea said, chuckling.

"Did we find the perfect parking spot or what?" A proud smile lit up Truckee's freckled face.

"But will you ever be able to get out of here?" Lucy mumbled. "You're a heck of a parallel parker, big man."

Lucy lowered the car window and waved to get the kid's attention. She suppressed the anxiety about her uncle's death, about the poisoning, and the suicide, and all that she didn't know. She would be in the moment, the here and now.

The colorful riot of delicious produce and lovingly displayed products in the market stalls were wonderful. The scent of pine and eucalyptus wafted from a table decked in fresh wreaths and gray-green mistletoe harvested from the oaks and sycamores that dotted local hillsides. The sound of Christmas and Hanukkah music being sung by a local children's choir was enchanting. Life was good, even when it felt really, really bad.

Bea and Lucy waited impatiently while Truckee fumbled for coins to feed the meter. Lucy offered up a couple quarters she'd pulled out of her pocket. Then she froze.

For an instant, she thought she saw Gary Mercer

walk out of a bagel shop across the street. He was with the new KLAK cameraman, Tom Rubio, who'd just come up from Miami. Lucy held her breath and strained to see them but they disappeared into the busy holiday crowd on the mall. Maybe she was imagining things. She rubbed her bruised head and again ran her fingers lightly across the jagged line of prickly stitches. Pain buzzed through her brain like a low-grade electrical current. Damn him, Mercer was getting to her. And Burleson, too. Did he know what the governor was hiding?

CHAPTER 18

Bea's offspring, Alyssa, and Dexter, finally crossed the street, packages in hand. Lucy ran to them, arms wide with hugs that she needed more than they did. After embracing Lucy, Alyssa skipped up to her mother for a quick peck on the cheek. Dexter was far too cool for that kind of public display.

"Okay, babies," Bea said, "what did you get your Mama for Christmas this year?"

"Only Lucy can see." Alyssa grinned, beads popped at the end of her cornrow braids. She was a stunning girl on the verge of womanhood with a face like young Halle Berry. "Look." Aly opened a red plastic gift bag so Lucy could see the contents. Inside was a *Best of Bob Marley* CD from the Starbucks collection and three OPI nail polishes, all pretty shades of deep red and wine.

"You think she'll like the colors?" Alyssa whispered,

eyes sparkling with pride at her choices.

"They're perfect. You've got your mom's good taste."

"Lucy Loose and Big Truck," Dexter called. He joined the group after going through quick ritual greetings with a couple of adolescent male friends from Santa Monica High that had crossed his path. Dexter was barely fifteen and would probably pass six-two by New Year's Eve but was as slim as a soda straw. His baggy, designer clothes made him appear like a walking stick swathed in fabric. He also had a heartbreaker of a face and bone structure to die for.

"Hiya, kids," Truckee said, giving them both high fives.

"Hey, Little Dex," Lucy said, looking up, way up. Little Dexter was rapidly becoming Big Dexter. That's what happened when you had a former LA Clippers point guard for a father. Kevin Jackson was Bea Middleton's first ex-husband.

He dug diligently in his backpack and unearthed a thumb drive in a clear plastic holder. "I finally finished editing it together. Here's the compilation of our class' short films. Sean Hayes never finished his, surprise, surprise, but everybody else is on here. You're a cool teacher, Lucy."

"Hey, thanks very much. I'm so glad you could be in the class!" Lucy said. It was a lot of work but wonderful to feel like she was giving back by teaching the next generation of kids interested in film and TV. "You guys were seriously the best group I ever had. Can't wait to see these Academy Award nominees!"

"A couple of us did a little more editing after the term ended. The stuff's really good and mine is Z-best!"

"Dexter, you are so full of it," Alyssa said, rolling her arresting hazel-green eyes. "He thinks he's the next Spike Lee."

"Well, who knows, maybe he will be," Lucy said. She gave Dexter's hand a squeeze.

"You don't even know who Spike Lee is," Dexter said, goading his little sister.

"I do too! I heard you talk about him to your stupid friends. I saw *Boyz in the Hood!*"

"Oh my God. That's John Singleton, not Spike Lee. You are such a dork."

"Get those skinny butts over here," Bea interjected, "and hush, both of you." She herded them all into the restaurant just before a whole group of little soccer players descended. At that moment Lucy wished fervently that one of those little munchkins belonged to her, but it wasn't to be. Injuries from the childhood car wreck that took her family had made it impossible.

"I have the station on the phone," Bea said to Lucy. Truckee forged ahead with Dexter and Alyssa to a choice table on the patio. "They can't find Tom Rubio and he's supposed to be on call. Do you have his cell number?"

"Yeah, I have it. It's on the share drive and it's posted plain as day in the newsroom."

"Well, they can't find it. I think there's a part-timer in there today because of the holidays."

Lucy pulled out her iPhone and located the number in her contacts.

"Wait, wait, they just found it," Bea said, pursing her lips in disapproval, "and he just walked in the door. False alarm." She clicked off her cell phone. "There was a message from Ernie, too. The network execs have been in a closed-door meeting since this morning. Food isn't even going in and out."

They looked at each other, clearly concerned. Lucy and Bea joined the others at a big round table as a waitress passed out menus and set down dripping glasses of ice water with lemon slices on the rim.

"Truckee," Bea said, "you know that nasty rumor going around town that Maxwell is going to be canned and our station's being bought up by a major? Well, looks like something's going on right now. Ernie's there and says it's like a meeting of the war council."

"We've been ignoring this possibility for a long time," he said and rubbed his forehead.

"They want a news director who can pump up the entertainment aspects of the station. We're the last holdouts to do more or less hard news. More people want to know about celebrity boob jobs gone bad and who just got thrown into rehab," Bea said.

"We run *Hollywood Focus* every night and *Entertainment Update* on weekends—isn't that enough salacious coverage?" Truckee asked rhetorically. "And they can pick up the gossip rags in line at the supermarket."

"Maxwell is the best," Lucy said. Losing their executive producer would be a real blow to everyone in the journalism community. "And our own Beatrice here is in line for the evening news director slot opening up."

"Sometimes I think we've been working on borrowed time," Bea said sadly. "Maybe I could teach journalism at USC full-time and be a news blogger on the side."

"I've got four kids to put through college. I don't know what I'll do if I lose my job," Truckee said, his mouth screwed into a tight circle. "I'd want to quit, walk out in support of Max, but how can I afford to?"

"Not much in the mood for the company holiday bash this year. But I RSVP'd for all of us," Bea said, with little enthusiasm. "Politics. We have to show up—can't burn bridges."

Lucy felt a profound sense of violation at the thought of becoming part of another parody of a news station. This is why they had all stayed at KLAK—because, amid the Bollywoodization of news stations in Los Angeles, they were still doing their best to tell the real stories, not the spin. With Maxwell Wedner gone, an era would be over, along with any opportunity to pursue stories in depth.

Without Max at the helm, Lucy knew that any new owners would want her to keep her on a short leash. She was not going to let that happen.

CHAPTER 19

It was Tuesday night and the KLAK-TV holiday party was in full *White Christmas* mode atop the Los Angeles Marina Hotel overlooking the wintry Pacific. The cloying scent of fake pine emanated from a display of plastic Christmas trees covered in fake snow at the entry to the ballroom. Strains of "Grandma Got Run Over by a Reindeer" blared from speakers inside. Lucy cased the place for food and drink. She snagged some stuffed mushrooms from a passing tray. Not bad.

Had the event been scheduled on a weekend as with most other companies, it would have cost double and the station was in major belt-tightening mode with the growing whispers of ownership change. Management remained mum about yesterday's big corporate meeting. Nevertheless, the employees and spouses were at the party and decked out in their finest holiday wear. They crowded around the stage in the slightly tacky, but who could tell with the lights down low, Marina del Rey hotel ballroom. For the beleaguered KLAK newsies, this was the event of the year.

Servers busily set up the buffet, while others circulated through the room in black tuxedos offering *hors-d'oeuvres* and glasses of champagne to the enthusiastic revelers. Partying was the last thing in the world Lucy felt like doing this holiday season but if she didn't show up, there would be phone calls. *How are you feeling? Come to our house for dinner? Poor, poor, baby . . . all alone.* She couldn't take the well-meaning sympathy. She tugged at the long sleeves of her garnet-red dress. Every year she meant to get something new but never quite got around to it. At least it still fit.

Suddenly her name boomed over the speakers, and the warmth of a spotlight hit her from the side. She wanted to duck beneath a table or run.

Maxwell Wedner, aka Max, the KLAK-TV executive news producer, was a tall, bald, professorial man in his mid-sixties. He stood on a dais in a Santa outfit, holding a wrapped gift in his hands. A blue velvet yarmulke replaced the Santa cap on his white-wigged head. Perspiring, and struggling to read a crumpled list in the glare of spotlights, his half-frame glasses perched askew on his long, narrow nose.

"And now, last but not least," Max called out, sounding like a smarmy talk show host. He held up another brightly wrapped gift. "My elves created something special for the leader of our photo department. We knew she was a hard-headed woman, but her collision with a camera last week really proved the point. Lucy Vega, come on down!"

Lucy tried not to hyperventilate. Attention was the last thing she was looking for tonight. The crowd clapped and whistled, growing more raucous by the minute as the D.J. cranked up Elvis Presley's version of "Hard Headed Woman." Every staff member received some kind of gag gift from management, and much of the evening's entertainment revolved around this tradition.

Max shouted over the crowd. "We were hard put to come up with any hardware more hardcore than a hard hat to thank you for all your hard work. So here it is, Lucy, for your future protection."

Truckee and Bea appeared and pushed Lucy up the steps. Santa tossed her the parcel. Opening it with the appearance of gusto she struggled to feel, she pulled out a purple bicycle helmet with a blinking light glued to the front. *Hard Headed Woman* was emblazoned in gold across the back.

"Oh! Look at this!" she said. "Thank you, Santa!" Lucy gave him a kiss, then strapped on the helmet. "I feel so safe now!" *If only it were this easy.*

The crowd clapped and cheered.

"The purple head award!" Brent, the very drunk intern, yelled.

"That's hat, Brent, not head," Bea whispered loudly in his ear. "But sounds like you sure as hell could use some of the latter."

He fell onto the stage at Lucy's feet. "God, Luce, I'm getting a hard-on just looking at you in that hard hat."

"Hard luck, Brentster," Lucy said, smiling. She stepped over his prone body.

"Somebody's got to get that boy laid," Bea said. "This

is getting pathetic."

"Merry Christmas and Happy Hanukkah, everyone!" Max called. "Your bonus IOUs are in the mail!"

The employees groaned. The band struck up the Village People's wicked old standard, "Y.M.C.A." In an instant, people jammed the dance floor singing and forming the letters with their arms. More trays of sloshing drinks circulated and the buffet opened. Lucy grabbed Bea's hand and pulled her into the relative quiet of the foyer.

"Hey, cool helmet," Bea said. "Goes great with that little red dress and those strappy heels. Jimmy Choo?"

"T.J. Maxx." Lucy primped ostentatiously. "No, wait, it might have been Tar-jay,"

"That helmet is sooo fine—trade you for the peacock?" Bea held up the stuffed plush bird Santa had given her. It was the "best-dressed reporter" award she'd won for the third year running.

"I wouldn't trade my *chapeau* for that turkey."

"A little respect, missy. This ain't no turkey. This is a network's time-honored mascot." Bea set the unwieldy peacock on a table containing a holiday floral arrangement. She broke off a poinsettia bud and stuck it in the bird's beak.

"I hear poinsettias are toxic to birds," Lucy said.

Bea shrugged her shoulders. "Tough not to see everything through a dark lens these days, isn't it?"

Lucy's eyes closed. "Hey, I'm sorry. I'm such a humbug, a Scrooge."

"Girl, you are not a humbug or Scrooge. You are so tough on yourself. No self-flagellation at this holiday party. The way the business is going, this could be our last one, so enjoy. You hear me?" Bea said.

"I do." Lucy chewed at her lip, immediately ashamed of casting a pall on the evening.

"So, what's up, girl? What're you dragging me out here for when the bar is still open and the karaoke is about to begin? Wanna do "I Will Survive" again? It was a moderate hit for us last year."

Lucy looked away and wished she could smile, wished she could get up there with Bea again and sing. There was no lightness in her soul right now, only fear and confusion.

A rowdy group of party-goers spilled into the foyer on their way to the restrooms. Several folks pounded gaily on her blinking helmet. She cringed but managed the appearance of holiday cheer. Her head was still sore and it didn't take much to make her ears ring—and not with Christmas bells.

"By the way, girlfriend, your mascara looks like Alice Cooper," Bea said.

Lucy dabbed her eyes. "It's supposed to be waterproof."

"Right, and Vitamin E gets rid of cellulite," Bea slapped her black velvet-clad thigh. She paused, then took Lucy's hand and squeezed it. "I'm being a jerk, just trying to get you out of your head for a few minutes. I'm also a teeny-weeny bit in the cups. Sorry, babe. I give you highest props for even being here tonight. In all seriousness, you know I'm there for you, always."

"And right back at 'cha, so let's stop apologizing to each other. Deal?" Lucy said.

They tapped champagne glasses and downed the contents. Bea pulled herself up tall and adjusted her dangly gold earrings as the foyer crowd thinned. "Okay, my dearest, I didn't want to talk shop tonight but I guess there's no point in avoiding it. I spoke with Sonja Gilhooley about an hour ago."

Lucy perked up. Gilhooley was the gatekeeper for major accident reports. "Thanks for reaching out to her. I didn't know that she's Truckee's second cousin."

"Scary small world, isn't it? And she looks just like him. She's got that Brunhilde-wearing-a-metal-helmet-with-rams-horns vibe going on."

Lucy rolled her eyes and chuckled at the thought. "So what'd Sonja say?" She pulled Bea over to a sofa away from the busy pathway between the restrooms and the ballroom. They put their empty glasses in a planter filled with glitter-caked sprigs of plastic holly.

"She couldn't get me a hard copy of the crash report on your uncle's Lexus," Bea said, "but she was at least able to read me the impound summary over the phone. I recorded it."

"I'm sure you informed her of that?" Lucy smiled.

"Slipped my mind, sister," Bea said, pushing buttons on her phone. "I'm emailing it to you right now."

A server headed toward the ballroom hustled by with a tray full of newly poured flutes of holiday cheer. Bea grabbed two glasses and handed one to Lucy.

Lucy took a sip, then set the drink aside. She was starting to feel a little too buzzed. "Did Sonja say anything about paint scrape at the points of impact?"

"The report said that the passenger side of the car had been seriously ground down from skidding inside the concrete tunnel and the driver's side door showed evidence of major impact with a black vehicle. From the paint chips, they think it might have been a late model Chevy truck, possibly a Kodiak or a Silverado. But could that have happened earlier? At airport parking or something?" Bea asked.

"Uncle Henry parks the Lexus at one of those expensive airport valet parking garages. Has used the same place for years. They know him and what he's driving. I called them this morning and they said his car was in perfect shape when he left at about eleven-thirty that evening."

"They have it on camera?" Bea asked.

Lucy nodded then looked over at Bea, her eyes suddenly burning with moisture. "Shit. Mercer has a big black truck."

Bea paused for a moment and pressed her friend's cold hand in both of hers. "So do thousands of other people."

Lucy's ring tone sounded and she checked out the incoming number. "S'cuse me for a sec. I've got to take this. It's my friend who works at Dynamic Chemical. I was talking to her on the phone in the hospital when you came to pick me up."

"Oh, yeah. The high school BFF." Bea drained half her flute of bubbly then pushed it aside.

Lucy cleared her throat then stood and took a step away. "Hey, Carly."

"Sorry to bother you at the Christmas party, kiddo," Carly said, voice low.

"No problem. I'm heading home soon. Thanks again for doing this, uh, research for me. Did you find anything?" Lucy began to pace.

"I did. Couldn't have done it without twisting my

husband's arm, though. He's a whiz at this stuff. Actually, Dynamic's firewalls aren't as sophisticated as you'd think for a business that must have secret formulas and all that kind of stuff to protect. But the ownership is the really interesting thing. We still on for tomorrow after work? Carly asked.

"For sure. I owe you big time."

"No prob. Get back to your party and I'll see you *mañana*."

Bye, Car." Lucy disconnected. She pressed the cell phone to her chest.

Bea pulled off a patent leather pump and rubbed her foot. Black toenail polish sparkled. "Anything?"

"Maybe." Lucy plunked back down onto the couch. "I asked her if she could track company ownership, clients, subsidiaries, executive staffing—that kind of thing. I couldn't see much on the web. She says she found something interesting. We're meeting tomorrow."

Removing her helmet, Lucy gently raked her fingers through her hair. "Anyhow, Beebs, I'm tired. I hate to be a party pooper, but I'm heading home."

"Okay, babe. Be careful. If there's substance to this thing with your uncle, which I'm not saying there is, but *if* it's solid, then we're not talking about an accident . . ."

"I know," Lucy said, eyes dark with runny mascara and fatigue, "we're talking about murder."

CHAPTER 20

Lucy retrieved her purse and cashmere wrap from the ballroom, tucked the goofy helmet beneath her arm, and slipped out the side door into the hallway. She dashed through the grand lobby toward the parking lot, hoping to avoid anyone she knew. She wasn't in the mood for more company.

The Mediterranean-style front entryway swarmed with parking attendants. Lucy pushed past the throng, head down. She'd never felt comfortable handing her keys over to someone she didn't know.

After a few minutes of forgetting where she had parked, she spotted her car at the end of a row near the edge of the dark marina. A heavy mist was turning into cold rain as she pressed the unlock button. The vehicle lit up like a soft, welcoming lantern against the inky harbor. Then she heard shuffling footsteps from behind.

An unknown male voice called out from close by.

"Lucy!"

Adrenaline hit her bloodstream. She whirled around. Where the hell was that pepper spray?

She jumped back as he reached out to touch her arm. It was the intern.

"I like the helmet" he said, disarmingly.

"You scared the shit out of me, Brent!" She wanted to clobber him with the damn thing.

"I'm sorry, Luce. Just wanted a word."

Brent Lucas swayed unsteadily on his feet. He was much taller and larger than she remembered—maybe six-three and two hundred pounds, maybe more, and definitely older than a typical intern. He worked at night with his nose in his textbooks and his ear to the police scanner. Right now, however, he more resembled a drunken frat boy. His wavy dark-blond hair dripped down his face and his eyes held a confused sense of despair. He smelled faintly of salt and stale booze.

"Listen, Brent, I'm not in the mood to talk. Why don't you find someone who can drive you home."

"Lucy, Lucy, Lucy," he slurred, "just give me a sec. Just a sec."

"We'll talk on Monday, Brent. You're drunk and you're making me uncomfortable. Go back to the hotel."

"I don't mean to make you feel uncomfortable. I only, I just wanted to apologize for being an asshole tonight. Drank too much. I'm an idiot—sometimes just don't know what I'm supposed to be doing these days. I'm a twenty-eight-year-old undergrad, and feel fuckin' eighty. Did three tours in the military," he held up two fingers then three, then gave up. "The last two in

Afghanistan. I got nothing in common with these kids in my classes. Nothing in common with anybody." He paused and looked out at the black water.

Lucy's irritation dissipated as she became aware of the earnestness in his wide blue eyes. Her voice softened, "I'm in a rough patch, too." She opened the car door, about to slide in.

"I know," he held the door for her, "and I'm sorry about your uncle."

"Yeah, life's a drag and a half sometimes, isn't it?" She sighed, sizing him up. A man who struggled, and admitted it, might be a pretty good guy at heart. "Come on, hop in. I'll take you home."

"But I'll mess up your car, I'm sopping wet. I, uh, kind of took a header into the fountain up by the valet stand."

Lucy chuckled. "I have dogs, chickens, and goats up at my family's ranch. They all insist on going for car rides, preferably after a dunk in the creek. They can't smell much worse than you do. Now get in. Absolutely no throwing up, though."

"Chickens swim?" Brent asked, trying fruitlessly to power up his wet cell phone.

"Yup."

"Like to see that." Brent hesitated, and then closed her door. He came around the hood, steadying himself, then crawled awkwardly into the passenger seat.

"Where's your place?" Lucy asked.

"Ocean Park, near 16th. Santa Monica."

"Good—practically my neighborhood."

"What if I would have said Huntington Beach?" Brent grinned.

"I would have dropped you at the bus stop," Lucy replied and returned the smile.

"Fair enough," he said, back to squinting at his phone. It remained lifeless.

"I didn't realize you were in the service. I know the transition can be tough." Lucy turned on the wipers and headed out of the parking lot toward Venice Boulevard. "What did you do there? Communications?"

"Shit, no." He stuffed the phone in his pocket. "I was in charge in Afghanistan, headed up a Special Ops unit with life and death responsibility for my teams. Now I'm just a shit intern." He squirmed in his seat, looking miserably uncomfortable. "I want you to know that I'm not a total jerk. I'm just having some momentary, you know, challenges. And I'm sorry. I'll get through it. Just a bad night."

Lucy nodded. She understood bad nights. Fifteen minutes later, Lucy pulled up in front of his small, stucco duplex. It looked well-maintained. Pink and fuchsia oleander was in full bloom and bougainvillea climbed the walls. He accidentally hit the button that rolled down the window then finally found the door handle. He opened the car door but didn't get out.

"So, you never said if you accepted my apology."

"Apology accepted. Now don't push your luck, Brentster. Get out of here and get something dry on before you catch cold. And put that phone in a bag of rice and maybe it'll dry out."

"Yes, ma'am." He struggled out of the Jeep and shut the door behind him, then turned and leaned against the car. "I like a woman who can take charge," he said through the window. "You'd do well in the Marines."

Lucy rolled her eyes. "I'd hate the military. Now get your butt gone before you end up owing me another apology."

Brent backed up then saluted. "Yes sir, ma'am."

Lucy waited as he started up the steps to his front door. Then he came staggering back. Had he forgotten something?

"You wouldn't, uh, want to come in and hang out for a while, would you?"

He licked his very nice lower lip.

"Thank you, Brent, but another time. Two drunk, needy people hanging out? We know what that leads to."

"Is that so bad?"

"I don't sleep with interns, no matter how old they are. Against the rules."

"You don't seem like much of a rule-follower."

Lucy laughed. "That's one rule I always follow. Now go to bed, by yourself, Brent."

"I need to kiss you goodnight," he said, beginning to lean through the window again.

"Not enough mouthwash in L.A. for that to happen." Lucy stretched over and touched his forearm, pushing him back. She sighed and raised her eyebrows. "I knew it, you're warm. I've vowed to only get involved with men who can't die."

"Like zombies?" His bleary eyes brightened.

"Not zombies. Their breath, if they breathe, might even be worse than yours. They always have such bad teeth. I prefer superheroes."

"They don't exist," he said, a little sadly.

"I know. See you Monday, Brent."

"Okay, uh, thanks for the lift." His eyes widened and

he dashed toward his front door.

As Lucy slowly accelerated away from the curb, she glanced in her rearview mirror. Brent was throwing up in the well-manicured hedge. She shook her head and chuckled. Then she noticed a light-colored sedan that had been waiting a little too long at the corner. It pulled out after her when she turned at a stop sign. Before Lucy could note the tag number, the car disappeared. She was getting more paranoid by the minute.

CHAPTER 21

The wind's moaning was deep and constant. The night felt like a living creature, rustling, breathing, and scraping through the streets, like those zombies Brent had mentioned. It had begun to pour in earnest by the time Lucy finally pulled in front of her garage. Branches of a spidery cypress tree next to her front porch undulated with eerie, grabbing arms in the illumination of her headlights. It was one of those times that made her vow, once again, to finally clean out the garage so she'd have room for the car. Lucy glanced around, looking for the light-colored vehicle she'd encountered on Brent's street. Nothing.

As she dug for the house key she glanced about the pretty complex at her neighbors' condos all decorated for the holidays. Lucy's own place looked sad and empty. Clutching a bag of groceries and the little potted

Christmas tree from the market, she pulled the key from the recesses of her purse to let herself in.

Hesitating for an instant, she thought she heard someone whispering her name. A chill ran down her spine. Not another parking-lot stalker—Brent had been enough for one night. As she climbed the steps to the front door, her eyes scanned the gloom but again, there was nothing. The jumpiness was probably just the residual effect of all of the painkillers they'd been pumping into her at the hospital, she rationalized. Then add booze to that. At home she rarely took anything stronger than vitamins, except lately. Lucy was relieved as the key turned in the lock.

Flicking the light switch with her elbow, she almost made it to the kitchen counter before the soggy grocery bag split and her groceries spilled into the sink. At least they weren't all over the floor. Why did she always forget her waterproof eco-bags when she went shopping?

Not ready to deal with the mess, Lucy draped her dripping coat over a chair at the kitchen table. She put the miniature Christmas tree on the counter and plugged in the string of white lights that decorated its stubby branches. That was better. She filled the teapot and turned on the stove to heat the water. In the pantry next to the back door, she rooted through the shelves for a container of Trader Joe's chocolate-dipped almond biscotti. Bingo. Six left. Then Lucy retreated to her bedroom and changed into fleece sweatpants and a gray T-shirt with a red moose on the front.

Her iPhone message notice chimed. She'd missed a call and several messages were waiting. Returning to the kitchen, she grabbed her cookies and brewed tea, then snuggled down into her cozy, gray chenille, L-shaped couch. The oriental-style rug she'd splurged on from Pottery Barn was soft beneath her bare feet. She pressed the voicemail function and listened.

Elsa had called to welcome her home from the hospital and encourage her to come up to the ranch for a weekend of potato soup and feather down quilts. Very tempting, but there was too much of Henry to face there. She heard Maddie bark in the background—she missed her furry baby. It was better for Mads to be at the ranch for now with Bugle, Howard the cat, the chickens, and the pygmy goats, Dorothy and Ozma.

Various well-wishers had left concerned messages, the UCLA Alumni Association had called asking for a donation before the end of the tax year, and then there was an unexpected call from Carly.

"Luce, I know you're at that party but you said you were heading home early. I decided this can't wait 'til tomorrow, so I'm on my way over. Actually, I'm just walking up to your front porch."

Lucy took a nervous bite of biscotti. She dunked the rest in her tea. What was the sudden urgency about? Then the doorbell rang. She spied Carly thought the peephole—the wind whipped at her curly rust-colored ponytail. Lucy quickly ushered her inside where they exchanged quick hugs.

Refreshments were offered. Carly opted for wine rather than tea which Lucy scurried to provide. The two women settled on the couch. Both were wound tight as springs—their movements fast and jerky, their faces grim. Carly wore workout clothes, like she had just returned from a yoga class.

"I'm thrilled to see you, but you're scaring me. What's with the midnight visit?" Lucy asked.

Carly took a long sip of merlot then dug into her backpack and pulled out a manila file. She handed it to Lucy who immediately opened it and began to peruse the contents.

Carly fidgeted in her seat, as if unable to get comfortable. "The more I thought about it, I knew you'd want to see this stuff right away. And I didn't feel like I could safely email anything." She took another swig of wine. "What you're looking at is a copy of the organizational chart you wanted. As you see, Dynamic Chemical is a subsidy of an international chemical conglomerate with headquarters in Mexico City. That was a new one on me."

Lucy studied the pages. "So, besides the main office in City of Industry, where you work, Dynamic Chemical has two subsidiaries in the states—one in Tucson and one outside of Las Vegas. They also have subsidiaries in Tijuana, Juarez, Mexico City, and in South America—Bogotá, Panama City, Lima, Cali, and Medellín, Columbia, right?"

Carly nodded. "The largest division is based in Lima, Peru. The Juarez portion of the conglomerate was headed by a guy named Carlos Ponce Alvarez. Don't know a thing about him except that he recently stepped down from that position and now supposedly works for the Mexican government in some capacity."

"Carlos Alvarez." Lucy scratched at her forehead. "I think he's a drug guy who the governor has refused to extradite. Oh, shit. This is not good."

Carly tapped at her phone and brought up an article

on the Alvarez brothers—Carlos and Luis.

She passed it to Lucy who checked it out then shook her head. "Not good at all."

"I messaged this to you for reference." Carly continued, "I couldn't find out who heads the other North American subsidiaries. Supposedly, all our companies manufacture legitimate pharmaceuticals. We even have a license to produce those organophosphate pesticides that poisoned the cattle but it's for very proscribed uses."

"So what do you think happened in the shipping department? Any clue as to how the mix-up could have gone down?" Lucy asked. Her tea remained untouched.

"As for shipping, a guy was brought in to our Los Angeles-City of Industry plant from the Mexico City plant to take over the dock from November fifteenth through the end of December. The regular guy's out for a while on disability. The papers were filed through the HR director and approved. All seemed copacetic."

"No other background information?"

"That's all the muck I could rake up."

The gusting wind roared through the neighborhood like a freight train. The women sat quietly, sobered by the dangerous potential of their discovery.

"I never should have asked you to get this stuff," Lucy finally said. "I should have been more careful. I was stupid."

"Lucy, I was dying to be an accomplice. My job is boring me out of my mind. I feel like I'm doing something important in helping you."

Lucy leaned over to hug her friend. "Carly, be watchful at work. Not a word to anybody."

"I have been, and will be, careful. I've got kids now,

can't be too wild and reckless." Carly smiled. "Keep me posted if you need anything else."

"This is plenty," Lucy said. "Gives me a pretty clear idea about what's at play here, and right now, it's scaring the shit out of me."

"We'll be okay, girlfriend. And, yeah, maybe I should start thinking about getting back into journalism. This has reminded me how much I love it. Thank you for that."

When Carly had gone home and Lucy returned to the kitchen to finally clean up the pile of soggy groceries, she felt leaden with dread.

Dynamic Chemical Company, the maker of both Dyna-Cide and Dyna-Feed, was linked to Mexican and South American pharmaceutical subsidiaries, and likely, drug cartels. If Carlos Alvarez was involved, his brother Luis probably was, too. This all had to tie together somehow. Henry had just returned from Mexico City the night of the accident. A mere coincidence? Lucy had been in the news business too long to believe in random twists of fate.

CHAPTER 22

Dynamic Chemical Company's complex of steaming white pipes, holding tanks, and chimneys was located on the outskirts of the sprawling Los Angeles suburbs. In an industrial area amid a flat, uninteresting collection of innocuous strip malls, depressed multiethnic blue-collar neighborhoods, and labyrinthine complexes of aging factories and warehouses, the place had the scent of sickness and pollution. Gang graffiti erupted on every paintable surface with the virulent tenacity of a mutating Ebola virus. War zone-like fences topped with razor-sharp concertina wire segmented the landscape. A high-tech stainless steel sign announced, *Dynamic Chemical Company*.

Mercury vapor lights, with their distinctive sulfuric hue, illuminated the parking area and adjacent loading dock. Just beyond the dock and next to the dumpsters was the unofficial employee smoking lounge. Several people were out partaking. Quiet conversation and an occasional peal of laughter wafted through the sour, chemical-infused air. Inside the dock's open overhead door, Carly Montgomery filled out paperwork to trace a misplaced shipment of four new Macs for the graphics department.

It was eleven-fifteen in the evening—the end of the coffee break for the sparsely populated night shift. Carly, a short, compact woman with curly strawberry blonde hair tied up in a loose bun, rarely worked overtime because, as her co-workers all knew, she had two small children at home to care for. But a last-minute HR insurance analysis suddenly had to be completed for the new top executive and put into a PowerPoint for an early presentation. She emailed it off to him and got an immediate reply not pertaining to the presentation. He directed her to check on the tardy equipment order before she shut down for the night. Carly huffed. She was in HR, not Purchasing, for heaven's sake. Next time she'd have to set the guy straight on her job description.

Carly reflected on the bit of investigation she was doing for Lucy and smiled. It had been years since she felt like her work was making a difference. Maybe it was time for a career change back into journalism.

A semi-trailer truck sat empty at the dock as she finished the paperwork. Two new art department social media assistants were starting and their equipment should have arrived several days ago. Finally, the last smoker returned to work and Carly was left alone. It was the first peaceful moment of a long day. She tossed the completed shipment tracing requisition form into the next day's basket of work for the clerk—was weird these forms weren't online.

It was dark and quiet in the holding area except for the lamp on the clerk's desk. High racks full of products to be distributed rose around her like aisles in The Home Depot. Carly stretched then slowly moved to collect her briefcase and jacket. She pushed the button to lower the huge rolling doors just as the shipping clerk had asked her to do. They clanked and grated closed. With the finality of a prison lockdown, automatic bolts fell into place.

Carly went to the employee exit door, looking forward to getting home and kissing her little sleeping angels. To her surprise, the exit was locked. She shook the handle, but it didn't budge. Strange. OSHA would have a fit. She grabbed the phone on the clerk's desk to call security. The line was dead. Carly reached into her purse for her cell phone. It was gone. Nervous butterflies irritated her stomach.

Then, she noticed the glint of another cell phone amid the papers piled on the clerk's desk. He must have accidentally left it behind. She felt relieved and foolish. Everybody forgets their phone on occasion. Lucy had freaked her out with talk of murder. She dialed Security at the front desk.

"Hi Austin. This is Carly Montgomery from Human Relations. Hey, I'm locked in the loading dock and I—"

She became aware of a motor firing up in the dark belly of the warehouse, then fast movement. Her momentary relief at reaching security blew out like a popped balloon.

Carly spun around, gasped and tried to run, but her

legs wouldn't move. Was it an earthquake? Would her kids be okay?

Silver tines flashed in the gloom. A forklift launched itself against the massive storage racks packed with heavy crates. In an instant, the towering structure began to disassemble and fall. Carly's mouth wrenched open in strangled terror. A hollow-eyed face behind the steering wheel of the lift was an apparition from hell. The engine roared. This wasn't an earthquake. Groaning, twisted steel crashed inches from her body, crushing the clerk's desk. Dust filled her lungs.

The security guard unlocked the hallway door. Carly stumbled toward its pale light, hands out, grasping, but the darkness swallowed her up with snapping teeth. Containers crashed and exploded, burying her in blinding pain.

*

Bea sauntered through the crew room door humming along with the six o'clock news theme music that grated from the engineering office across the hall. Holding a tin of crumbly Christmas cookies in her hand, a mysterious smile curled the corners of her mouth. "I'll bet you can't guess who I just had a little chat with—again," Bea said.

"I can't imagine. You're annoyingly perky so the station is probably still in business. That rules out the CEO."

"Would be happy to give that asshole a piece of my mind." Bea offered the cookies in Lucy's direction. "Have one. They're stale but they'll give you enough of a sugar rush to get you home."

"Thanks, I'll pass." Lucy looked suspiciously at her

friend. "So, what's going on?" She plugged the camera batteries into the charger then turned and sat down on the wood bench that spanned the row of lockers. She pulled open the door to hers and perused the contents. Yoga pants, a tired box of DayQuil, and one black rubber boot fell out onto the floor.

Bea continued to hum, unfazed.

Lucy shook her head and laughed. "Oh, jeez. Okay. Michael Burleson called. Am I right?"

Bea sat down next to Lucy. "Called to confirm for next Wednesday night at *Chez Mimi*."

"Why are you getting so excited?" Lucy asked. She stuffed the fallen debris back into her locker and slammed the door, hard.

"I'm not excited."

"Beebs, the guy's a burn-out. And you know what your therapist said about your compulsion to rescue emotionally immature men."

"Ah, c'mon. Why so critical? We all have our little issues. And it's not like I actually would ever date him."

"Does sleeping with him count as dating?"

"Lucy, stop. You know I don't go for Robert Redford types. The guy congratulated us on the great piece we did on the livestock extermination. And he specifically asked about you. Wanted to know if you got the flowers he and the governor sent when you were in the hospital."

"They sent flowers?"

"I told him you didn't get them. Actually, you were unconscious so I took them to an anniversary party I had to go to later on that night and I forgot to tell you."

"Bea!"

"Hey, I'm just kidding. I never saw them. Anyway,

what are you going to wear?"

"Well, I don't know. My Galliano is at the cleaners, so is my Vera Wang." Lucy stared as the yoga pants caught in her locker door. "He seemed pretty impressed with himself. Could be a long evening. Maybe I'll beg off."

Bea put the cookie tin down on the bench with a clang, exasperated.

"Beg off? Forget it, my friend. It'll be a lonely existence if you don't start opening up to people, particularly eligible male people."

"I've heard this lecture before from you. And even if I was interested in having a relationship, it wouldn't be with an adrenaline-junkie war reporter, probably with all the emotional depth of a . . . shot glass."

"He has been nothing but nice to you."

"He was totally arrogant."

"He dragged you out of that damned pit you fell into! Got himself all covered with blood. Disgusting."

Lucy felt her brows furrow. "He did, like, rescue me?"

"Yes, he sure did, he and Truckee—it was a nasty business, believe you me!" Bea began to pace and banged on the lockers for emphasis. Then she abruptly stopped.

"All right. Okay. I'll cool it for now. I know I'm a pushy broad but we should definitely meet with him."

"And I'm stubborn as hell," Lucy said, an apologetic tilt to her head. "I wouldn't miss dinner with you and Media Mike Burleson. I know he wants to grill me on my uncle. We might need something from him at some point. Just let me know when and where. I'll be there."

"And looking fine?"

"At least no sweats, or yoga pants," Lucy

promised.

Bea smiled. "That's more like it."

The two women hugged in truce.

"Oh, I almost forgot," Bea said. She pulled a white envelope from her pocket and handed it to Lucy. "This was left for you at the front desk about an hour ago. They were going to put it in your box but I said I'd bring it down."

"Thanks."

Lucy tore open the envelope, and began to read. A small article that appeared to be from a website of some kind—the San Bernardino County eGazette, was dated today. Attached was a note from Carly Montgomery's husband, Keith. She gasped in horror as the story became clear.

"What is it?" Bea plunked down on the bench again and pressed the lid back on the cookie tin.

"My source at Dynamic Chemical, my friend, Carly," Lucy's words were barely audible. "She was almost killed in a loading dock accident last night." Lucy passed the article to Bea.

Bea skimmed the news. "That's appalling. I am so sorry."

"And she . . . she may never walk again." Lucy licked her lips and tried to clear her throat. "She has twins, barely toddlers." Lucy leaned against her locker, pale and shaken. She looked into the envelope and discovered another small piece of paper. She read the note, and stuck it into her pocket.

Bea dropped her voice to a whisper as the new camera operator, Thomas Rubio, walked in. "You don't think that . . . I mean, loading docks are always fairly dangerous places."

"I don't know what to think." Lucy's head spun. Grabbing her coat from the bench, she stood up and shrugged into it.

From the far end of the room, Thomas Rubio, a small man with dark features, came toward them. Despite his stature, he had a wiry strength with the camera and gear that belied his size.

"Hi, Tom," Lucy said. They exchanged greetings and then Bea and Lucy continued to talk in subdued tones as he made his way across the room to the assignment monitor.

"I wonder who else knows about this subsidiary business," Bea asked.

"I have no idea. I mean Carly only shared it with me and I only told you. That's it."

Picturing Carly brought a lump to Lucy's throat. It was from more than fear, it was guilt raising its incriminating finger. Had her requests for information from Carly almost pounded nails into her coffin? On the scribbled piece of paper, Carly's husband, Keith, asked Lucy to meet him at their house in the Santa Clarita Valley Friday night, after work. He wrote in his note he suspected this was not an accident. *Do not mention this to anyone,* he demanded.

Bea handed the article back to Lucy. "I mean with subsidiaries all over the place and especially in Juarez and Medellín," she said, appearing to ruminate on the possibilities. "Conjures thoughts of drug cartels and organized crime, doesn't it? It just screams bad news!"

Lucy looked sadly out of the room's only narrow window toward the parking lot then turned to Bea.

"Let's state the obvious," she said. "If Dynamic Chemical Company manufactures pharmaceuticals and food additives, illegal drugs could well be a sideline."

"Or a main line, especially if an Alvarez brother was an executive," Bea murmured.

"Medellín has really cleaned up. It's not a bad place anymore," Tom said.

Lucy and Bea's heads turned in unison. Neither of the two women had noticed that Thomas Rubio was still at his locker.

"Is the station planning to send a crew down there?" he asked in his lilting continental accent.

"No, they're not," Bea said. She gave the man a disapproving look.

"I'm sorry, Miss Middleton. I really wasn't listening to your conversation. Just heard Medellín mentioned. I was in Columbia in the Peace Corps. It's really a beautiful country. It makes me unhappy that everyone still thinks only of murderous drug dealers when they talk about the place."

"I prefer the days when thoughts of Columbia elicited the aroma of rich Columbian Coffee from Juan Valdez," Lucy declared. She wondered if Thomas even knew what she was talking about.

"I really have to be outta here," Bea said. She glanced at her watch. "I'm taking that extension course at UCLA tonight and I've got to pick Dexter up from b-ball practice, like, right now."

"Okay. Later, Bea. I've gotta run, too."

"You gonna be all right, Luce?"

Lucy nodded. "Of course. Give the kid hugs from me."

"Somehow Rubio doesn't seem like the Peace Corps type to me," Bea whispered just before she left. Tom stashed his camera, closed his locker and came over to Lucy, a worried look on his face.

The sound of Bea's heels clicked away down the hall.

"How are you doing, Thomas? Is everything all right?"

Lucy was head of the camera department and, along with executive producer, Max, she was responsible for hiring Rubio away from a top Orlando television station. His audition tape looked fantastic and his recommendations were impeccable. Lucy was surprised, however, what a difficult time he was having getting up to speed here in L.A. Nothing he turned in came close to what he had presented on his tape.

"Everything's fine, Miss Vega. I'm getting around the city okay. My family and my wife's family are from San Francisco, so we like being back out west. We weren't too crazy about Florida. My wife hated the humidity in the South, and the bugs."

Lucy smiled. "It's not too often someone chooses to give up a gig in the Sunshine State."

Tom smiled, and nodded his head. "I, uh, I . . ." he hesitated.

"What is it?"

"I don't think Miss Middleton likes me. I think maybe I offended her tonight. I really wasn't eavesdropping."

"Don't worry about Bea, she'll get over it," Lucy reassured him. "She's just a little stressed, got a lot on her mind."

"About the story in Columbia?"

"There's no story in Columbia, Tom. We've got

enough stories here in our own back yard to cover.

"By the way," Lucy continued. "I thought I saw you over on the Third Street Promenade yesterday with an old, uh, friend of mine, Gary Mercer."

Hi eyes widened. "Mercer? I don't know a Mercer."

"Ah, maybe I was mistaken. First half hour out of the hospital, I was probably hallucinating."

Tom Rubio nodded and stepped toward the door, nervously rubbing his hands together.

"I hope you are feeling much better now."

"Yes sir, I am." Lucy smiled at him. "Glad you were able to cover for me. Thank you."

"It was my pleasure."

Lucy hoped Rubio would finally kick in and start working at a little higher level. She certainly wanted to give the guy the benefit of the doubt. She sensed that he was feeling insecure and somewhat lost. Big moves were tough for most people.

"Listen Tom, if there is anything I can do for you, just let me know. Don't hesitate. I want to see the job work out for you here."

"Thank you, Miss Vega."

"Please, call me Lucy. In case you hadn't noticed, we're a very laid back, informal group here, okay?"

"Okay, Miss . . . I mean, Lucy. Good night now."

"Good night, Thomas. Now wipe that worried look off your face!"

He smiled and then stumbled awkwardly out of the room. Thoughts about Thomas Rubio and his mediocre camera work quickly vanished as Lucy thought about the painful, upcoming meeting with Carly's husband.

CHAPTER 23

Although it was barely five o'clock when Lucy arrived at Carly and Keith Montgomery's neighborhood, the last vestige of pale winter light had disappeared beneath the horizon. The attractive new Santa Clarita subdivision was obviously filled with young families. As she drove along the street she passed a mind-boggling array of Christmas and Hanukkah decorations. A family of inflatable snow people with tennis ball noses and oversized plastic sunglasses sat in the yard next to the Montgomery home—a two-story, Spanish-style stucco dwelling at the end of a cul-de-sac.

Lucy pulled to the curb and turned off the ignition. She looked up at the dark porch—Christmas lights hung unlit from the gutters. Sitting for a moment in the darkness, she could already feel the warmth ebbing from the interior of the car. It was time to meet Keith

Montgomery and find out what happened on that loading dock.

After ringing the bell, a stocky, gray-haired woman opened the door. With her came the delicious scent of potatoes, onions and pot roast.

"May I help you?" she asked. Her eyes were red and puffy.

"I'm Lucy Vega, a friend of Keith and Carly's. I think he's expecting me."

"Oh yes. I'm Mary Montgomery, Keith's mom. Come on in, dear," she said, patting Lucy's arm warmly. "I apologize that this house is such a mess. We've had quite a time here." She wiped her damp forehead with the edge of her apron.

"I'm so sorry, Mrs. Montgomery," Lucy said, swallowing hard. "This is so horrible."

"It is, indeed, but I'm very glad you're here. Keith's in the family room."

"How is Carly doing? They wouldn't let me talk to her."

"She's got a good attitude, never one for feeling sorry for herself. Keith will fill you in on the rest. My daughter, Ruthie, took the kids grocery shopping, so they won't be bothering you. Oh, how rude of me—may I take your coat?"

"Oh, no thanks. I'm a little chilled tonight."

"It's sure a cold one. Please, this way."

Lucy followed Mrs. Montgomery down a dim hallway into a large family room. It was a chaos of toddler paraphernalia.

"Right in here," she said, motioning to Lucy. "Keith, you have a visitor."

Keith Montgomery, dark-haired and gaunt, sat at a PC next to a playpen. When Lucy entered he stood up immediately and offered a hug. He had an open, pleasant face and a practical, no-nonsense way about him that Lucy had always been drawn to.

"Hello, Lucy. Thank you for coming. Nice to see you again. I'm sorry this has to be the circumstance of our meeting." He glanced over his shoulder at the computer. The top of the monitor was piled high with toddler pull-up undies. "I'm working at home for the next few weeks. I don't know how I'm going to get anything accomplished." He managed a half-smile. Please, sit down."

A space was cleared on the couch for Lucy. She draped her coat over her shoulders and savored the coziness of the room. Keith planted himself across from her on a broad rocking chair. Lucy could envision Carly sitting there rocking her babies. After high school they had gone their separate ways—Lucy to UCLA and Carly off to Stanford. Although the times they had spent together in recent years was sporadic at best, there would always be an enduring bond of friendship that made their occasional meetings as comfortable as if they had seen each other yesterday.

"I'm glad you invited me to visit. I just want to say . . . I am so sorry." She struggled with the words. "What happened is just horrendous. How is she? What did the doctors say?"

Keith took a deep breath and scrubbed his hands through his short-cut hair. "She'll walk again, hopefully. Her legs are pretty much screwed together, and the tissue damage was bad. There will be months, maybe years, of rehab."

"Lucy let out a slow sigh. "That accident could have killed her."

Clearing his throat, Keith leaned forward, elbows balancing atop bony knees, eyes glistening and watery. "I wanted to talk with you about her accident, because we don't think it was an accident."

Lucy chewed at her lip. Tense silence was heavy in the room. Then Lucy said, "Would you share your thoughts with me?" Her gut agreed with Keith but she didn't want to believe it. Had she recklessly set her friend up for catastrophe? A knot of guilt and horror pulled tight in her chest.

"Information security systems is my field. I consult for major businesses and teach at Cal Tech," Keith said.

"Yes, I remember that." Lucy said.

"Carly talked me into helping her get the information on Dynamic Chemical Company for you," he said. "I advised her against it but you know how insistent she can be."

Lucy's smile was faint. She was preparing for the worst. "She told me she had . . . twisted your arm."

Keith nodded. "There wasn't much info but it was interesting. I'm sure there aren't many people in that company who have access to the facts of their South and Central American connections. Carly sure didn't have a clue." He sat up straight and rubbed his neck, kneading tight muscles with his fingers. "I've never done anything unauthorized like this before, illegal hacking. My wife convinced me it was critical information, important to solving your uncle's, uh, murder. I guess I need to be reassured again that we did the right thing, because she'll be struggling to walk for a long time."

The blood pounded in Lucy's head. "You think someone tried to . . ."

He glanced over to the kitchen to see if his mother was within earshot, and then whispered, "Yes, I think somebody tried to kill my wife."

Lucy pressed her chest. Keith was confirming her worst fear.

Keith's gaze turned to the computer monitor. The screensaver displayed colorful, languidly swimming tropical fish. Then he looked back at Lucy, his hazel eyes raw with fear. His voice lowered to near inaudibility. "Right now I'm scared to death. Would they, whomever *they* are, try again? Or worse—would they go after one of the kids, or my mother?" He buried his head in his hands.

"I'm really freaking out," he said. "I mean, I'm definitely the worrier of the family. But this time I think I may be right. What happened is just too bizarre. Those boxes and racks were pushed by a forklift. The investigator said they just fell, were stacked poorly, but Carly said she saw someone and he purposefully rammed those storage units, causing them to crash."

"Could she identify this person?"

"Just a shadowy face is all she saw. Cops are pretty much blowing it off." Keith drew himself up straighter. "This may sound nuts, but I'm selling the house and we're moving. I've had an offer in Singapore I turned down a year ago but they keep asking me. The money is great. The kids would grow up in an international environment. I have to get us away from here. I have to protect my family."

"Keith, 'I'm sorry' doesn't begin to express what I feel." Tears welled in her eyes. "The information you and Carly discovered could be very important. It could be the key to everything."

"What do you mean—*everything?*" Keith pressed.

"I'm not sure I even know yet—but my uncle's death, Carly's so-called accident, the organophosphate poisoning. Something's very wrong at Dynamic Chemical. I'm going to get to the bottom of this. I promise."

"No, wait!" Keith sprung up and began to pace the floor. A baby started to cry from upstairs. Keith's mom padded up the steps. "What I mean is, I asked you here to tell you that if you push any harder, we could all be at risk, including you. Whatever's going on, it's not worth another life or limb. Whatever it is, or was, it's over now. Done. Nothing will take away the poisoning of this state, or bring back your uncle, or make Carly's learning to walk again any easier. Please, Lucy, for all of our sakes— back off. Leave it alone."

Lucy stood up and wiped the moisture from her eyes. Her head felt like it was being squeezed in a vise grip. Her stitches itched like fire. Keith and Carly's life had been blasted apart because she'd asked her friend for this favor.

"Do I have your promise, Lucy? For the sake of my family?" Keith asked, eyes pleading, frightened.

"Keith," Lucy said, "you can't ask me to turn away. It's not right. They shouldn't be allowed to get away with this."

"But I *am* going to ask you. Lucy?" His eyes narrowed and he chewed at the inside of his cheek.

Lucy stomach churned with nausea. Carly and her

family had paid, so had her uncle, and who knows how many others. "I can't lie to you, Keith," Lucy said. "The lid is off the box." She stood and put on her coat.

Keith shook his head is frustration and disappointment. "Okay then, I'm going ahead with plans to move. As soon as we can. Carly will be on board."

Lucy's shoulders fell. She looked drained and exhausted. "I'm so, so sorry."

Keith reached out and touched her arm. He sighed deeply, resignedly. "Lucy, it was our choice to help you. We're not faultless here, we knew what we were doing. I just didn't expect this—disaster."

"Me either. Take care, Keith," Lucy said, almost gagging on the powerful emotions she was feeling. "Tell Carly I love her, and kiss the kids." She walked down the hallway and out the front door.

"Be careful, Lucy," Keith called from the darkened doorway. "I know my wife would support you in this, despite my protests. Do it for her, then. Find these assholes, but don't sacrifice your own life in the process."

She stopped for a moment, not looking back, then fled into the dismal night.

CHAPTER 24

A cold, misty rain slicked the streets with a glassy finish. Lucy carefully navigated out of the neighborhood and stopped at a light on the outskirts of Montgomery's subdivision. In front of her, the highway bustled with commuter traffic. Headlamps raced by, creating a fluid streak of illumination.

A high, metallic squeal of brakes sounded. Lucy's eyes darted to her rearview mirror. An SUV was skidding up behind her, threatening to roll over her like a big, black bowling ball.

A flash bang of adrenaline cut through Lucy's chest. She couldn't escape into the intersection. Too many cars, coming way too fast.

The SUV fishtailed out of control. *This guy isn't going to stop.* One hard tap and he'd smack her into oncoming traffic.

Lucy wrenched the steering wheel hard and accelerated, landing on up on a sidewalk in the midst of a front-yard Christmas display. An illuminated plastic donkey flew into the air and landed on her hood with a thud. It dimmed, flickered, then went out. Thankfully, she had spared Joseph, Mary, and baby Jesus.

The SUV behind her smashed her rear taillight before nearly colliding with a telephone pole. Motorists on the clogged highway were oblivious to the near disaster coming at them from the side road. Lucy shuddered, her heart hammering. She jumped out of her car and dashed toward the other vehicle.

"Are you all right?" she cried, knocking frantically on the dark tinted window.

To her shock, the driver hit the gas and tried to maneuver around her car, nearly running her over in the process. She smacked her palm on the windshield. *Bastard.* "What the hell are you doing?" she yelled. "Are you crazy?" She wanted to grab a reindeer and do major damage to the guy. Then she recognized the face behind the steering wheel. "Thomas Rubio? What the—I don't believe it! It's Lucy. Are you all right? What are you doing driving like that?"

The window slowly lowered. Rubio's lips wrenched into a smile that looked like bent wire. "Miss Vega, I mean Lucy. I'm fine, and I'm so sorry. The streets are very bad. I guess I'm not used to winter driving yet."

"I can see that."

"I forgot the rain lifts the oil up and makes everything so slick," he said.

An open camera case glinted on the seat next to him. The lenses and accessories were in disarray on the floor.

Apparently, he drove as badly as he photographed.

"God was watching over us. Are you okay, Miss Lucy?"

Gee, nice of you to ask. "A little shaken, but I've had worse. What a coincidence—you plowing into me out here. You live in this neighborhood?"

"No, but nearby," he said, coughing. "I just had to drop my wife off at a friend's house. You live here? It's a very nice area."

"I have a place in Santa Monica." Lucy pushed dripping strands of hair out of her face. *To hell with this little conversation.* "Listen, we'd better exchange insurance information." She bent toward the window.

For a moment, Rubio sat quietly in the dry comfort of his car, not even inviting her to climb in out of the rain. He didn't reach for documents in the glove box.

"I have a terrible problem," he began. "I accidentally let my insurance run out when we moved here. But don't worry, I'll pay for all of your repairs. Just give me the bill. And you won't have to file a claim. That will be good, no?"

A car pulled up behind them and honked. Lucy signaled them around. Several other horns joined the grating chorus. "Dammit, we've had an accident here, people. Give us a break!" she yelled.

"We'd better clear out," Rubio said. "Or we'll cause more problems. Yes?" His eyes flitted left and right.

"Okay, Tom. We'll deal with the insurance thing Monday morning," Lucy said. She glanced at her Jeep, which straddled the sidewalk and shook her head. "Drive more carefully. And you're crazy to be on the road without insurance. What if you killed somebody?

An innocent person would be dead and you'd lose everything you have."

"I've been very foolish. I am so sorry and I'm glad you are all right," Rubio called as he eased onto the road ahead. "See you Monday." His window snapped shut.

Lucy waved, feeling more than a twinge of resentment as he went merrily on his way. She was still stuck in a Christmas pageant. A family of faces peered out through their front window. Lucy gave them a quick wave. A little girl of about three pointed at the donkey and wailed. You could hear her even through the closed window. *Oh, terrific.* Lucy grabbed her cell phone, ran for her car and called the auto club, her mind filled with thoughts about her family, her uncle, and the fragile precariousness of life.

✳

Monday morning brought a slight warming trend as temperatures rose into the high fifties—still considered arctic by Southern California standards.

"I kind of like the cold, wet weather," Lucy said. "Nice change."

Truckee brought a big box of sweet rolls and coffee into the staff office. It resembled a YMCA locker room with an equipment cage, a big table with mismatched office chairs in the center, and a kitchenette that was a step above the coffee island at a Jiffy Lube. News programming played on several widescreens affixed high on the walls.

"I admit it," the big guy said, "I'm a total whiner where the weather's concerned. If it's not sunny and seventies for more than two days, I'm ready to move to

Arizona and retire in the desert."

"Ah, you love it here and you know it," Lucy bit into a doughy maple-glazed buttermilk donut, which was incomparably better that those light, airy crispy things everybody raved about. She couldn't suppress a slight moan of pleasure.

"No way, I'm ready to move on. L.A. sucks. The traffic drives me nuts," he complained.

"Uh-huh. Seems like I heard those very words before when you passed on that job in Atlanta," said Lucy.

"The humidity down there gives me heat rash."

"What about the offer in San Diego last year?" Lucy took another chomp of donut and swooned again.

"San Diego—I can't stand the Padres." Truckee grinned as he grabbed for a second cheese danish.

Lucy sat down at the table and fired up her laptop. She licked the crumbs off her fingers. Truckee settled onto the aging, overstuffed, faux-leather couch next to the office door.

"So, what's happening with your friend Carly's injury?" Truckee finished off his second danish then reached for a bear claw.

Lucy rubbed her forehead. "Cops don't buy her version of the story. The dock supervisor says there's no evidence of foul play, but OSHA's being called in. I called them."

"Good. Are you and the husband—"

"His name is Keith," Lucy reminded him.

"Are you and Keith getting carried away? It's tough to come to grips with his wife getting hurt. He'd want to hang the responsibility on somebody with deep pockets. I don't blame him. Hell, she's pretty much a paraplegic."

Lucy slammed her coffee cup down with a thud. "Yeah, it's horrible, but it was not an accident. She knows stuff they don't want her to know. I'll prove it to you, to everybody. Be patient. Trust me, big guy."

Truckee slurped a swig of coffee and shrugged his heavy shoulders.

The fast *clip-clip* of high heels sounded in the hallway. The metal door to the office burst open and Bea appeared, eyes blazing.

"So, did you all have a nice weekend?" She whipped her scarf off so violently she accidentally smacked Truckee in the head. He glared at her but she didn't offer an apology.

"Saw the Lakers beat Golden State," Truckee said, tearing into another pastry. Powdered sugar went up his nose. He sneezed with a gale force blast. "Gotta stop eating this shit."

"No kidding," Lucy said. She rolled her eyes. "And my weekend was the pits, thanks for asking." Lucy watched the browser open on her computer screen. News of military disasters, celebrity hook-ups, and political shenanigans paraded across the screen with jarring graphics.

"Mine was a disaster, too," Bea declared. She shrugged out of her bright red designer raincoat and tossed it onto a chair. "I had to work Saturday and Sunday with Rubio. The visuals he gave me were so hideous that I ended up doing voice-over stock footage. Lucy, you have *got* to get rid of that man."

"At least he didn't total the rear end of *your car*. And if I hadn't recognized him, I think he would have fled the scene."

"What? You're kidding?" Bea exclaimed. A little wind leaked out of her outraged sails.

"The auto club had to tow me out of a Christmas manger scene and it took them almost two hours to show up. The kids who live in the house were all crying because I'd mangled the donkey and flattened an archangel. And on top of that blasphemy, get this—he's not insured."

"Aw, jeez. Well, it's time to take action," Bea said. "Fire his bony, incompetent ass."

"All right," Lucy replied as she punched up her electronic address book. "I've been meaning to call the news director in Orlando to see if he could give me some insight into making this guy productive. I also wanted to personally curse him out for sending us such a disaster."

"That's more like it!" Bea said, cheering up.

"Forget the 'in'—just see if he can figure out how to give Rubio some basic sight." Truckee chuckled at his own joke. "Hey, Beezy, can I get you a cup o' joe?"

"That would be sweet, big man."

Lucy checked her watch and continued to scan through the address files. "Ah, here's the info. The Orlando station news director's name is Alan Klein."

"I remember him," Bea said. "We met once at a conference in Miami. Short, cute, kinda looks like John Stewart."

"I'd say more like Seinfeld's Larry David but with more hair." Lucy grabbed the phone and dialed his direct office number. Klein picked up immediately.

"Hi, Alan. This is Lucy Vega, head of the photography department at KLAK in L.A."

Hey, nice to hear from you, Lucy. What's going on out on the left coast?"

"Well, we've got a problem. I have some questions about your guy Rubio, the one who started with us about a month ago."

Klein hesitated for an instant. "I'd be happy to help you, Lucy, but Thomas Rubio is working in Atlanta. He's a Southern boy, a Georgia Tech grad, didn't want anything to do with the West Coast. I just spoke with him a week ago. He's doing great. Bought a nice condo in Buckhead."

"Now wait a minute." Lucy pressed the spot between her eyes, hard. "Are you saying the Thomas Rubio who worked for you, with the audition reel from the Hurricane Alice disaster and AIDS in the Cuban immigrant population, went to Atlanta?"

"Yep, that's right."

"What the hell?" Truckee growled from just over Lucy's shoulder. He handed Bea her coffee, which she gratefully seized.

"Can you email or fax me a picture of him, like his station I.D. or something?"

"I'll call HR right away and get that over to you," he promised. "Actually, let me text you a photo I have on my phone of him at our local baseball team playoffs. That'll be faster."

Lucy suddenly sensed a possible broader connection. "You do business with anyone named Gary Mercer, by any chance?

"Oh, sure, he was a freelancer for us for a few months. Good photographer. Left Florida a couple weeks ago, heading back to L.A."

Lucy gasped, puzzle pieces were shifting but maybe there was some mistake. "Any chance of getting his picture, too?"

"No problem. Keep me posted on all this, okay?"

She and Alan spoke for a few more minutes then she hung up the phone.

"Lucy, what's going on?" Bea asked.

"I don't freaking know. And you won't believe this one—Gary Mercer has been working as a freelancer in Orlando with Rubio!"

"Mercer?" Bea scowled.

"And Klein says Tom Rubio went to Atlanta, not L.A."

"Holy shit," Truckee said. He choked on his coffee, put his cup down and finally stopped eating.

CHAPTER 25

"This is bizarre as hell," Truckee said as they awaited the text message from Klein. "You think Mercer masterminded this identity switcheroo to screw with us?"

"I wouldn't put anything past that asshole," Bea said.

"He's in this up to his eyeballs." Lucy checked her phone six times in less than a half minute. Finally, the message came though.

The face in the baseball jersey holding a hot dog did not belong to KLAK-TV's Thomas Rubio, and the tall man in the row behind him, was definitely Gary Mercer.

Lucy sprinted back to the crew room. Bea and Truckee followed in her wake.

"Wait a minute, Lucy," Bea called. "Slow down, let's talk about this."

But it was too late. All they could do was to try and

keep up with her. Lucy went directly to Rubio's locker. The door hung open. His coat and equipment were gone. "He had his camera on the seat when he hit my car last night. The stuff from the case was all over the floor. I wonder if he was spying on the Montgomery's . . . or on me!"

She turned, pushed past Bea and Truckee and sprinted for the door to the parking lot. Ernie entered the station and barely avoided a collision as Lucy shot by him.

"You see Rubio out there?" she called over her shoulder.

"On his way over toward the vans. What's up?"

Lucy bolted across the parking lot. She spotted Rubio at the same time he spotted her. He turned and ran all-out away from the parked news vans, the camera tucked beneath his arm. The guy was fast.

"Rubio!" she yelled. "Who the hell are you, Rubio? Did Mercer put you up to this, you fucking liar?"

Lucy chased him through the lot but he had too much of a head start. By the time she caught up with him, he was already firing up his car. It was the same one that had rear-ended her. He backed out of his space and gunned it toward the main gate, and toward Lucy.

Tires screeched as he blasted straight at her. His engine growled like a demon lawnmower. Lucy's nostrils stung from the scent of burning rubber. For an instant she was paralyzed, then she dove for all she was worth away from the blur of the oncoming vehicle.

Rubio swerved back toward the gate and sped out of the studio lot. He missed Lucy by inches. She gasped for breath, collapsed in a puddle of gravel and oily water.

Her hands were scraped raw and blood oozed through the knees of her khakis. Bea, Truckee, and Ernie ran up beside her, panting.

"Oh my God, are you okay?" Bea crouched at Lucy's side.

"I think he was actually trying to take you out," Truckee gasped.

"No shit." Lucy puffed and struggled to stand. Truckee grabbed her beneath her arms and lifted her like a feather. "A rather extreme reaction to avoid paying me for wrecking my car, wouldn't you say?"

"I got the license plate number. I'll have it run through the DMV," Bea said as she scribbled the number on her hand with a Sharpie.

"Car's probably stolen," Truckee said.

"I'll take a pic of fake Rubio's station I.D. and text it to Klein, see if he recognizes him," Lucy said. She slumped against Truckee. He wrapped his arm around her shoulder as she began to shake from the receding adrenaline rush.

"And I'll send it to my cousin over at LAPD. Maybe she can do something with facial recognition software," he said.

"Sounds good." Lucy grimaced and examined her bloody palms. "We'll get this asshole."

"Somebody's got to tell me what's going on here," Ernie said, hands open in bewilderment.

Lucy pulled the iPhone out of her pocket and brought up the photo from Orlando.

He read the text, studied the photo, then looked up, eyes wide. "If this is the real Rubio, then who the hell was that?"

✳

Late the next morning, Lucy pushed through the heavy back door into the KLAK-TV building. She hadn't slept and her head pounded. She'd knocked back a couple of Advil but they'd stuck in her throat. She helped herself to a long swig of water from an open bottle on the guard's desk then wiped the spout with the sleeve of her sweatshirt. "Thanks."

"Feel free to help yourself." He smiled. "Tough night, babe?"

She nodded. He waved her through security then turned his attention back to the lascivious graphic novel on his desk.

As Lucy trudged down the hallway to the crew room, camera in hand and gear bag banging against her hip, Truckee emerged from the men's room. Tucking in his red plaid flannel shirt, his hands were buried so deep down his pants that the shirt tails must have ended around his knees.

"Hey, Truck," Lucy said as she rounded the corner to her locker. Although the hand that had taken the brunt of the fall in the parking lot had loosened up a bit since her first assignment that morning, it still felt like it was cast in concrete. Just moving her fingers was painful. Her wrist was sprained, too. Running on empty, she couldn't wait to stow the camera.

"Anything yet on the fake Rubio I.D.?" she asked.

"Should be coming any time now. Truckee helped Lucy put her gear away. "You doin' okay?" he asked.

"Hangin' in. The road rash sucks."

"Maxell's looking for you, by the way," Truckee said with a dramatic roll of his eyes.

Lucy took a deep, wary breath. "What's he want?"

"Well, he said—*tell her to get her pretty little ass down here the minute she gets in.*"

" 'Little'? He said that?"

"Not exactly, but in so many words. I mean, not the 'pretty little ass' part. You know Max, always so civil," Truckee said.

Lucy smiled. "But you're so much more colorful. He probably wants to give my butt a big, fat raise."

"Don't think that was the mood he was in," Truckee said.

Lucy winced as she peeled the leather gloves off her injured hands. The bandages tore at the fresh scabs like crows on carrion. She knew what Max wanted to talk about, and she didn't look forward to it. That added to the pain.

Truckee slammed his locker door shut. "Chiliburgers in the cafeteria today. I've got the beano. Join us if you're still employed."

"Thanks for the words of encouragement," Lucy called over her shoulder. Truckee chuckled.

She shuffled slowly toward Maxwell's office, ready to walk the plank.

❋

"Go on in, sweetheart," said Esther Levine, Maxwell Wedner's long-time administrative assistant. The woman was a throwback to gentler times. She was the kindly elementary school secretary who handed out late passes, forgotten lunchboxes and soothed scuffed knees. Dressed always in floral prints, her hair was a fuzz of blue-gray curls. Her trifocals hung from a chain around her neck as she scrawled reporter's names onto an electronic assignment board. No one was ever less L.A.

"He's more than a little crabby today," she whispered across the desk to Lucy.

"The hell I am!" Max growled from his office.

Esther pursed her lips, shook her head and dropped the tone of her voice even lower. "Those upstart young executives from New York are driving him crazy this week."

Lucy didn't have time to respond before Maxwell was at his door. He ushered her into his windowed corner office with a view that spanned from Century City's cold, corporate high-rises, to the ocean in the distance. She'd had a great relationship with Max over the years. She loved the guy. He wouldn't suspend her, or fire her—would he?

"Have a seat, Lucy." He pointed to a well-worn leather chair in front of a broad desk covered with a riot of papers, DVDs, news clippings, Post-its and two laptops with multiple monitors. Esther shut the door behind them.

"So, Max, what's up?" Lucy asked.

Maxwell sat down behind his desk and leaned intently toward her. His tie hung down like a big blue tongue.

"Lucy, you know I have nothing but respect for you, in every way, but what you did yesterday was out of line. Taking off after a potentially dangerous man, on your own—you could have been killed. The head of security played the tape for me. Rubio, or whoever he is, missed you by inches. I was horrified. And what if he'd been armed? Jesus. What were you thinking?"

Lucy sat up straighter and tried to stop the overwhelming urge to squirm in her seat. "Okay. You're right," she said, squirming like crazy. "When I heard Mercer was working down in Florida, and a face I'd never seen before turned out to be the real Thomas Rubio, I reacted. Sometimes that's just what you've got to do. I went with my gut."

"You should have called the police immediately. Let them deal with it. Am I correct? Instead, you almost got killed. Your colleagues could have been injured, too. And meanwhile, mystery man is long gone."

Max's usually soft gray eyes had gone laser. Lucy's head pounded. She wasn't about to fight with him. She knew he was right, damn it. "Something in me just took over. I just lost it. I'm sorry."

"Impulsive action—it's both your gift and your Achilles heel. You know that, don't you?"

She sighed. "I've been told that a few times." She was more like her mother than she wanted to admit. She looked into Max's watery eyes above his ever-drooping half-frame glasses. He wasn't just her boss—he was her friend.

"Okay, Max. I was wrong. I wanted to confront that asshole face to face. He's mixed up with Mercer who put me in the hospital for a week. This fake Rubio could be tied into my uncle's death and to the livestock poisoning. The bastard lied to me, cracked up my car, and tried to run me over. I'm taking this very personally. Maybe I shouldn't, but I'm only human."

"I think you sometimes forget that fact," Max said.

"What do you mean?"

"You've been under a lot of stress lately and you've never missed a beat. Maybe you need some time away from all this, to recover, renew." Max took his glasses off and proceeded to clean the lenses with a Kleenex.

"Jeez, you've been talking to Bea. I don't need time off. Work keeps me grounded." She fought back tears and the burning in her throat. "It's all I have right now. I can't just rattle around the house, I'd go crazy."

"Time off does not need to mean rattling around the house." Maxwell shrugged and dropped back in his chair, placed his glasses on a tattered file folder. "I also want to make one more point."

Lucy looked up and bit her lip.

"If . . ." he leaned forward again, his brows drawn with concern, "if there are some things I should know that you're not telling me, if there's a story you're working on—please level with me. You should not be playing vigilante Lone Ranger."

"What are you talking about?"

"If you have a lead on anything unusual regarding Mercer, the fake Rubio, the poisoning, or any of that stuff—I expect you to tell me. We'll involve the proper authorities. I am worried about you, Lucy. I want you safe and healthy because I want to keep looking at the world through your lens for a long, long time. Okay? Do you understand what I'm saying?"

Lucy gulped. "Yes, of course."

"I'm not sure you do." He reached over and patted her hand. "Go have lunch. You're off for the afternoon, by the way. That news conference on garbage pickup at the pier you and Ernie were scheduled to cover, was canceled. In the meantime, Lucy, think about a vacation.

Again, taking some time doesn't mean you have to be bored to death. You're a creative woman—there must be somewhere you'd like to go—take photos for that children's book on the relationship between kids and animals you've always wanted to do. How about Turkey or Hong Kong—somewhere different, exciting?"

"Okay, Max. I'll think about it." Lucy didn't want to hear more of the travelogue.

"I'm glad we had this talk, Lucy. We understand each other?"

"Yes, we do." Lucy cleared her throat and disappeared quickly out the door.

CHAPTER 26

Lucy decided to meet Truckee and Ernie for lunch, even though the talk with Max had pretty much wiped out her appetite. At least she hadn't been suspended, or worse yet, fired. If she didn't fill in her friends on the gist of her come-to-Jesus meeting with Maxwell, the rumor mill would start to spin, as it frequently did in their little KLAK-TV community. Truckee was second only to Bea in turning those wheels. Ernie was third.

She spotted her colleagues in a far corner of the cafeteria. It was well after 2:00 P.M., and thankfully, the lunch crowd had thinned considerably. Lucy passed up the famous chiliburgers and ordered a bowl of chicken soup with a bag of oyster crackers. The soup slopped onto the serving tray as she made her way over to the two men.

"Finally," Truckee said. "I thought you stood us up."

"I'd never do that to two of my favorite boy toys." She unloaded the wet tray and left it on a nearby table.

"This here old boy toy wants to know what's up with Max. We having your last supper?" Truckee sank his teeth into at least his second chiliburger. Remnants from the first littered his shirt.

Ernie chuckled and choked on his chili fries.

"Wife's got him on a paleo diet—can't handle this junk food anymore," Truckee said.

After the coughing and gagging subsided, Lucy spooned a couple of long slurps of her chicken soup. Guess she was hungry after all.

"Okay, guys—here's the short, sweet summary. Max has enough on his plate with all this corporate buy-out crapola so I feel too guilty to hit him with my suspicions over my uncle's death. He told me he wanted to stay up on everything. But I mean, why worry him when I have absolutely nothing solid? Yet."

"Max is excellent at invoking guilt," Truckee said. "The Jews are almost as good at guilt as us Catholics."

"Catholics have it, hands down," Ernie said. "Once the Jews start building confessionals and handing out rosaries, maybe we can talk guilt."

"Aside from that, he thinks I should take some time off and just chill. Pressed me hard." She watched the oyster crackers wilt in the soup bowl, then crushed them to mush with her spoon.

"Good idea," Truckee said.

I'll second that," Ernie added. He dabbed at his chin with a crumpled napkin.

"I told him I'd think about it. And of course, he was pretty upset that I went after fake Rubio. Should have called the cops."

"He's right, technically," Ernie said. "But he wasn't there. He would've done the same thing. We all took off after the guy."

Truckee nodded. "Max just doesn't want anyone to get hurt. We're not LAPD. Our job is to report what happened, not intervene."

"Again, technically speaking, I couldn't agree more," Lucy said, "but we all know that line gets crossed, particularly if someone's in danger."

"We've had this conversation tons of times." Truckee tossed a handful of well-used napkins on his empty plate. "Bottom line—we all have to live with ourselves. Right? We take the objectivity as far as we can, we do the job, we believe in the job, but then sometimes—boom. You throw yourself in front of a car or tell some politico to go fuck himself. At some point, you choose not to be the machine."

"Hear, hear." Lucy raised her glass of water. "Listen, I have a question. Who talked to the rail yard manager the night the pesticide got mixed in with the feed?"

"I did." Ernie finished off his last bite of chiliburger and popped two of Truckee's beanos into his mouth. "I can't remember his name, but I'll check my notes. No, wait, it was Bud Martinez. Seemed like a straight arrow. We had a nice rapport. He was Mexican—Oaxacan, actually. He seemed very old school, very by the book."

"And what about that temporary supervisor who killed himself?"

"Sergio something. Cops figured he did it because he screwed up big time. Plus, his immigration papers weren't in order. I heard they were forgeries."

"Sergio has a girlfriend here, right?" Lucy asked.

"Yep, Hollywood, east side." Ernie licked his lips and stared at the dessert menu posted on the wall.

"You talk to her?" she asked.

"Everybody talked to Esmeralda, or tried," Ernie said. "She pretty much cried the whole time, denied he'd ever leave her. She's seven months pregnant and cares for his eighty-year-old mother who has Alzheimer's. On top of that, they've got his six-year-old son from a first marriage. I felt really sorry for her."

"Maybe all that responsibility and the prospect of losing his job put the guy over the edge," Truckee said.

"Yeah, maybe." Lucy smiled at Ernie, feigning innocence, badly. "Hey, you know, we're off this afternoon, Ern. The press conference was canceled."

His eyes narrowed. "I have a lot of research to do right now, Lucy. I'm moderating a panel on green energy sources at Loyola Marymount University tomorrow night. Did you know they use more solar energy than any other university on Earth?"

"That's awesome. But Ern, where did you say the girlfriend lives?"

"No, Lucy." His mouth set in a stubborn line. "Leave it to the LAPD."

"Please, Ernie—just this teeny tiny favor?"

He rolled his eyes, groaned, and punched up his iPad to check the address. "Lives on Highland, near Big Lots."

"If Sergio trusted his girlfriend, Esmeralda, with the care of his son, his mother, and was having another child with her—she must know a whole lot about him," Lucy said. "Maybe the cops just weren't asking the right questions. "It'll take fifteen minutes to go over there. If nobody's home, I'll just forget it for now and help you with your research. Truck, wanna come with us?"

"Fat chance," he said. "Sorry I have to leave you two but some of us actually have to work this afternoon. *Adiós,* Vargas, and good luck." Truckee smiled and lumbered out of the cafeteria.

"So, Luce, what do you think you're going to find out from her?" Ernie crossed his arms on his chest like a man unwilling to budge.

"I don't know. I just want to be open to possible puzzle pieces. I don't think she was properly looked at by anyone, even you, my good man."

Ernie sighed and dug into his pocket for car keys. "Okay. You may be right, but we got to be back by 3:30, *and* you help me for two hours with research."

"Deal!"

"Plus, two hours of babysitting—weekend of my choice."

"Oh, come on . . ."

"Those are my terms."

"You're a tough one." Lucy pushed her soup bowl aside. "I hope your kid is a lot more fun than you are."

Together they made a beeline for the parking lot. Lucy drove while Ernie tried calling Sergio's girlfriend. He only succeeded in leaving her a voicemail.

CHAPTER 27

Esmeralda Nogales lived on the second floor of a five-story, pea-green, stucco apartment building on the edge of downtown. Someone had made a valiant attempt at upkeep, but despite fresh paint, the place still looked tired and worn out. A heavily Hispanic neighborhood, it included a smattering of student apartments and seedy retirement villas. Struggling but optimistic art galleries, family restaurants, and a few hip cafés pushed their flowering possibilities through the crumbling concrete sidewalks. Crack houses and massage parlors still held their ground, but budding gentrification stirred the air.

Ernie parked across from the apartment building. The street was empty as they climbed the steps to the front door of the complex. They walked into the lobby past a wall of mailboxes toward a main stairway. The floor was littered with discarded flyers for cheap insurance deals, bail bondsmen, and yellowing penny-saver newspapers still rolled in their rubber bands.

Up stained carpeted stairs, through moldy-smelling dim halls, they made their way to Esmeralda's second-floor apartment. A Spanish language telenovella chattered from a television inside. Ernie tapped on the door and called out an introduction.

The bright light behind the peephole darkened, several locks disengaged, and the door opened. Big brown eyes peered out from just over the extension of a chain lock.

"You no *policía?*"

"No, *señora,* like I said on the phone, I'm from—" Ernie didn't get the sentence finished.

"I know you!" Her eyes widened. "I know you from the TV. Mr. Ernie Vargas. You left a message."

The door slammed shut with a jingle, then reopened immediately, chain disengaged. "I like you. You're good. Not as handsome as the other guy, but *muy* better."

"Uh, thank you," he said, not sure about the handsome comment.

"Were you here before? I don't remember much about that first week after the terrible thing happened to my Sergio." Fresh tears sprang to her eyes.

"We did speak, but there were many others, too," Ernie said. "It was a very difficult time for you. I regret that to do our jobs we often push into people's lives at very painful times."

Esmeralda nodded and wiped her eyes.

"We didn't get a chance to talk much then. I hoped I could have a minute of your time right now."

"Please, come in." Ernie and Lucy followed Esmeralda

into her tiny apartment. She was an attractive woman in her early thirties. Hair in a dark, swingy ponytail, she wore a gray couture knock-off maternity sweat suit over a fresh white T-shirt. A gold crucifix hung around her neck and small gold hoops pierced her earlobes. She turned off the TV then turned to her guests.

"Everybody wanted to talk, talk, talk, but now nobody cares anymore. Maybe you do. I was, what you call it—hysterical for a while." She sighed, then realized that another news person was also present along with Ernie. "And who is this? A new reporter? Very pretty."

Ernie winked at Lucy. "Forgive my bad manners, *señora*. This is Lucia Vega. She's a photographer but she's not here to take pictures today. We'd just like to talk, to follow up on a couple things."

"Missus Vega, *buenos días*. You don't look so Mexican. What else are you?" Esmeralda stopped herself and blushed. "Forgive me! I'm hooked on those genealogy shows—love all the stories."

"No problem, I'm hooked on them, too. I'm half Mexican and half Norwegian."

"Azteca and Viking." She chuckled. "I like that."

"Kind of an unusual pedigree," Lucy said.

"A *mucho* pretty one. You should be a news anchor, or maybe weather."

"Thank you. You are very kind, but I truly prefer the photography."

Although Lucy took it as a compliment from Esmeralda Nogales, she couldn't count the times people offered their incredulity that a decent-looking woman would want to work behind a camera instead of in front of one.

"Yes, I know what you mean," Esmeralda said. "Getting the makeup done, and hair, nails, and a good dress everyday—who needs it, huh? You like the jeans and sweatshirts. Me too."

"Exactly." Lucy tugged at her UCLA hoodie and stole a quick glance at her short, unpolished nails.

"Please, sit and be comfortable." She gestured Lucy and Ernie to the couch and brought herself a chair from the kitchen. "I offer you something to drink?" Her English was heavily accented but very good.

"No, thank you," Lucy answered. "You are very kind, but we just finished a late lunch."

"Okay. I think I'll grab a glass of water." Esmeralda ducked into the kitchen; a cupboard door squeaked then she turned on the tap. This gave Lucy and Ernie a moment to look around, unattended.

The apartment was neat and clean. The wall across from the sofa was filled with framed family photos next to a wooden crucifix. Toys and games were contained on several shelves next to the television. A basket of crocheting sat on the coffee table where Esmeralda had evidently been working on a deep purple shawl. An anatomy textbook yawned open next to the yarn work. In a far corner, a very old woman slept in a recliner, quietly snoring through her open mouth, dentures askew. She was covered by a navy blue afghan.

As she came back into the living room, Esmeralda noticed Lucy admiring it.

"I sell my sweaters and shawls at a shop down the street, and I make most of our clothing. In Guadalajara, my mother and grandmother were seamstresses." She nodded toward the slender old woman. "Mama Yasmina won't wake up for another hour or so. She can sleep through anything."

Esmeralda finally sat down on the kitchen chair. "You have questions?" She sipped her water.

"Ms. Nogales, could you simply tell us about the time leading up to Sergio's disappearance? And how long has he been your boyfriend?" Ernie asked.

Her face flushed. "No, no, he no boyfriend. We been married seven years. They want to make us look like we immoral. Then they don't have to listen to us, take us seriously. Sergio is a citizen and I have a green card, we legal. Terrible slander! I wish I could sue."

"How did the press get that information so wrong?" Ernie asked.

"They talked to my mother-in-law while I was trying to explain to our boy what was happening. I don't know what Mama Yasmina said to them. They printed some corrections a week later on page twelve of the Metro section but who would see it or care by then? I was so hurt. We are a proud family."

Lucy stole a quick glance at Ernie as Esmeralda took a long gulp of water.

"But more important," she continued, "a better man never walked the earth than my Sergio. Whatever he was involved with was only because he try so hard to take good care of his family. I am in school to be a nurse," she pointed to her anatomy textbook, "and I work at night, too. Mama is very ill with a mental disease—Alzheimer's, and our son, he have a heart condition, and we have another baby on the way." She rubbed her pregnant belly and tears welled in her eyes again.

"All that's a big load to carry," Lucy said.

"*Sí,* but my Sergio's a strong man and we a strong family. On his father's grave, I swear to you, he would never kill himself. Never. We are devout Catholics. And he would never, never, abandon his family. Mr. Vargas, Miss Vega—he was murdered. I'm sure of it. Please help me, no one is listening."

Lucy felt a hard pang of empathy. No one seemed to be listening to her about her uncle's death, either. Were the two connected somehow?

"Could you tell us what you remember about that night, *señora* Nogales?" Ernie continued.

"Okay, sure. My Sergio, he got a call about 3:30 in the afternoon from his supervisor, Mr. Fredericks, telling him he had to be over there at the rail yards in San Bernardino at 5:30 sharp. Sergio works overtime and substitutes around the county a couple times a month so this wasn't no big deal. I packed him a thermos of coffee, a couple burritos and he left here at four o'clock in our SUV. I swear to you, if my husband had made that terrible mistake, mixing the poison with the livestock food, he would not have run away, he would have faced up to it.

"The boy is not your stepson?" Ernie asked, checking his facts.

"No, no, I tell you, he our son, me and Sergio. He came from my body, at Cedars-Sinai hospital. His name is Michael Jordan Sanchez Nogales, after the basketball player. Sergio love the Chicago Bulls, never got into the Lakers or the Clippers. Michael Jordan—at first I didn't like it, but we finally decided that it's a good strong name, and very American. Don't you think so?"

"Absolutely," Lucy said. She had the distinct feeling

that Esmeralda was telling the truth, as much as she knew it.

Esmeralda composed herself, blowing her nose into a pink tissue. She glanced at her watch. "I have to pick him up from preschool soon, at Saint Barnabas."

"*Señora* Nogales," Ernie said, "we won't take up much more of your time, but do you remember what your husband was wearing that night when he went off to work?"

"Sure, mostly the same thing all the time. An olive green, what do they call them . . . a jumpsuit, one piece, and a black knitted cap with a Bulls logo, black boots, and gloves, too. Was very cold that night."

Esmeralda began to struggle with tears again. Her shoulders hunched and her chin dropped to her chest. Ernie patted her hand.

"*Señora,* do you know a man by the name of Luis Alvarez?" Lucy asked.

Esmeralda's brows drew together and she slowly looked up. "Yes, yes, I know a Mr. Luis Alvarez."

Lucy glanced at Ernie then back to Esmeralda. Would this be their break? "Can you tell us about Mr. Alvarez?"

"Okay. Well, I work part-time in the cafeteria of the old people's home just around the block. A couple of times I've had to bring food to him when he was too sick to leave his room."

"He lives in a retirement home?" Ernie asked.

"*Sí, señor.* He had a bad stroke. He probably close to ninety, so it's very serious when they get the flu or something like that."

Lucy's excitement deflated like a balloon bursting

in her chest. Luis Alvarez was a moderately common Hispanic name.

Lucy and Ernie stayed only a few more minutes before thanking Esmeralda Nogales for her time. They returned to Ernie's car.

✳

"Well that conversation was pretty damn interesting," Lucy said, as they approached their vehicle.

"Would you drive?" Ernie asked. "I want to break out my laptop for a minute."

"No problem," Lucy caught the key fob Ernie tossed to her. "What's the scoop on Sergio's supervisor, Fredericks?"

Ernie moved toward the rear of the car as Lucy unlocked the doors. "He called Sergio to work that night after receiving a phone call from central dispatch telling him they needed a replacement at the San Bernardino-Riverside facility. Beyond that nobody knows where the request originated."

Ernie pulled his laptop from the trunk then crawled in next to Lucy.

"All that stuff about the INS," he said, powering up the notebook, "and Sergio being her boyfriend, not her husband, and their son being a step-child—that was all from a press conference out of the governor's office. Looking back on it, seems like we were almost purposefully misled."

"If she's telling it straight, and I think she is," Lucy said, "the spin the politicians put on this story is pretty outrageous. The supposed INS problems, the implied promiscuity—we nod our heads and think 'typical of *those* people.' "

"And I'm Chicano—one of *those* people, and I bought it, hook, line, and sinker," Ernie said. "I owe her much better reporting."

"We both do. We owe everybody our best job. Just because we're of Mexican heritage, doesn't make us any less prone to falling for stereotypes than anyone else."

"No kidding," Ernie said, smiling. "And, my little *señorita,* because of my lack of sensitivity, I'll release you from your research commitment when we get back to the station, but don't expect any movement on the babysitting front."

"I love the babysitting part, actually." Lucy chuckled as she pulled out into traffic.

CHAPTER 28

Lucy's phone chimed. She groped for her cell but her eyes refused to unglue so she could see who it was. Her bedside lamp was still on and Lori Lansens' novel, *The Girls,* had slipped to the floor. It was three o'clock in the morning. Remembering the last middle-of-the-night phone call she had received from the news room, her chest swelled with cold panic.

"It's Lucy." Her voice was tight and cautious.

"Sorry to phone you so late, or early. How are you?"

It was Brett the intern. His tone was irritatingly conversational.

"What the hell is going on, Brett? I'm not on-call. You know this kind of thing scares the shit out of me."

"Hey, I am so sorry, truly. I almost didn't ring you because I figured you might freak."

"I'm not freaking," Lucy said, grinding her teeth and

freaking.

"Okay, fine, but I thought you'd want to hear about this. You know the woman you and Ernie talked to this afternoon, at her place over off Highland?"

"Yeah, Esmeralda, and how do you know about that?"

"I, uh, heard Ernie talking about it to Bea."

"You were snooping?"

"No, I wasn't snooping but I do have ears and if something's in my range, I can't help but hear it. I'm an intern but I am also a news reporter. I try to keep a reasonable level of awareness about what's going on around me."

Brett's attitude was shifting from apologetic to pissed off.

Lucy took a deep breath and tried to soften her own attitude. Maybe she was treating Brett like Michael Burleson had treated her initially—assuming she was inexperienced and in need of his divine direction. But Brett had been to war and back. He was no boy. He was learning the ropes in a new arena, one that wasn't easy, where the rules were soft and not always what you thought they should be.

"All right, you weren't snooping. Ernie can be very loud and animated when he gets excited. I'm sorry. Anyhow, what's up?"

"Are you sure you want me to tell you? Maybe you'd rather go back to sleep."

"Okay, Brett. Spill it. You probably have a good reason to call, so I apologize."

"Accepted. So, I just heard on the police frequency that the apartment building where that Esmeralda woman lives—it's burning. Big time. Like tons of alarms. Thought you might wanna get over there and check it out yourself. I mean there's a team already on their way but I thought you might be interested."

Lucy gasped at the news.

"Yes, thanks, Brett. Sorry I was a bitch. I owe you one." She disconnected, grabbed random clothes and flew out the door, half naked, dressing as she raced to her car.

✳

Lucy was lucky to find a parking spot four blocks from the scene. Fire trucks were arriving and sirens screamed. The KLAK-TV satellite truck hadn't shown up yet but KTLA's white van just pulled around the corner. She waved at the driver of the competition's rig. He called a greeting out the window. Everyone knew everyone in the local news business.

The night sky flickered a bloody red as she jogged closer to the inferno. People of every age and ethnicity were out in the street in their pajamas and all manner of bedclothes, speaking in many different languages. Probably all were asking the same questions as they watched the disaster unfold. Lucy ran toward the burning building and tried to get close before the police cordoned off the area, which would make access difficult, if not impossible.

Firefighters drenched the roofs of adjacent buildings, trying to keep the flames from spreading. The air was heavy with acrid smoke. Lucy's eyes stung and watered. Sparks showered like falling stars and helicopters circled the area. High-pressure hoses streamed thousands of gallons of water into the blazing structure. Despite the all-out attempt, it didn't look like the battle was going to turn out well.

Several EMT units arrived as two singed, gagging men crawled out of a basement window. They staggered and collapsed onto the sidewalk, their hair smoking. Med techs jumped out of the closest ambulance and rushed to the victims. Lucy wondered if Esmeralda and her family had found safety. She didn't have their phone number, so she texted Ernie and asked him to try and reach her. *Stat.* They had spoken with Esmeralda in the afternoon, and tonight, her home was burning. There had to be a correlation. Was this more of Mercer's handiwork? But she's a devastated, pregnant widow with a small child and an aging mother-in-law. What could be gained by killing them and wiping out a neighborhood?

A young African-American police officer jogged up to Lucy. "Hey, lady, you need to get outta here. Now! This place could go up any minute. Natural gas shit."

Lucy flashed her press credentials. "I'm covering this story, sir."

"Sorry, Miss Vega, but those creds aren't gonna keep you from getting hurt. You gotta move back to the end of the next block. This is seriously dangerous. Could blow."

"All right. Okay," Lucy said. She couldn't hide the frustration in her voice.

As she turned to retreat, she spotted a familiar silhouette amid a thick bed of tangled oleander and bird of paradise blooms in a nearby yard. Could it possibly be?

"Dexter Middleton Jackson! What in the hell? What are you doing here?" Lucy hurried toward him and hoped the cop wouldn't try to tackle her.

Even in the darkness, she could see his eyes widen to twice their normal circumference. The proverbial deer in the headlights. Then a second form emerged from the dense foliage—a short, skinny kid with spiky blond hair that reflected pink in the firelight. It was Sean Hayes, Dexter's friend from the film class Lucy taught, the erratic student who had never finished his final project.

Lucy slipped into the greenery after them. She tripped on a sprinkler head. "Damn. What in the world are you two doing here? Does your mother have any idea you are out at this time of night, Dexter? Don't even bother to answer that." Lucy shook her head in disbelief.

Dexter was struck dumb.

"Hello, Ms. Vega," Sean said cheerfully.

"Hello, Hayes. So nice to see you across the street from a building that's about to explode. Let's get the hell outta here, then I want some answers from you two."

She grabbed each of them by their baggy T-shirts and dragged them down the block, camera and gear bag in tow.

Out of breath, Lucy stopped just beyond the KTLA van. "Okay. Talk to me. Now."

"Well, we, uh . . ." Dexter was still as incredulous at seeing Lucy as she was at seeing him. "Uh, I was staying overnight at Sean's and we heard about this fire on his dad's police band. And, you know, I thought I might want to do documentaries . . ."

"And I needed to finish my project for your class," Sean piped in, "so we thought this might be a good opportunity."

"Dexter, when your mom finds out about this, the

only documentary you're going to be doing will be called *Home Alone: Locked in Your Room for a Month.* And Sean, it's about two weeks too late to hand in a project."

"I thought maybe . . ."

"Not an option," Lucy said. "Now how did you two get here?"

"I drove," Sean said. He smiled like he'd just swallowed a goldfish—a very unpleasant grimace. "I have a license. Passed the exam yesterday."

"Yesterday? Congratulations and God help us. You know you can't drive after 11 P.M. for another year." Lucy pressed her palms against her aching temples.

"My dad's a trucker and I've been driving his 18-wheeler since I was twelve. Takes me cross-county with him in the summers and I drive while he sleeps or watches old episodes of Seinfeld."

Lucy crossed herself even though she wasn't Catholic. "You drove an 18-wheeler—here?"

"No, my mom's Civic," he said. "Pops won't let me drive the truck in town."

"Small mercies," Lucy whispered and looked heavenward. "All right, you two, I'll take you home. Let's move out before we get arrested, or killed." On the top floor of the burning structure, a string of Christmas lights exploded like gunshots, one at a time.

"We were the first ones here," Dexter said. His pride was obvious at beating the fire trucks and news teams but tempered with appropriate humility at being caught in the act. "They say that the people who start fires like to stay and watch their work. I learned that from an old *CSI*—the Vegas one, not L.A."

"Marg Helgenberger was hot, for an old babe," Sean

said. "Like you, Ms. Vega."

"Cut the crap, Hayes. You're busted," Lucy said.

Hayes' eyes widened with a look of exaggerated innocence.

"So, boys," Lucy continued, "you got pictures of everyone who was here when you arrived?" She knew she'd have to take a look at that footage and tried to keep overt enthusiasm out of her voice.

"That was the first thing we did, after the establishing shots, of course," Dexter said.

"All right. Grab your stuff. Let's go back to the satellite truck and take a look at the contraband you've come up with."

The boys looked at each other, grins spread across their young faces.

"Sweet," Sean said, knuckle-bumping his friend.

Lucy glanced up to see the police officer who had earlier ordered her out of the area, approaching rapidly.

"Let's boogie," Lucy shouted. She and the boys dashed toward the KLAK news truck. It had just pulled up a half block ahead. Behind them, an explosion rocked the neighborhood. The concussion knocked them to the ground. Glass shattered, car alarms started to blare, and people cried out in terror and confusion.

"Holy shit!" Sean shrieked. He spit out a clot of dirt and grass. Dexter and Lucy struggled to stand, Sean tried to follow but his legs tangled in the baggy pants that had fallen to his ankles. They each grabbed one of his arms and staggered through the throng of onlookers, cops, and news personnel toward the KLAK-TV truck. Sean's pants were left in their wake but fortunately, his boxers managed to stay on his scrawny butt.

Breathless, Lucy pounded on the truck door. In a moment it was opened by a frizzy-haired, fortyish engineer, slightly overweight, wearing rumpled khakis and a pajama top he'd clearly slept in.

"Lucy. Hi, babe. What're you doing here? Just can't get enough of it during the day?"

"Hi, Dave," Lucy motioned to the two frightened teenagers she had in tow. "I have a personal interest in this story, and I also discovered a couple of my students who are aspiring news people—if they survive the tenth grade. This is Sean Hayes. He lost his pants somewhere down the block, and Dexter Middleton Jackson, Bea's eldest."

"Bea's boy. Well, shit. Come on in, kids. Nice to meet you. We're just about to do a live feed. Sit down and help yourself to some of that guacamole. Soda's in the fridge."

Another explosion rocked the neighborhood. The air shimmered from the heat and compression.

"Ah, shit," the engineer said. His two main monitors went fuzzy, then rebooted and came back up. "This is one nasty fire."

"We don't want to bother you, Dave. You got your hands full, but could I use the small editing bay for a minute to look at some vid? These kids may have some footage we could to use as cutaways, so I want to see it."

"Help yourself, Luce. I won't be using it. They have broadcast quality equipment?"

"Yep, we donated five of our old Sonys to the SaMoHi program a few years ago."

"Cool. Dudes, if your stuff is good, maybe you'll score some casheroo tonight," Dave said. He sat down at the control panel and put on his headphones.

Potential cash? Sean and Dexter turned to look at each other, not believing their ears.

On the engineer's monitor, the reporter fidgeted with her microphone. In the background, acrid black smoke and fiery tongues rose from the roof of the building adjoining Esmeralda's. The devastation was spreading. Dave struggled to get the feed online.

Lucy took a deep breath. "Okay, rookies. Before you start thinking money, let's take a look at what you have." She slid into the editing booth with the two boys looking over her shoulder. Dexter handed her a flash drive.

"You use Avid NewsCutter here?" Sean asked.

Lucy nodded her head and began a slow scroll through the video. "Good, you got some nice wide shots, establishes the location. Okay. And look at that second blaze erupting. Nice image, very intense. We'll show that to Dave." She could feel the boys' excitement.

The kids had grabbed cutaways of police cars arriving, just before the fire trucks came wailing down the street.

"A little soft focus there," Lucy said, "always gotta pay attention to that. Will ruin a great image."

Dexter and Sean nodded like dual Bobbleheads.

The boys nailed a couple good shots of people fleeing their homes, bleary-eyed and frightened. Then there was a close-up of a little boy in Spiderman pajamas holding a gerbil in one hand and a suitcase in the other. Bingo. The image spoke.

Lucy further studied the freeze frame. Just behind the boy with the gerbil, Esmeralda, bloodied but standing had wrapped Mama Yasmina in a shawl. Her son clutched her nightshirt in his little fist.

Thank God they're okay. She felt faint with relief.

"Okay, my bad children, I think you're gonna score some *dinero* tonight after all," Lucy said, her spirits rising. "Your mamas will probably confiscate this ill-gotten cash, but you'll have a hell of a demo reel."

The boys fist-bumped each other again, breathless with success.

CHAPTER 29

During the early morning hours, the fire leaped across multiple structures like a wolf spider after prey. Two adjacent apartment complexes and a convalescent home were consumed. By 9:00 a.m., the blaze had been reduced to ash and smoldering cinders. Black soot coated the palm fronds high above and acrid particles floated through the bright crisp air as the fronds beat against each other in the breeze.

The police and firefighters were able to evacuate residents of the adjacent buildings in time. This included moving the elderly and ill from the nursing home to nearby hospitals and shelters. Esmeralda's apartment complex, ground zero for the inferno, did not fare as well. Of the seventy-three residents, many lost their lives. The number was still mounting. Lucy wiped moist eyes with the back of her hand. Did their conversation with Esmeralda somehow lead to this?

Recovery personnel continued to sift through the steaming debris, in search of bodies. Lucy had to clamp a hand over her mouth to keep from crying out as one of the firefighters carried a small, tarp-wrapped figure toward the temporary morgue tent on the sidewalk. She grabbed her camera and recorded the firefighter's pitiful task.

An unexpected blast of wind dislodged the morgue tarps. They billowed up like dark mourning capes and revealed the tragedy beneath. More than twenty body bags awaited the medical examiner. A policewoman rushed over to help load the small, blackened figure into a bag marked *Child* in yellow letters.

Lucy heard Keith Montgomery's pleading words in her head: *Leave it alone, Lucy. It's not worth another life.*

Mid-morning, Bea, Truckee, and Ernie provided relief for Dave and his news gang. Lucy was already on scene and decided to stay. Hayes swore to her he'd very responsibly get himself and Dexter back home as fast as the speed limit and traffic conditions would permit.

The KLAK team's assignment was to pull together an aftermath story for a noontime special report. The crew spent several hours interviewing victims and responders. Lucy shot footage of the smoldering ruins and edited in more of the kids' visuals of the fleeing residents. Upon completion, Lucy, Bea, Truckee, and Ernie gathered in the truck to review their news piece. They also watched other station's reports on multiple monitors while they waited for the fire inspector's press conference. Arson was the word on the street.

Not long for such tight quarters, the crew grabbed folded stadium chairs and followed Truckee outside the van and onto the sidewalk.

Ernie hung back, his eyes bloodshot. "Luce, you believe in coincidence?"

"Wish I could but no good journalist does. And we're very good, Ernie."

"The question is then, why would someone torch this place? It makes no sense." He blew his nose into a wad of tissue from the Christmas-themed box of Kleenex tucked under his arm.

"We're not dealing with a rational person or people. Anybody who'd do this is beyond screwed up," Lucy said. "Like Mercer." She closed her eyes and took a deep, slow breath. "Listen, Ern, when we get back to the station, let's really examine Dexter and Sean's footage, blow up faces in the background, see if there's anyone familiar. The kids got here just as the police and the first-alarm firefighters arrived. Maybe the jerk-off stuck around to watch his handiwork."

Ernie nodded and sneezed. "Great idea. Let's keep it close, for now, only our team until we have something."

"Agreed," Lucy said. She and Ernie joined the crew who were still outside, now sitting on their canvas chairs and sipping coffee from paper cups.

Birds chirped in the bushes. The hum of the nearby Hollywood Freeway and the gargle of radio dispatch emanated from numerous vehicles and hand-held devices. All blended into white noise in the background. The air smelled of melted electrical wire and plastic, tinged with the bite of burned flesh. Lucy felt the odor sink into the pores of her skin. A host of baths wouldn't wash it away. She tasted it on her tongue. Strong coffee couldn't blunt the brutal flavor.

Lucy rested her camera on the ground next to an empty chair. She sat down, spent, and accepted a cup from Ernie. "Any word on the fire inspector's press conference?"

"*Nada,*" Bea answered. "They may have to push it until after lunch."

"If we're gonna put this baby together by noon," Truckee said, "we've got to get shaking." He looked at his watch and plucked at his bushy red beard.

"Noon is obviously not going to happen." Ernie's cell phone chirped with the strains of "Lullaby and Goodnight." Everything about him said sleep-deprived daddy.

"Vargas." He listened, scowled, cursed, and disconnected.

"What?" Bea frowned as the KTLA truck hurled by them with the Santa Barbara station van in its wake.

"Press conference at City Hall, in twenty."

"It was supposed to be here, at the scene." Lucy grabbed her equipment.

"What can I tell 'ya?" Ernie said. "Let's boogie."

Truckee lowered the satellite receiver on top of the truck then pulled out through the throng of official vehicles onto Highland before heading south toward Santa Monica Boulevard. They passed Lucy's Jeep. She saw a parking ticket stuck under the windshield wiper. Shit.

Ernie sat in front with Truck and talked to his wife on the phone. Lucy and Bea rode in the rear, hanging on for dear life as Truckee beat a red light.

"So, what's your very talented juvenile delinquent up to today?" Lucy asked, referring to Dexter.

"I still can't believe that kid. Those two little jerks could have been killed, or mugged, or in a car accident, or who knows what. Teenagers. I don't know how I'm going to survive. And a young black man out in the middle of the night with a canvas bag full of expensive camera equipment? Sweet Jesus. No sense of his own vulnerability. He was sound asleep when I left but he's supposed to detail my car, with a toothbrush, and have three sweet potato pies baking in the oven by the time I get home. And that's just the start."

Lucy couldn't help but smile. "Ten years from now, we'll laugh about this when he gets his first Emmy."

Bea shook her head, dismayed. "So, Christmas Eve at our place Friday night? Seven o'clock as usual with your famous cranberry salad."

"Christmas Eve—in two days?" Lucy sighed. How could she be so out of touch?

"Yes, dear one, it's almost here."

Lucy felt as if she were on another planet, observing the surroundings, the seasons, the days—all from afar. Her uncle dead, cattle slaughtered, Carly crippled, and a neighborhood burned. Could she make it stop? Make him stop? Mercer was a key. Mercer, and Mexico.

Bea grabbed the grip handle over the door as Truckee flew around a garbage truck. Lucy tightened her seatbelt. She sank back in her seat and gazed out the window as they passed the Staples Center. Cirque de Soleil was setting up their white peaked tents in the massive parking lot.

"Slow down," Ernie said, "I'm getting car sick." He

gagged a little for effect then blew his nose, loud and long.

"Here's a puke bag," Truckee tossed a crumpled McDonald's burger bag Ernie's way.

"You're always such a hoot." Ernie sneezed several times in succession. "This damn cold."

Bea cracked open the window, letting in a cool stream of fresh air if Los Angeles Basin air could be referred to as fresh. "Ever consider taking a sick day, Ern, so you don't contaminate the rest of us who are struggling to remain semi-healthy?"

"He doesn't think we can function without him," Truckee declared.

Ernie frowned at the big guy. "That's because I'm the brains of this operation."

Everyone groaned.

Truckee slammed on the brakes and the groans turned to shrieks. He barely avoided rear-ending the NPR radio news Honda. It had stopped abruptly, likely on its way to the same press conference. Horns blared as a homeless woman pushing a Vons' shopping cart stopped in the middle of the street to fix her wig and give everyone the finger.

"We're never going to make it in time, folks." Truckee drummed on the steering wheel. The homeless woman trundled by the truck and made obscene gestures with her tongue. Truckee returned the favor. She winked and showed him a toothless grin. "My kinda man, sheee-it," she yelled and slapped her ass.

"You're quite the babe magnet, big man," Bea said dryly.

Truckee snorted.

Ernie's cell phone rang again. He had a quick, quiet conversation with the caller. "That was Max," Ernie said. "We're okay—the news conference has been pushed back another hour. Everybody's stuck in the same mess."

"Let's bring up what Dexter and Hayes shot while we're waiting," Lucy said. "And with the extra time we have, maybe Truckee can slow down and *not* get us killed."

He grunted and wove his way through the downtown traffic toward City Hall with only a few close calls and nasty outbursts of profanity.

Lucy, Bea, and Ernie huddled around a monitor in the editing bay. Lucy brought up the kids' digital video and scrolled through, freezing frames at every crowd scene. She blew up crowd shots to rough, grainy close-ups. Nothing, nothing, and more nothing.

Then there was something.

"Enlarge that one again," Ernie said. He adjusted his glasses. The lens had finally been replaced.

Lucy selected a face with her cursor. "This one?"

"Not that guy, the one behind him." Ernie leaned closer to the screen. Bea moved over to give him a better view.

A dark, shadowy face emerged, blurred and heavily pixilated. Lucy didn't recognize the man.

Ernie squinted his eyes and examined the face, then nodded. "That's the guy who manages the train depot in Riverside. Was in charge the night the poisoning went down."

"The one you talked to, who seemed like a good guy?" Lucy recalled an earlier conversation.

"Yeah, that's him. Bud Martinez. Said he lives in

Sylmar."

"What the hell's he doing in Hollywood in the middle of the night?" Lucy worked to get better resolution on the image. Her pulse raced. "I think we share this with the arson investigators, ASAP."

"Frame grab and email it to me," Bea said. "I'll get it to the fire chief. Texting him right now: *need to meet after the news conference. Possible lead.*" She pressed send.

Lucy smiled and wiped perspiration from her forehead. *Maybe a break in the case? Merry frickin' Christmas.*

CHAPTER 30

When Lucy opened the glass doors of *Chez Mimi*, she was distracted and bone tired. Her whole body hurt from crashing onto the pavement to avoid fake Rubio's car. Her hands, stiff and scabbed, still smarted from road rash. But she'd promised Bea that she would show up and be charming. Maybe after a few drinks, she could do it. Given what appeared to be Burleson's cozy relationship with Governor Scanlon, she was determined to glean some useful information so the night wouldn't be a complete waste.

Lucy left her coat at the coat check and ran her hand gingerly across the smooth fabric of her simple black jersey dress. She'd promised Bea no sweatpants or T-shirts. The only jewelry she wore her mother's pearl earrings and a gold heart on a long chain Uncle Henry had given her given her when she'd turned fifteen, for her *quinceañera*.

The maître d' approached like a terrier ready to nip. "Excuse me, ma'am, you're here for Mr. Burleson?"

Lucy nodded.

"This way, please." The black-clad fellow led her toward a shadowy brick archway that partially obscured an intimate, candle-lit, dining nook.

Michael Burleson rose to greet her. In a brown cashmere sweater and well-worn jeans, his sharp, handsome features gave him an air of sophistication despite a nose that looked like it had been broken several times and hair that he likely cut himself. His smile was warm and genuine.

"Lucy, thank you for coming. A pleasure to see you."

"Thank you for inviting us. Bea's on her way."

She winced as they shook hands. He stopped, turned her hand over in his palm and inspected the damage.

"Ouch, how did this happen?" Burleson asked.

His touch was warm and light. Lucy bit her lip and withdrew her fingers. "A fall in the station parking lot." She sat down on the chair he'd pulled out for her and buried her hands in her lap. "Am I starting to appear rather accident-prone to you?"

"I think you're just somebody who gives it all she's got. Accidents happen when you're in there taking chances."

"I guess they sometimes do," Lucy said. *How right he was.*

"But first of all, how's the head? Last time I saw you, you were out cold."

Lucy flushed. "Just a mild concussion. I was in and out of the hospital pretty fast. Thanks for the flowers, by the way. I didn't actually see them, but Bea said they were lovely. Very kind of you."

Michael smiled. "Something to drink?"

The waiter, a stiff, proper-looking man with diamond stud earrings, came to the table and took drink orders. Lucy requested a glass of Chardonnay. Michael asked for sparkling water.

"Not joining me?" she asked.

"I'm on the wagon. Permanently. But I never let it keep others from enjoying what I seem to be unable to indulge in without destroying myself."

Lucy nodded. "I respect your candor—good for you. By the way, thanks for pulling me out of that livestock pit. My colleagues told me what happened. Not one of my better moments."

"It's the least I could do after you put me in my place for questioning your professionalism," Burleson said.

She felt heat rise in her cheeks. "I way overreacted, and you were just trying to help. If this dinner is about making amends, it wasn't necessary."

"It's not about making amends. Well, maybe a little bit." Burleson looked away and picked at the cuff of his sweater for a moment, then stopped and raised his eyes to meet Lucy's. "I was being an arrogant asshole. Assumed that you didn't have a lot of experience and that you needed my invaluable assistance."

Lucy took a healthy gulp of wine. "I've been in the business for more than a decade."

"And your work shows it . . ."

Before Michael could finish his sentence, Bea bustled up to the table. She wore a pale pink silk print blouse and charcoal trousers. Shopping bags were clutched in both hands.

"Hey, sorry I'm late." She kissed and hugged both Michael and Lucy.

Lucy knew that punctual Bea was late for a purpose. She'd bullied Lucy into this dinner convinced that Burleson held a key to their investigation and Lucy would find it. Bea also pointed out that Burleson was mega-hot and Lucy was in dire need of a few sparks. Ridiculous. She trusted twice-divorced Bea's instincts on absolutely everything but relationships.

"Actually, I got here early," Bea continued, "but had to run across the street for a sec to pick up a birthday present for my niece, and guess what? They were having their annual shoe sale, and well, I just got caught up in it for a few minutes. I have big feet, size tens . . . all right, elevens and they had a ton of things I had to try on."

"Is it any wonder Beatrice wins the best-dressed reporter award every year?" Lucy said. "How many pairs did you walk away with this time, super-shopper?"

"Just four—sandals don't count. I'll show them to y'all later."

Michael stood and held the chair for her then sat back down.

"Can I bring you something to drink?" The waiter stumbled over one of the bags and gritted his teeth. "May I check these packages for you, ma'am?"

"Oh, all right." Bea looked down at his shiny, Italian loafers. "But I don't want to go back and find you trying them on."

"Ma'am, you've ruined my fun," he said dryly and retired with the bags.

"And I'll have what my girlfriend here is having,"

Bea called.

Lucy smiled and shook her head in dismay. "Can't take you anywhere civilized."

The waiter returned quickly to fill Bea's glass with Chardonnay. He left the bottle on the table.

"So," Bea said, "it's sweet of you to invite us two poor working girls to dinner. But do tell, what are you doing in L.A.?"

Burleson ran his hand through thick, gold hair that grayed at the temples. A silver ring set with a large piece of turquoise flashed. "Well, actually, this is home. I was born in beautiful downtown Burbank."

"A Burbank boy? Who would have guessed," Bea said. "I picked you for Montana or Colorado."

"Nope, a homie. Still have aunts, uncles, and cousins in the area, plus a ninety-six-year-old spitfire of a grandmother who gets cranky if I don't visit. Grew up next door to the Scanlons, just off Burbank Boulevard."

"Scanlons? As in Governor Scanlon?" Lucy asked, surprised. She knew from watching Burleson and the governor at the livestock extermination they were familiar, but this was much more than that.

"Uh-huh. George was my big brother Patrick's best friend. I was around two years old when we moved to Burbank from Minneapolis and we've always stayed close to the Scanlon family. Good people." Michael offered Bea warm, dark bread from the linen-covered basket. His hands were strong and compact, his knuckles calloused.

"It's a tragedy how the organophosphate poisoning fiasco put the skids on his political career," Bea said, then attacked the breadbasket with gusto.

"I agree. Very unfortunate," he said.

"He was the best governor we've had in a long time," Lucy added, as Michael refilled her glass.

"Definitely presidential material," Bea said, "but that may be history after this mess." She popped a hefty hunk of bread into her mouth but continued talking unfazed. "Well, moving to a happier topic, I hear you got a nice multi-project deal with CNN."

Burleson rubbed at the hint of golden stubble on his chin. "It's actually not CNN. They're not my biggest fans. I've got some private funding with a PBS partnership, so I'm finally going to be able to do one of my own projects. In fact, I'm heading to Mexico next week to start on the first documentary."

"The one you didn't want to talk about the last time we met?" Bea's perfect eyebrows rose.

"If I was rude, I apologize."

"Not rude, more like grumpy," she said.

"So why are you going to Mexico? Lucy asked. "My mom's side of the family is from Guadalajara. Love it there but rarely get to go."

"Yes, tell us about your project." Bea perused her menu and stole a quick glance Lucy's way.

Lucy noted a moment of hesitation on Burleson's part. He squeezed the lemon into his water and took a long drink. Was he editing down just how much to tell? Probably.

"Okay. Well," he began, "the impetus for the documentary started here in L.A. George, Governor Scanlon, has been gung-ho for me to get involved with a story he's interested in. The State of California received a major grant several years ago to help promote economic development in southern Mexico. It's a big state/ federal partnership program. Supposed to encourage agricultural projects that are alternatives to the drug production industry."

"I think my uncle was overseeing part of that project," Lucy said. The feral hairs on the back of her neck now stood on end.

"Ah, I'm so sorry about your uncle. The governor briefly mentioned to me what happened."

Lucy nodded and wondered what else the governor might have mentioned. "So you're off to Mexico City?"

"No actually, I'm going to a little outpost called Tingo Tia."

"Tingo, what?" Bea asked. She had gone through most of the bread and signaled to the waiter for more.

"It's on the edge of the Sierra Madre del Sur, about a hundred miles inland from the Pacific. I'll be working with an amazing former priest, Juan Jesus de Anza. We met many years ago when I was on assignment in Central America. He was a theology student committed to liberation of the indigenous populations. Today, he has this entire township growing cacao—chocolate beans. The project's financed through something like a micro-grant but it's the next step up—bigger money involved, but still, run as a non-profit. Call themselves the Mixtec Trail Chocolate Company. The area used to be totally dominated by heroin poppy production but much less so now."

"Sounds like quite a success story," Bea said.

Burleson nodded. "It is, indeed."

Lucy glanced at Bea then back at Burleson. "Ever hear of a man named Luis Alvarez in connection with any of this?" She saw his eyes narrow, sensed a guarded change in his demeanor. "But I doubt he's in the chocolate business."

Burleson chewed at his lip, then took another drink of water. "Hmm, yes, Alvarez. I think he's a politician of sorts." He paused and seemed to consider his answer. "I think, uh, I'm pretty sure he's the former head of the Mexican National Agricultural Police."

Lucy drained her second glass. She rarely had more than one. "Agricultural Police. You mean the people who make sure nobody grows illegal crops?"

"That's right," Michael replied.

"The fox minding the hen house. So you know a fair bit about Alvarez?"

"Not at all." Burleson slipped on round, metal-rimmed reading glasses and picked up a menu. "Actually, I know very little about him. Why are you interested in this guy?" His eyes met Lucy's.

She'd been pushing too hard and knew it. "He may tie into something we're working on."

Bea interrupted, drummed her shiny nails on the table. "My girlfriend here gets a little intense sometimes, in case you haven't noticed. But I'm starved. I love country French food. Are we ready to order?"

Michael smiled at Bea. "What looks good to you? The bouillabaisse is excellent, so is the chicken, *Chez Helene.*"

"When did you say you were leaving for Mexico?" Lucy asked, ignoring the food talk.

"Next week." Burleson's eyes were glued to the list of specials on the chalkboard.

"I think I might have the trout. Sounds healthy.

That, or a steak. Rare. Not as healthy but so good," he said. "And save room for the raspberry *chômeur*—poor man's pudding. Nobody makes it like Mimi."

Lucy still hadn't touched the menu. "Are you taking an American crew with you?"

Burleson was unable to put her off, even to order. He shifted his attention to her stormy blue eyes. "Initially, I'm going down with a language and cultural interpreter who lives in L.A. He's native to the region, just finished his Master's in the Chicano Studies program at UCLA. I'll be hiring on several of my former CNN colleagues when we start production. It can be dangerous down there and it's pretty much off the grid. I can't see bringing anyone in who's not sophisticated in volatile situations ripe with political unrest."

"Oh, really?" Lucy wondered if the volatility was mostly a projection of Burleson's substantial ego.

"I can see your mind working," Michael said. He took off his reading glasses.

"I'm that transparent?"

His brows knit together and he leaned forward, eyes sharp and bright. "I'm not patronizing you, Lucy. As talented as you are, working in a quasi-war zone takes a whole different kind of smarts that have nothing to do with videography and news gathering."

She refused another fill-up of her wine glass. "L.A. doesn't have any quasi-war zones?"

Michael sighed and shook his head. "It's different, it truly is."

Lucy smiled across at him. "You're probably right." She finally picked up the menu and wondered what she would be ordering this weekend in Tingo Tia.

CHAPTER 31

Well past midnight, a light misty fog sparkled beneath the streetlights as Burleson eased his usual car rental, a Ford Explorer, up to the gate outside the governor's mansion in downtown Sacramento. He'd been expected to arrive an hour earlier but the plane had been delayed. A sharp-eyed guard waved him through the gate. He parked at the rear of the mansion then headed toward the back-entrance portico. As Burleson was about to ring the bell, the door swung open. Governor Scanlon stepped outside, bundled in a down jacket and ski cap. He gripped a crushed pack of cigarettes in his hand.

"Greeted by the chief executive himself! Was hoping you'd be by the fireplace with a couple of hot toddies on the warmer." The two men embraced, and then Michael pulled his coat collar up around his ears. They were numb with chill.

"I thought you quit that hard stuff," Scanlon said, a flash of deep concern in his eyes.

"Shit, yes. All I can handle these days is a strong cup of coffee so wipe that worried look from your face. A hot toddy's just a euphamism for a welcoming environment in the wintertime, okay?"

"Sorry," the governor said. "I just can't think about you starting in again. Scares the hell out of me."

"I swear to you, I am done with booze, George. Done. I'm coming up on one year sober."

"Okay, okay, very fucking good. Dammit. That's great, kid. Come on, let's take a little walk. They tell me the house is clean but I'm more paranoid than usual these days. Plus, I need a smoke."

"Cigs'll do you in, too, my friend."

"True, very true. But they didn't destroy my marriage, fuck up my job, and ruin my confidence and self-esteem, like the booze did to you."

Burleson forced a smile and sighed. "Also very true."

The men walked down a wet pathway toward a grove of great palm trees. Two of Scanlon's bodyguards tried to make themselves inconspicuous nearby. It was an idyllic winter's night—evocative and deeply silent. The business at hand, however, was anything but peaceful.

"So," the governor's breath puffed in pale clouds, "you had dinner with her. What do you think she knows?"

"Not sure, but she was definitely fishing. Asked me if I'd heard of Luis Alvarez."

"Shit! How did she get his name?"

"I think a friend of hers from Dynamic Chemical Company mentioned it to her. I don't know what the context was."

"Who's the friend?"

"Jesus, I couldn't ask her that. Would've been an immediate tip-off."

"We'd better find out, fast." Scanlon studied the burning ember at the end of his cigarette. "Is Bea Middleton onto this?"

"I'd say definitely. And maybe a couple more of their colleagues."

"Damn. Probably Ray Truckee and Ernie Vargas. If Lucy Vega gets in any deeper, she's in major danger, they all are."

"From what I could glean during our conversation, I'd guess that she totally believes her uncle was murdered and that you know all about it." Burleson pulled at his collar again, tried to sink down into his coat like a turtle.

"Damn girl's right. Said as much to me before we took off in that helicopter during the cattle extermination. Shit. Fuck."

"Any other significant comments, sir?"

"No, those are my standby cuss words. Oh, also 'hell' and 'bastard.' The wife puts her foot down at anything beyond that."

The two men sat on a wood slat bench that overlooked the mansion's park-like grounds. The moon peeked from behind scudding clouds and then disappeared like a closing eyelid.

"For a minute during dinner, I almost thought she was going to ask to go to Mexico with me."

Scanlon's eyes narrowed. He pounded his hands together to generate some warmth. His cig flickered in the darkness. "She can *not*, under any circumstances, be allowed to show up down there. Don't get me wrong, Lucy's a wonderful girl—smart, talented, very attractive, but impulsive as hell." He looked up at the low wintry sky and shivered. The temperature was dropping. "I just don't want to see her hurt, or worse."

"Don't worry. I'm sure I convinced her that it would be a waste of her time." Michael bit his lip.

"Good, good. So you'll just go about your business in Tingo Tia, work on your documentary and feedback anything you hear about Luis Alvarez and his cronies. You're my undercover eyes and ears."

"Absolutely, and you won't regret funding this project. I owe you big time."

"I owe you, too, for agreeing to take this on. And you be careful. Damn careful. You hear me, Mike?"

"I hear you, Scan the Man."

"Scan the Man? I'm the governor now, for God's sake. A little respect. You ever gonna let me forget high school?"

"Nope. Name of fame. South Burbank football legend."

"You always were a pain in the butt, little brother."

"I know."

"Hot coffee?" Scanlon asked.

"Straight up," Michael threw his arm around his old friend. "Let's go."

The two rose together and headed back toward the mist-shrouded mansion.

CHAPTER 32

After a high-energy Christmas Eve meal with Bea's family and neighbors, including truly amazing sweet potato pies courtesy of Dexter, the night culminated in caroling with their Baptist congregation. Their church held holiday services at the Forum where the Lakers played before they moved to Staples Center. It was packed, enthusiastic, and could almost make the most hardened of quasi-Protestant agnostics want to become a Baptist gospel choir member. This was the early service, kids were everywhere, and the Christmas pageant was equal parts laugh out loud and heart melting.

After all the action, Lucy was relieved to be up at the Malibu ranch with Howard the cat, Bugle the beagle, and Maddie the golden Lab mix, all on the couch together in front of the fireplace. Elsa was in Phoenix for the week with her daughter and grandkids, but she had put up a pretty Christmas tree and had hung a wreath over the mantel of the big stone fireplace. Lucy was grateful for the holiday decorations; this was a year she couldn't have done it herself.

With a cup of peppermint tea in hand, she paged through the wonderful Annie Leibovitz photo book Bea had given her for Christmas and listened to the St. Olaf College holiday choir concert on PBS. Because of the school's strong Norwegian Lutheran tradition, and the fact that a major residence hall was named after her grandfather, Ragnar Arnesen, her father had always hoped she'd attend there. Lucy sometimes regretted that she hadn't signed on. She imagined herself learning to play broomball on the ice, and majoring in Norwegian, or the philosophy of Søren Kierkegaard. She could have lost her virginity to someone named Sven or Leif, and God forbid, in the basement of Arnesen Hall.

Another life. She hadn't been in the best shape psychologically at the time, and the thirty-degrees-below-zero wind chill she experienced when she made the college visit, sealed the deal for UCLA in all of its cultural diversity and sunshine.

A ringing phone cut short her Norwegian maiden fantasy. She extricated herself from between Maddie and Howard and went into the kitchen to grab her cell. Probably Bea calling to say Merry Christmas and thanks again for the Cirque de Soleil tickets.

"And Merry Christmas to you, too!" Lucy said brightly into the receiver.

"Lucy?" the voice was several octaves below Bea's. "It's Michael Burleson. Merry Christmas."

"Well, this is a surprise," Lucy said. Was this coal in

her stocking or a supposed gift from Santa's little helper, Beatrice Middleton?

"I thought I'd take a chance and call you. I had Bea's number and she gave me yours at the ranch. Said you wouldn't mind."

Lucy rolled her eyes. "Oh, uh, not at all." Bea knew she'd mind, big time.

"I'm driving down from Sacramento, and am just about to Thousand Oaks, heading up the Camarillo grade as we speak. Got a nice bottle of that Chardonnay that you liked the other night and a disgusting bottle of ginseng green tea for myself. Thought we could share a little holiday cheer. I won't stay long but since I'll be literally driving past your place in about twenty minutes . . ."

Silence. Did she want to see him again?

"Lucy, you there?"

"Yes, yes of course, sure. Come on by. I'm just sitting in front of the fireplace reading and listening to some music, thinking about binge-watching *The Vikings*. The TV series, not the football team."

He laughed. "Very nice on a rainy holiday night."

"Yeah, it feels cozy here. Christmassy, in a not depressing way."

"Just what I could use right now. You sure you don't mind?"

"No, it's fine. I got a couple of pieces of sweet potato pie left over from Bea's Christmas Eve dinner. Sound good?"

"You have no idea."

Lucy gave him directions and jumped into a frenzy

of house picking up and personal grooming—meaning a quick shower, a clean pair of jeans and an old green sweatshirt with a big snowflake on it. She had a thing for ugly holiday sweaters. Bea would be proud of her for actually accepting a spontaneous invitation from someone of the male species. She had to admit it was nice to have a tiny bit of company tonight, but what did Burleson want? This visit couldn't be just a stab at alleviating holiday loneliness. Whatever his intentions, he knew more about her uncle's death than he let on. She needed to dig deeper. Maybe this unplanned drop-in was a gift after all.

It was pouring hard as Burleson pulled his car up to the ranch house. When Lucy heard the gravel under his wheels crunch to a stop, she went to open the front door. Burleson jumped out of his car and ran toward the porch, his blue rain parka flying, a wet grocery bag in hand. The *El Niño* season was relentless this year.

"Come on in!" Lucy held the door open as he dashed into the entry hall, dripping water onto the stone floor. "Wow, what a deluge."

Maddie barked twice and made a half-baked attempt at a growl. Bugle yawned, and then they considered their guard dog duty done. Both went to snooze next to the hearth after accepting a friendly ear scratch from the visitor. Howard disappeared completely, as cats tend to do in the presence of strangers.

Michael left his boots by the front door. Lucy hung his coat on a hall peg and brought the groceries into the kitchen. He followed her, looking wintry in black jeans and a fisherman's knit oatmeal-colored sweater. His hair looked like it had been combed with a garden rake and he tried to smooth it down. Lucy laughed at his unsuccessful efforts.

"Making fun of me?" He grinned and planted a light kiss on her cheek. "Merry Christmas and thanks for letting me stop by."

Lucy frowned and pushed him away. "Hey, back off cowboy, if you think you're getting anything besides tea, pie, and religious music tonight, you're sorely mistaken."

"Hey, I'm sorry, I'm sorry,' he said, holding up his hands in protest. "That was just a totally impulsive display of holiday cheer. Nothing else. Okay?"

"Okay. I'm sorry, too. I'm being very Grinchy. Thank you for the wine, and what else is in there?" Lucy emptied the contents of the soggy bag onto the kitchen counter. "Mmmm, a loaf of La Brea Bakery's fabulous walnut cranberry bread. I've got a chicken Caesar salad in the refrigerator. I'm suddenly starving. You hungry?"

"Yep, sounds great. Beats Mickey D's on PCH hands down."

Lucy chuckled. "Grab the teapot and a mug for yourself out of the cupboard." She dumped romaine and croutons into a bowl.

They put dinner on a tray and brought it out to the big pine coffee table in front of the fireplace. She and Uncle Henry had done this so many times. God, how she missed him. Maddie came over to sniff the visitor. Michael stroked her graying muzzle, received a lick, and then the old pup returned to her resting place next to Bugle.

"So, were you up in Sacramento visiting our esteemed governor?" Lucy asked, impatient to start digging.

"Yes, but mostly I was up north to stop by and see

my two girls. They're with their mom for the holidays in Davis. Awesome kids. I miss them. This is a tough time of year."

"How often do you get a chance to visit?"

"Not often enough. They're both in college back East and we're, well, rebuilding our relationship. I was the kind of idiot dad who thought a job and a career, ostensibly for their benefit and care, was more important than time spent with them. Then, of course, an alcoholic doesn't make a very good role model."

Lucy nodded her head and poured him a cup of hot, minty tea.

"I'm trying to make up for lost time, but at this point, it's coming more from my needs than theirs. But, we do the best we can, right? We all screw up and have to live with our choices. Life goes on."

"At least you have some great kids and if you keep working at it and love them, things will probably turn out all right, eventually."

"I sure hope so. Gotta keep the faith." Michael took a bite of Caesar salad then wiped his mouth. "Mmmm, this hits the spot, as Granny Burleson would say." He took a long swig of tea then turned his attention toward Lucy. "And how about you? How are you doing this Christmas evening? It's been a tough year."

Lucy sat back into the couch. She was again disarmed by his forthrightness. He actually seemed like a nice guy. It was much easier to keep up the necessary walls when he was an asshole.

"Well, today I've been counting my blessings," she said. "My friends, an interesting job, financial security, but there's a part of me that's perpetually sad and probably always will be. My uncle was the last link to my family." Lucy could feel the niggling edges of a panic attack beginning to pull at her insides. Her heart pounded. *No way, not tonight,* she told herself. She took a deep, steadying breath and wiped wet eyes.

"But trying not to be a total victim and doing good work—that keeps me going right now. So," a wan smile flickered on her lips, "the real question for me right now is: Are we going to be working together, or at odds with each other?"

"What are you talking about?" Michael asked.

"You know exactly what I'm talking about. My uncle's murder, Dynamic Chemical, Alvarez, the governor, and Gary Mercer. That's what I'm talking about."

"Oh, man," Michael scrubbed his fingers through his hair. "Holy shit. You do not want to get involved in this, Lucy. I promise you, it's being handled."

"I'm already involved. And I don't think it is being handled. I think it's just being covered up, and I also think you know why."

Michael glanced over at her, a very worried look on his face. He gulped down his tea.

"If you thought you were somehow going to keep me from becoming involved in this thing, you are mistaken. And don't look so distressed—I'm a great partner, so relax." She smiled at him. "Ready for some sweet potato pie, darlin'?"

CHAPTER 33

Detective Frank Martin of the Orlando Police Department pulled on his tie and opened the buttons around a beefy neck that was never meant to be bound by a collar. The sinus-infection color of the walls and the low ceiling in the interrogation room always made him slightly nauseous. An ancient HVAC system worked fitfully at circulating damp, musty air. The environment that was supposed to make the suspects miserable, worked the same nasty magic on the detectives. He was beginning to sweat, unlike the perp—the slender, cool, magazine cover-boy across the table.

The arrogant GQ asshole oozed condescension from his quasi-sincere smile to his slow, ultra-courteous way of conversing. After twenty years on the force, Martin's shit-detector was as well-honed as a set of new steak knives. Gary Mercer sounded good, but he was full of crap.

Seated at the metal table in the center of the small room, Mercer was handsome and annoyingly confident. He dressed conservatively in expensive gray Italian trousers and a navy linen jacket over a crisp, white shirt. It was curious attire—most photogs were slobs. A Rolex's alluring face smiled on his wrist.

Martin studied his paperwork and then pushed it aside. He tapped his pen on the table. Jorge Cardenas, also known as Thomas Rubio, was wanted in Southern California for attempted vehicular manslaughter and was also a person of interest in an arson investigation back there. He seemed to be linked to the man across the table. Orlando's top local TV news director, Alan Klein, had talked off the record to the detective about this dude's possible involvement in all the Cardenas/Rubio California shit, plus maybe a murder of his own.

"Mr. Mercer, can you tell me how long you worked at KLAK-TV in Los Angeles, and in what capacity?"

Mercer's hands folded respectfully as the detective began to press him about his relationship with Jorge Cardenas. "Yes, sir. I was there for three years, the last year as head of the camera department." Mercer surreptitiously pulled down his shirt cuff to cover the forked tongue of a snake tattoo that wrapped around his right wrist. Although Martin gave no sign of noticing, he saw the ink. The devil snake, the world's first liar. Maybe Mr. Clean wasn't so clean cut after all. On the other hand, everyone seemed to be displaying decoration these days. It was the Rolex that really caught his attention— quite the bling for somebody working camera at a local television station. Hell, the timepiece probably cost more than his condo. LAPD folks said Mercer had come from money but had been disowned.

"I understand you had a falling out with KLAK," Martin said. "Particularly with one of your colleagues, a Ms. Lucy Vega."

"This is true." Mercer hesitated for a moment. His eyebrows raised and then he sighed and shrugged. "I don't know how to say this delicately."

"Then say it indelicately, Mr. Mercer."

GQ-man shifted in his seat and stole a quick glance at his fancy watch. His body language said, *I'm rich, and busy, and have I got a good one for you.*

"Actually, sir, I resigned because of sexual harassment."

"Really?" Martin's eyes widened for an instant then he reached for his papers and made a note.

"Yes, on her part, not mine." Mercer folded his hands back onto his lap.

This was not at all the picture the KLAK news chief had painted of the relationship. "In what way did Ms. Vega, uh, harass you?"

"It's uncomfortable to talk about, especially as a man, but she was obsessed with me, even stalked me. I suppose I should have gone to management about it, but I really didn't want to incite the whole mess that would've resulted. Plus, in the end, it only would've been my word against hers. When I found out that I got the job here in Florida, even though it was just freelance, I jumped on it."

Martin tapped his pen on the table again. He observed that for someone uncomfortable with the subject of harassment, the guy seemed eager to spill. "So, you came to Florida to escape Ms. Vega's advances?"

"That, and the earthquakes."

"Of course. Ms. Vega and the *temblors*. Give you a tropical storm over that shakin' and bakin' any day, right?"

"At least you can see the hurricanes coming," Mercer's eyes narrowed.

Martin's narrowed right back. "So, how well did you know Mr. Cardenas, also known as Thomas Rubio?"

"I only knew him here as the guy who cleaned the newsroom early in the morning. We barely spoke. Sorry. Wish I could be more helpful, sir."

"Did you know he posed as a news photographer in L.A.? Stole an audition reel from one of your local colleagues to get hired there. I wonder how he managed to get his hands on that stuff. Alan Klein said you had access to the tape library."

Mercer studied his fingernails, then offered up a contrite face. "I have no idea how this Cardenas guy got the material. But what's really secure anymore, right?"

Martin loosened his tie further. "So, you never assisted Cardenas in any way?"

"No, sir. Absolutely not."

The sleaze-ball was bright, good-looking, convincing, and was probably guilty as hell—the epitome of a hardcore sociopath. Mercer was just the type of dickwad he'd love to put away.

"I hope you catch the prick," Mercer said, face somber.

"We will." Detective Martin wished like hell that he had even a shred of solid evidence on which to collar this liar.

✳

Bea swung her silver Beemer into a space in the LAX short-term airport parking garage and turned off the ignition. Immediately, Lucy checked her watch. She jumped out and pulled a duffle bag, a carry-on backpack, and a camera case from the rear seat. Bea hoisted herself out of the warm car and stretched, cat-like.

Just before six in the morning on the second day of January, the temperature hovered in the high 40s, which was unseasonably cold for SoCal. At least the rain had stopped; the sunlight dazzled, and the air was clear. Lucy took in a long breath and admired the view for an instant. The snow-covered San Bernardino Mountains on the horizon were spectacular. On a good day, this was one of the most beautiful cities in the world. On a bad day, well, you couldn't see much beyond the yellow haze.

Bea yawned. "When I said I thought you needed a vacation, a little change of scenery, I didn't mean reclaiming your roots in the Mexican wilderness. I meant, Hawaii, Bora Bora, umbrella drinks at Club Med Grand Caymans or something like that. Definitely not rural Mexico, wild with government rebels and drug runners."

"But the indigenous cultural experience is always the part of vacationing that I like the best." Lucy left the stunning view behind and practically jogged across the pedestrian bridge toward the terminal. The fresh scent of the morning became tinged with jet fuel.

"This is all so sudden." Bea's high-heeled boots *clacked* on the terrazzo floor.

"You know I've been thinking about heading to Mexico since we had dinner with Michael Burleson,"

Lucy said.

"Well, I guess I repressed it." Exasperated, Bea sighed and grabbed her friend's carry-on bag. "Let me get this. I don't know why you're racing. Slow down. You know how much I hate any kind of morning exercise . . . unless he's at least six-four and . . . well anyway, you've got over an hour and a half before boarding, and the Aeroméxico counter looks empty. They said the plane's only half-full, right?"

"I'm racing because I'm nervous. Maybe I made a mistake—I'm on my way to Tingo Tia, on a hunch. Who's ever even heard of the place? Where the hell is my Xanax?" She rummaged through her pockets. "I hate to fly."

"Lucy, don't go. I can't help flashing on the Rubio imposter coming straight at you with his car. He tried to kill you! It's all too dangerous and unpredictable now. Maybe you can still get your ticket changed to Cancun."

The recollection of that moment of terror in the parking lot, and her subsequent promise to Max that she wouldn't be a Lone Ranger caused Lucy to pause. Then she picked up her pace even faster.

"I'm going, so let's stop talking about it."

Lucy spotted one of the coffee shops outside of the secure part of the terminal.

"Starbucks?" she asked Bea.

"Sure, but no caffeine for you, girlfriend."

"Okay. A cup of decaf and a raspberry scone. Split it?" Lucy asked.

"You're on," Bea said. "I can't believe you wouldn't even let me stop at Dunkin' Donuts on the way."

They ordered their snacks and found a table with

high stools that overlooked the incoming runways. Early on a Sunday morning, especially post-holiday, the traffic was light. A Southwest Airlines 737 glided in for a landing, its wheels touching down with a puff of smoke. From a speaker nearby, Peggy Lee crooned the silvery sad tones of "Is That All There Is?" as Lucy finally found the meds in her backpack. She shook a pill into her hand and popped it into her mouth, swallowing with a grimace. The two women sat quietly together and waited for their coffees to cool along with their anxiety levels.

"Okay," Bea said. She broke the silence with a noisy slug of latte. "I'm just really worried, we all are. You'll be down there in Tingo whatchamacallit, by yourself."

"I'll be with Burleson and his crew."

"And he knows this?"

"Not yet." Lucy smiled.

Bea rolled her big brown eyes. "Okay. You've made up your mind, so I'm not going to say anything else."

"Good, thank you," Lucy said.

"Except be careful. Insanely careful."

"I will."

"And you have your cell phone and charger?"

"Yes, mom, and a credit card, my toothbrush, and clean underwear."

"Excellent. But I have one more thing to ask, something for you to just consider," Bea said.

"I thought you weren't going to say anything else," Lucy took a big bite of her half of the scone. It was hard as a rock.

The grinding of metal-on-metal sounded as a rail-thin Hispanic girl struggled to levitate the roll-up gate of the souvenir store next to the coffee shop.

"This is serious, Luce. I've been wanting to talk to you, but I've been too uncomfortable to put it out there. As your friend, I have to ask."

"You know there's nothing you can't talk to me about."

Bea paused and waited for a noisy group of flight attendants to hustle by. Then she took a deep breath. "Okay. You're not going to want to consider this, but do you think your uncle could have been involved in anything . . . illegal?"

"Illegal?" Lucy choked on her coffee. "You mean like drug-related?"

"Yeah, anything like that?"

"Absolutely not." Lucy's back stiffened. She pushed her cup away. "It's not like the possibility hasn't crossed my mind just in the natural course of thinking about all the possible options, but Henry Vega was a good man. Truly good. The best." She dropped the remains of her scone into a napkin and started crushing the pieces to sawdust. "He would never have been involved in anything unethical or illegal, particularly drugs that hurt kids. Wouldn't happen. Impossible."

"Okay." Bea massaged the pressure point between her eyes. "I just want to make sure that if you're going to do this, you're looking at the painful possibilities. All of them."

Lucy nodded and admitted only to herself that this was one horrific possibility that she had not, until this moment, even considered.

CHAPTER 34

The door to the 737 closed with a sucking *thunk,* a sound deep and dense like the steel teeth of a bank vault, or the doors to the maximum-security prison Lucy had once visited on an assignment. Or, she thought, fighting what felt like the chest-splitting onset of a massive coronary, or like a coffin. Black, airless, and final. She hated to fly. No, she much more than hated it. Control issues, her therapist always said. Damn right control issues, Lucy admitted as she tried to keep the electricity in her wildly firing synapses from bringing down the plane.

Lucy Vega, the dark-haired woman with pale blue eyes, all calmness on the surface, popped another Xanax and swallowed it with what saliva she could work up in her dry mouth. Overhead, the tepid stream of bacteria-filled canned air slowed to a trickle and the lights flickered as the jet lumbered toward the runway.

In the aisle, the flight attendant's lips moved as they droned through the seatbelt drill. Lucy sank deeper into her medicated meditation, preparing to come to terms with her imminent, fiery death as she plunged from the sky.

She once had gone into full-blown panic attacks when faced with flying—body numb, palsied, and silently screaming inside. But since therapy, hypnosis, and drugs, flying now only invoked sheer horror. As the acceleration began and the sky whale miraculously lifted into the bumpy ocean of air—engines whining, wheels folding into the belly with a metallic, scraping grind— she was at least relieved that the seat next to her was empty. Turbulence often caused her to randomly put a death grip the on the arm, or whatever appendage was most prominent, of an unsuspecting seat mate. She finally took to warning the passenger next to her that this could possibly happen. Then she'd usually have to endure the "you could be killed more easily sitting in your own living room watching TV," lecture. As if rationality meant anything. Once in a while, she'd get the thin, haunted smile of a fellow traveler teetering on the same precarious edge, but there was somehow no comfort in their shared experience. On a lucky day, the passenger would look at her like she was insane, which she admitted she was in this department, and start negotiating for a change of seat.

After a picture-perfect takeoff, which was still hell, the flight crew began the drinks and peanuts ritual, the only food they would probably offer on the cross-border trip.

"Some water, please," Lucy croaked to the flight attendant, a middle-aged woman with a patient smile. It took a while, but the small cup finally appeared. She drained it in one gulp.

Now high over Southern California on the way to Mexico City, the plane was climbing through a spectacular skyscape of cumulus clouds. The view of the earth and atmosphere at this elevation was the one and only occasional pleasure for Lucy in flight. As a photographer, she had to admit that there were moments of sheer wonder that lifted her above the debilitating fear. Then she'd come crashing down again.

Struggling to remain hyper-vigilant in case she had to save the plane from disaster, the medication finally kicked in and took her to a twilight sleep distanced from thoughts of impending doom. The turbulence was just riding a horse on a rugged trail through the mountains; the screaming baby was a hawk calling in the distance; the powerful motors droned with the cyclic sound of ocean waves crashing rhythmically on the shore.

Miraculously, the hands of her watch reached the three-hour mark. When they touched down in Mexico City, she was breathing more easily, relief buoying her out of the 737 and into the busy terminal. Next was a forty-five-minute trip to Tingo Tia in a plane the size of a flying noodle.

It was almost over, and then it would really begin.

✳

Tingo Tia, home to approximately 2,500 souls, sits on the edge of the coastal rain forest and the foothills of the Sierra Madre del Sur in Mexico's State of Guerrero. Lucy learned from the loquacious pilot of the tiny twelve-seat flying amalgamation of loose bolts and tin, that the area had long been dubbed the *Zona Amapola*—the Poppy Zone. Tingo Tia and surrounding villages constituted the number one pipeline for production and trafficking of black tar heroin entering the U.S. This was a tidbit of information Burleson had been alarmingly sketchy about when describing his documentary.

The Tingo Tia airport terminal was an unenclosed baggage holding area, covered by corrugated plastic sheets, with a modular trailer adjoining. The courteous transportation agent/luggage handler/ticket seller and taco chef, helped Lucy secure a government-sponsored taxi.

She climbed into a *Road Warrior*-esque cab and dragged her camera and backpack into the back seat with her. The driver stashed her duffle bag in the trunk. Sallow-skinned with a startling gold grille on his teeth, he was in his mid-twenties and wore wrap-around reflective sunglasses and a Beyoncé T-shirt. The taxi itself was an old Toyota, which probably hadn't been cleaned since the day it was purchased—or otherwise acquired. Each of the fenders was a different color of primer, held together with layers of gray epoxy and silver duct tape.

Lucy hung onto the door handle as the vehicle lurched out of the taxi park and passed so close to an old man riding a burro that she could smell the animal's breath. If this was an official taxi driver, God only knew what the non-government authorized cabbies were like.

"*Hermano viejo loco,*" the driver cursed at the old man.

It wasn't the old man who was crazy. The taxi hit a

deep rut, fishtailed in the gravel and kept accelerating. Lucy had thought the plane ride was bad. The car shot through the countryside like a bullet train, zooming by slow-moving wagons of produce, and anything else impeding its way, without regard for no-passing zones or any other traffic signage.

Sweating and her heart pounding, Lucy was more than thankful when they finally pulled up to the Fiesta del Rio, touted in an internet ad as the best hotel in town. She could, however, smell the *río,* and the burro's breath was preferable. All contributed to a perfect fiesta for malaria mosquitoes or the Zika virus. She was already starting to itch and visualize babies with small heads.

Lucy paid her fare with pesos and was left standing in the dirt with her baggage. She hauled her belongings through an archway choked with hot pink bougainvillea and into a tiny office.

At the counter, she could see into the hotelkeeper's dark apartment. An old episode of the '70s TV hit, *Dallas,* dubbed in Spanish, played in black and white. Near the television, she spotted unkempt male feet with long toenails in rubber flip-flops atop a threadbare, greenish velour footrest.

Lucy cleared her throat a few times to get his attention but finally had to call out for assistance.

The man groaned as he pulled himself from his lounge chair and emerged into the pale light of the lobby. *"Buenos tardes, señorita."*

"Buenos tardes, señor." Lucy's Spanish was rudimentary but functional.

Bald and skeletal, the proprietor had to be in his late ghties. An equally aged macaw was perched on his shoulder; white droppings dripped down the back of the man's Hawaiian shirt. The bird flapped off his shoulder perch, landed on the counter and pecked at Lucy's fingers as she tried to fill out the registration form.

"She a real *pistola, sí?*" The hotelier watched, amused.

Lucy finally managed to remember how to say something like, "I am going to kill your bird," in Spanish. The macaw was ordered back onto the man's shoulder where it eyed Lucy with yellow, beady eyes and avian disdain.

The ancient proprietor looked youthful compared to his brother Tito, the bellman, who was followed by an arthritic Chihuahua. Flecks of whitish spittle oozed from the corners of the old man's mouth. Lucy tried to dissuade him from helping her, but he insisted on carrying her pack while she took the camera case and duffle. She imagined him having a coronary on his way to her room, and then she would be morally obligated to perform CPR. Whoa.

Tito was spryer than he initially appeared and was kind enough to smash several of the largest, slowest moving cockroaches that skittered across the floor when she flipped on the light switch. She gave him a generous tip, patted the dog's head—who was much nicer than the macaw—and then shut and locked the door behind her.

After a moment's perusal, she was not sure whether she wanted to be locked in or out. In fact, looking around at the dingy brown and orange furnishings, complete with a bullfighting poster over the bed and the matador sword aimed toward her pillow, she noted a rip in the window screen large enough for a serial murderer several accomplices to crawl through. In the corner, two kangaroo rats, who undoubtedly carried the hantavirus, plotted how they were going to chew into her luggage and leave poisonous black droppings on her toothbrush. An orange shag rug lay on the floor like a Muppet carcass.

As Lucy threw her bags onto the bed, she wondered again if the decision to take on Tingo Tia alone been just a wee bit hasty.

CHAPTER 35

When Lucy awoke, it was ten o'clock in the evening. She had fallen asleep for two hours with her bags still clutched in her hands. She felt an imprint of the luggage tag etched into her cheek. Her whole body ached from the awkward position she'd slept in.

Faint strains of a guitar reverberated from somewhere nearby. She crawled off the bed and scanned the floor for critters then tiptoed to the window and peered down the street. A little cantina looked to be open. She was famished. Nervously venturing into the bathroom, which was, thankfully, fairly clean, she washed her face, pulled her hair into a ponytail and changed into khaki shorts and a pale blue T-shirt. She was relieved to find both the hotel staff members and their pets missing from the lobby.

A half-block walk from the hotel, Lucy entered a

small, tidy, family-run restaurant called *El Fresca*. A dark-eyed, teenaged boy ushered her to a table with a view over the inky river. The evening was soft and balmy. White lights were strung in nearby trees and brightly colored native animals cut from tissue paper hung languidly from the ceiling. There were no other customers.

Lucy ordered cheese enchiladas with rice and black beans and an ice cold Modelo Negra, her favorite Mexican *cerveza*. She downed it quickly.

As she enjoyed her dinner and perused a Mexican tour book touting the charms of the State of Guerrero, she became aware of a looming presence, too near for comfort. Her gaze shifted from the pages of the book to the cowboy boots on the worn linoleum floor, then followed the boots up the jeans to broad shoulders and a familiar face.

"Mr. Burleson," she said. "How are you? *¿Cómo está?*"

His deep blue eyes sparked with anger.

Not much of a drinker, Lucy felt a little beer buzz. Just as well, it'd take the edge off the conversation she'd been dreading. "Join me?"

Burleson's face was stony, he crossed his arms over his chest. "Lucy, this was not a good choice."

"But I love enchiladas, and these are excellent." Lucy took a big bite and accidentally breathed in part of her meal. She couldn't finish her sentence as she choked. Her eyes watered like a broken faucet. She grabbed her beer bottle and swallowed what was left of the liquid to clear her throat. It didn't help much.

Burleson offered no sympathy.

"What an amazing coincidence to meet you here," she croaked, refusing to be openly embarrassed by a near call for the Heimlich maneuver.

"News travels fast. And I've known Tito for years."

"Ah, yes, he seems nice. And the dog is kind of cute." Lucy signaled the boy for a second bottle of Modelo. "Want anything?"

Burleson shook his head and remained standing.

"Well, I'm here to help you out, thought you could use a camera." Lucy still cleared her throat.

"No, thanks. We talked about this, Lucy. The place we're headed is way too dangerous."

"I know, I know, everything you do is dangerous." She shrugged. "Plus, I don't have to share all my plans with you, do I? No, *señor*."

"You shouldn't have come."

She smiled up at him. "And you rather neatly forgot to mention the magnitude of the drug dealing going on here. It was all about chocolates and alternative economies, wasn't it? Sweet."

"What are you doing here, Lucy?"

"Finding out why my uncle was murdered. What are you doing here?"

"You know I'm doing pre-production on a documentary on alternative economies. That's the truth."

Lucy looked up at him, eyes narrow. "And I'm conducting an etymological study to see how long it takes a pupa to turn into a fly on the pile of shit you keep dumping on me."

They glared at each other.

"A plane leaves for Mexico City tomorrow at noon,"

he said. "There's only one flight a day and if you're smart, you'll be on it." Michael turned to leave.

"If you're smart," Lucy said, "you'd admit that it would be to both of our advantage if we worked together." The beer, fatigue, and residual edge from her flight anxiety meds began to take over. The room began to slowly spin. "Then you could at least keep an eye on me, save me if I get in trouble."

He glanced back at her.

She gave a cryptic smile. "Think about it, Mr. Burleson. In the meantime, I'm returning to the Psycho Hotel across the street to get some rest, if that's possible." She drained the last drop of *cerveza,* tossed pesos onto the table to cover the meal, and pushed past him.

Burleson angrily punched numbers on his satellite phone. After several tries and no connection, he stuck the phone back into his pants pocket and headed for the door.

"The signal's much better up past the hotel at the top of the hill," the teenage waiter told him as he bussed Lucy's abandoned dinner plate.

"*Muchas gracias.*" Burleson nodded and marched off into the darkness.

❊

The night was calm and quiet except for the hum of cicadas and an occasional call from a night bird. A dog barked in the distance. Burleson was at the top of a hill overlooking the Fiesta del Rio hotel. The lights of the small town glimmered like the remains of exploded fireworks below him. Beyond the town, there was no ambient light and the sky was a black velvet pincushion of silvery stars. The benign beauty of the region disguised whatever malignancy crawled beneath the surface.

The air began to cool and the wind rose, gently blowing inland from the ocean, a hundred miles away. He should have begun to relax, but instead, Burleson battled the frustrating certainty that Lucy Vega was along for the ride, and if anything happened to her it would be on his head. He pulled the satellite phone from his pocket and dialed again. The young waiter was right, the signal looked better.

Governor Scanlon's voice sounded clear and close as if he were in the next room. "Mikey B, my boy, how was your trip down? Everything copasetic?"

"Everything's just, hey, going fine. Except for one little snag," Michael replied, not wanting to share the bad news but knowing he had to.

"What's up?"

"The girl is here."

There was silence then, "What? No way."

"Uh-huh, way. And she's not leaving. She's a goddamned pit bull, won't let go. I'll try to hit the road before she figures out where I'm headed."

"Shit," Scanlon said, then paused. Burleson heard him drum his fingers in the background. "I owe her uncle. She has to be protected. Pay whoever needs to be paid to keep her off your trail. There's a good chance that Alvarez and his band of merry assholes know who she is. That could really complicate things for her. And us."

Burleson ground his teeth. He didn't want to think Alvarez and his goons could be aware of her arrival so fast, but hell, through Tito, he'd known within a half hour that Lucy'd checked in, how many bags she had, and the brand of shoes she was wearing.

"This place has the vibes of a rat's nest. I hope Father Juan Jesus de Anza pans out to be the good guy I think he is. It's been a lot of years since we knew each other in Chiapas. But he was a fine priest then, a good man, his heart was with the people. He's the key to our access here."

"All the more reason to support him and his efforts to make an alternative economy viable in the region," Scanlon replied. "In the long run, it will protect California's interests, and that of our entire country."

He sounded a bit too oratorical to suit Michael's irritated mood. "Okay, gov. I'll try to get the hell out of here as soon as possible, leave her behind. My cultural interpreter is supposed to meet me at eight tomorrow morning. And what about the CIA coverage we're supposed to have?"

"Your driver and two of his people have been contracted."

"They're contractors? Not regular operatives?"

"My guy in D.C., he's high up on the Agency's food chain, says they've worked for us before in Guerrero and did a good job. They're solid," the governor said.

"Okay. We'll load and go first thing in the morning. If Lucy figures out where we're off to, it'll take her a couple days to set up any kind of private transportation. Public busses only make the trip twice a week. Hopefully, she'll be on her way back to L.A. in no time."

"From your mouth to God's ears," Scanlon said. He ended the call with politically correct, hollow-sounding words of encouragement.

CHAPTER 36

The following day dawned as humid and heavy as a wet beach towel. The oversized T-shirt Lucy had slept in was damp with perspiration and her head ached. Her bags and clothing had fallen off the bed and onto the floor. She didn't want to think about what might have nested in her belongings during the night. Were those rat droppings she saw next to her socks?

Lucy slid out from between the sheets, which she had carefully inspected the night before, and headed for the shower. Tepid water beat down on her tired shoulders.

After tying her wet hair into a braid, she slipped into the clothing she had worn the previous evening, slung a small purse and digital camera over her shoulder, and went out to the front steps of the hotel.

Hummingbirds buzzed around a bright red feeder just outside the office. On a bulletin board, a poorly photocopied list of restaurants in Tingo Tia was posted. A map of the town was so faded by the sun as to be unreadable. Lucy sat down on the steps and pulled out a local information pamphlet she'd picked up at the front desk. It offered no map. Lucy sighed.

An attractive Hispanic man in his late twenties, with jet black hair, gathered into a ponytail longer than hers, ambled slowly up the steps. Lucy pretended to pour over her reading material as the guy approached. He was probably a local but he wore a UCLA Bruins basketball jersey and baggy shorts.

"*Buenos días, señorita. ¿Usted una turista?*" He asked if Lucy was a tourist. His voice was nice, deep and soothing.

She looked up from her pamphlet and realized that she was actually yearning for some conversation, even if it would be in broken Spanish. She was feeling isolated and unsure of what was to come.

"*Sí, no hablo mucho español.*" Despite her half-Mexican heritage, she was far from feeling fluent in the language.

"Oh, you're American," he said in perfect English.

His smile was friendly, and his caramel-colored eyes sparkled. Lucy couldn't help but smile back with a wide grin.

"Yes, visiting from Southern California. And you? Are you from Tingo Tia?"

He nodded. "I was born about thirty miles southwest of here, nearer the coast. Been in L.A. since I was sixteen. This is my first trip back in ten years. I'm Gregorio Hidalgo, by the way." He offered his hand. His grip was firm and assured.

"Nice to meet you, Gregorio." Lucy stood up from the step she was sitting on. "I'm Lucy Vega, also from L.A."

"Yeah, go Rams," he said. "What is it, six degrees of separation?"

"Yep, it's a small world." Lucy tucked her tour book into her purse. "So what brings you back to your old 'hood, if I may be so presumptuous as to ask?"

"Just finished my Master's in Mexican Culture and Political Systems at UCLA." He plucked at his Bruins shirt. "A few weeks ago I was offered work with an American film company doing a documentary here. I'm going to be their language and cultural interpreter."

Lucy's eyes widened for an instant. This man was working with Burleson. She could feel her heart begin to race.

"I'm a UCLA alum too," she said.

"Then we're *compadres,* for sure."

"So, what will you actually be doing as a cultural interpreter?" *Besides helping me get a spot on Burleson's bus to Pitacallpa.*

"Translating and connecting with the locals, explaining stuff, that kind of thing. I speak several of the indigenous languages—Mixtec, Zapotec, and Nahuatl. Very few outside these tiny communities are fluent." Gregorio drew himself up with a touch of pride.

"Wow, your communications skills will be quite an asset."

"I was raised speaking Mixtec until I was around ten. After that I began using more Spanish, then English, of course."

"You aren't, by any chance, working for Michael Burleson, are you?"

Gregorio's eyes widened. "Yeah, you know him?"

"Oh, uh, yep. I'm on the film crew too." She didn't know how those words popped out of her mouth so easily. Wishful thinking, maybe. He'd find out soon enough that she was not on Burleson's list of favorite people, let alone his crew.

"Hey, great." A smile lit his face again. "I didn't think anyone else besides me was coming down 'til next week. I'm a day early, was supposed to stay at a B&B across town, but they were booked. This place kind of sucks, but it had a room. You see the bird?"

Lucy nodded and rolled her eyes. "He almost took off one of my fingers." She shifted from foot to foot. "Did you, by any chance, run into Michael last night? Or have you seen him yet this morning?" She wanted to ferret out their plans so she could determine her strategy.

"No, he's in the capital, Chilpancingo, 'til later this evening. Film permits, something like that. Waylaid by bureaucracy."

"Oh, good. I mean good that we'll see him soon." The knot in Lucy's stomach began to loosen. She wouldn't have to face Burleson right away.

"What kind of work do you do?" Gregorio asked. He glanced up at angry cumulus clouds that churned over the distant southern Sierra Madre.

Lucy's eyes followed his. Big weather was on the way. Would that affect their journey to the outlying village? "I'm a cinematographer. Work in TV news, actually."

"Very cool." Gregorio hoisted his daypack onto his shoulder. "How 'bout we get some breakfast?"

"Sounds good. You know the restaurants?"

"I know what used to be here. We'll find something

decent. Did you get your expense money?"

"My what? Oh, no, not yet. But I have plenty of pesos for now. Actually, he wasn't expecting me this early. I sort of surprised him."

"I'm sure he was happy to see you."

"Oh, you have no idea." Lucy licked her parched lips.

"Let's go, I'm starving," Gregorio rubbed his lean, flat stomach. "I know a little place that's probably still in business. Great *huevos rancheros* with salsa and strong coffee."

"Lead me to it." Lucy began to feel a glimmer of hope after a long night of discouragement.

CHAPTER 37

Several blocks beyond the Fiesta del Rio hotel, Gregorio and Lucy walked along the edge of a dying business district littered with the remnants of small shops and squalid housing. Filthy, destitute children, some as young as toddlers, lay listlessly in doorways or in crumpled cardboard boxes.

"What is this horrible place?" Lucy whispered. The level of poverty, neglect, and despair was far beyond anything she had seen in the States, where there was at least an infrastructure in place to assist people in need, particularly children. "Who do these kids belong to?"

A hardness came into Gregorio's voice. "Nobody— they're baby drug addicts, orphans, runaways. I could have been one of them. They haven't been as lucky."

"What do you mean?"

"My mother died of typhus when I was a baby and

my father was murdered by *guerillas* when I was eight. My cousin says I watched from the doorway while he was tortured. I don't remember any of it."

Lucy stopped for a moment, blindsided by the account of this atrocious experience. He recited the words as if he were giving a book report, a dispassionate commentary on someone else's life.

"How horrible. Did they catch the people who killed him?"

I'm trying to catch the people who killed the man who raised me like a father. Her throat tightened and she held back tears. She and Gregorio were both orphans.

"Never caught them. They never do. A Catholic priest came and rescued me. He took care of me and made sure I went to school."

Lucy and Gregorio walked a while in silence.

"So how did you get to the U.S.?" Lucy asked. She noticed a long, ragged scar on his arm.

Gregorio shifted his daypack to the other shoulder. "When I got older, they sent me to a Catholic boarding school in Mexico City. Then I won a scholarship to UCLA. One of my teachers had graduated from there and encouraged me to go for it. Helped me fill out the forms, get references, and all that stuff."

"Then off you went into a brave new world?"

"You got it. Pretty mind boggling but I survived and did well." He chewed on his lip and gazed about. "It's very bizarre to be back."

They turned a corner onto an even more depressing street if that was possible.

"Sorry, I gave you much more than you wanted to know. It just sort of . . . flowed out. I'm sorry."

"No apology needed. Must be very strange to be back here, all sorts of memories stirring up," Lucy replied. She knew she couldn't even begin to imagine how difficult it would be.

Impatiently, Gregorio pushed away several children who followed them, begging for money.

Lucy winced. "They're just babies, shouldn't we give them something?"

His eyes darkened. "It won't help, they'll only spend it on more drugs, or the bigger kids will steal it."

"I know, but . . ." Lucy sighed. She pulled out her camera and began to take pictures. It was why she got into news work, to begin with—to tell the story, show the pain, to help people, and yes, to save them.

"This neighborhood is the definition of hopeless," Gregorio said. "It's where the throw-away children come to die of neglect, malnutrition, disease, or O.D. on whatever they can get their hands on. This is why peasants will work for the drug lords."

Lucy nodded and continued shooting.

"And that's why Michael Burleson's friend, Father Juan Jesus de Anza and his village of Pitacallpa, are worth doing a documentary about," Gregorio said. "They show us successful economic alternatives to heroin and cocaine production. They show us hope. I guess that's the reason I'm here."

Goose bumps raised on Lucy's arms. The depth of his passion moved her. Who is this Juan Jesus de Anza and where is Pitacallpa? Did any of this tie in with Alvarez or Mercer?

"I'll look forward to meeting Father de Anza," she said. If she thought Tingo Tia was a backwater, she wondered what the village de Anza lived in would be like. Had her uncle been there? Did he know this Catholic priest? Did they work together?

She hated herself for the niggling doubt Bea had planted regarding her uncle's integrity. How could she think like this about Henry Vega? He was the finest person she had ever known.

In her peripheral vision, Lucy sensed movement. A young girl, maybe ten, appeared from nowhere, like a sylph, a subtle disturbance in the air. She leaned gracefully against a corner storefront where she caught the shade of a dusty pepper tree. Not yet pubescent, she carried herself like a woman years older. No gawky, childlike motions, no excess of spent energy.

Lucy pulled out her camera and began snapping photos of the girl. She was elegant, even with her dirty, scuffed legs, filthy clothes, and long, tangled hair. She slowly approached Lucy and Gregorio. Her small hand opened like a sea anemone, ready to possess an offered coin. Her fingernails were bitten to the quick but her skin beneath the grime appeared clear, her lips were full, sensual, but split down the middle by a thin scar. When she looked up at them, Lucy gasped, the child's eyes were like dark holes, devoid of emotion.

"Come on, Lucy, let's go," Gregorio said, moving away and motioning for her to follow.

Lucy unhooked a little silver travel angel she always clipped to her purse, a charm she believed helped her cope with her fear of flying. Its blue rhinestone eyes had long fallen off. She folded it into the girl's cool hand. A transient light flickered in the child's eyes, like a firefly you thought you might have seen on a summer night in a deep wood.

Several older children watched the transaction, faces intense with radar-like awareness. As they began to move toward Lucy, the girl turned and ran. The others rushed after her.

"Lucy," Gregorio said, anger in his voice. "Children have murdered each other over less."

"I took her picture, I wanted to give her something."

"*You* wanted to give her something—it's not about you."

Lucy felt the sting of his disapproval and the shame at her mistake. In giving the girl a trinket she had put the child's safety at risk. But maybe she would fight to keep it, maybe she would prevail.

"I saw something in her eyes for an instant."

"Kindness can be so cruel to those without hope. I know the scope of this is something you may not be able to understand."

"Maybe at some point, we can do something."

"Americans. Senseless optimists."

"I guess it's both our best quality and our curse." Lucy glanced back to where the woman-child had disappeared.

Gregorio shrugged and they moved on.

As Lucy snapped pictures, capturing the obscene tragedy of this neighborhood, of this life, the children followed them like hungry ducks to breadcrumbs. But soon, the older, more dangerous-looking denizens of the district began to slink after them. Lucy jogged beside Gregorio through back alleys until they reached the other side of town.

The commercial center of Tingo Tia was a collection

of Spanish-style stucco storefronts with wrought iron balconies around a tree-filled park, the *Jardín de Benito Juárez*. It honored the only indigenous person to ever become president of Mexico. A big square colonial-style bank, *Banco de Guerrero,* built of white stucco with arched, church-like windows, sat in the corner like a heavy cash box. It was flanked by a medical clinic, several elegant jewelry stores, cafes, clothing shops, and art galleries. A spectacular Romanesque cathedral of carved stone, with gilded spires and intricate stained glass windows, rose into the cloudy sky from behind the bank.

Most of the citizens were dressed in simple, cotton clothing. Others, the minority, made their way down the street in expensive foreign suits, carrying slim briefcases.

A farmers' market had stalls set up in the square where vendors hawked produce, baked goods, local crafts, puppies of unknown breeds, and every kind of chili pepper one could imagine. Knock-off designer clothing, accessories, and electronics were in abundance. The contrast from the previous neighborhood was staggering. Lucy guessed this was the drug money side of town.

"The restaurant is over there—Paco's Cantina." Gregorio pointed to an outdoor patio filled with small tables, surrounded by pots bursting with red geraniums and flowering succulents.

They crossed the busy street, dodging cars, bicycles, and small motorbikes before they settled into the sunny courtyard. Lucy and Gregorio both ordered up the *huevos* with *mole* and strong coffee with hot milk, *café con leche*.

"So, how are we all getting to Pitacallpa? Just the three of us for now, right?" Lucy mopped up the eggs and beans with a warm tortilla. "I didn't get all the details before I left L.A." Lucy hoped she could glean a bit of information on Burleson's upcoming plans.

Gregorio took a long slow drink of his coffee before answering. "Ahhh, I feel like a human being again. Sorry I was so edgy back there—cuts close to home."

"You know the turf, and I screwed up." Lucy lifted her coffee cup and took a sip, closed her eyes. The empty-eyed girl-child, who opened her hand like a sad little flower, was not easily going to leave her alone.

"Last I heard, the van takes off for Pitacallpa in the morning, around seven o'clock from the B&B. Takes ten or twelve hours to get the village, depending on the roads. The Catholic priest Michael talked about will be expecting us." Gregorio waved to the server for more coffee. "I'll see if we can get you a room at the B&B with us for tonight. Burleson left me a message to go over and make final arrangements with the driver, too. You worried about the trip?"

"Oh, no, not at all." *Right. No worries.* "Gregorio," she continued, taking a chance, "have you ever heard of a man named Luis Alvarez? He's supposed to be known around here. I guess he's a local politician or something."

Lucy was momentarily distracted by a dusty police car that cruised slowly past the restaurant.

Gregorio put his coffee down abruptly and motioned for Lucy to hold off the conversation as the waiter approached with refills. He splashed coffee into both their cups and left an extra pot of cream.

"Where did you hear about Luis Alvarez?" Gregorio

glanced over his shoulder. The server had vanished into the kitchen.

Carly's broken limbs flashed through Lucy's mind. "Somebody mentioned him as a person we should, uh, talk to for the video."

Gregorio poured cream into his fresh, steamy cup of java. "Luis Alvarez is head of the agricultural police that patrol this region of Guerrero—*Policía de Agricultura de Guerrero Alta*—PAGA, for short. They enforce the laws against growing coca plants and heroin poppies. PAGA's highly involved in controlling the illegal drug trade."

"Oh, so he's a good guy?"

Gregorio was deathly silent. He pushed his coffee cup away. Then, at last, he whispered, "PAGA killed my father and blamed it on the *guerillas*. I know it. It's their style. They've controlled the area for a long time. They're dangerous, Lucy. And Alvarez is the most dangerous of all."

Lucy suppressed a shiver. So Alvarez was both head of PAGA and also had serious connections with Dynamic Chemical Corporation in L.A., the company that manufactured the pesticide that contaminated the livestock. The revelation was more than Lucy had bargained for. She looked out across the street as another police car turned the corner.

Gregorio smiled. It felt thin and forced. "Not to worry, *señorita*. Alvarez has huge respect for Father de Anza. No one will mess with us." He signaled to the server for the bill, then turned his full attention to Lucy. "Tell me about your family. I've droned on far too much about my tales of woe."

Lucy sighed. "More tales of woe." She pushed her

plate away. The cruiser, with a PAGA logo on its side, crawled by again. Lucy was seized with an uncomfortable feeling that they were being watched and that far from being safe, they were already being messed with.

***

Gary Mercer sat in his idling open-topped Jeep a block away and puffed on a filterless cigarette. He wore a pair of snug designer jeans, and an Armani golf shirt the color of blood oranges. His Ray-Bans reflected Lucy in the distance. He watched how her fingers closed around the creamy coffee cup, how her eyes narrowed as she breathed in the scent and gulped down the hot caffeine. That mouth could probably suck the skin off a zucchini.

How in the hell had that whiny do-gooder, Gregorio Hidalgo, found Lucy Vega? And how the hell had she found her way to Tingo Tia? He didn't like the comfortable way they talked together. He had underestimated her. Dangerously underestimated her. But women disappeared in the *Zona Amapola* routinely.

"Count your days, Lucille," Mercer whispered, aware of the ache rising between his thighs. The hunt was the aphrodisiac.

A shirtless young man, brown, chiseled, and taut as a wire, jumped into the Jeep next to him and tossed a gym bag into the back seat. Mercer dropped his cigarette stub out the window. He made a tight U-turn and roared away from town, into the foothills.

"Gonna trash us some bitch?" The young man grinned. His too-perfect white teeth glimmered in the sunlight. The tongue that flicked from his mouth was narrow and split down the center.

"Later, baby. Gotta trash something in L.A. first."

Mercer pulled a fat, half-smoked joint out of the ashtray. Toked it up.

"Can I fly the plane?" the young man entreated, wild-eyed and excited.

"Make it worth my while, and I'll think about it." Mercer rubbed his swollen crotch.

The split tongue went to work.

CHAPTER 38

At a Pemex gas station a half block from the bed and breakfast that Gregorio had helped Lucy move into the previous evening, Michael Burleson and Gregorio assisted several local men in loading luggage and gear on top of a thirty-year-old Volkswagen minivan. The cumulus clouds of the previous morning had turned dark and ominous. Although the rainy season was still months away, the infamous *El Niño* weather system again turned the norm on its head.

Gonzalo Pogo, the van's pudgy, gap-toothed driver, covered the baggage with a plastic tarp and tied it down with bungee cords. "All loaded, have gas, ready to go, *señors.*"

He held open the side door as the passengers climbed into the van. Burleson slid into the front seat, Gregorio was behind him in the middle. Two local Mexican men in their late thirties chatted quietly together in the very back. They were introduced as Jupe and Augusto, Gonzalo Pogo's cousins, on their way to a small village near Pitacallpa.

"What about Lucy?" Gregorio asked.

Burleson's face registered complete surprise. "What? You know Lucy?" Then he heard her voice.

"I'm sorry I'm late, *señor!*" Lucy called out. She ran down the street with her luggage banging against her legs.

"*No problemo, señorita,*" Pogo said, and moved to assist her. As Michael leaped out of the front seat, mouth agape in disbelief, Pogo hoisted her duffle and backpack onto the roof. He expertly rearranged the load and strapped everything down again securely.

"Hey, Lucy, I was afraid you were going to change your mind," Gregorio said, clearly glad to see her. He moved over to make space next to him in the middle seat.

Burleson's jaw muscles bunched and unbunched. "How do you two know each other? And where do you think you're going, Miss Vega?"

"To Pitacallpa," she said matter-of-factly, and hauled her camera case into the vehicle.

"This is my van. I paid for it, so I choose the passengers, and you're not coming with us," Michael said, his arms folding across his chest. Lucy ignored him and climbed in next to Gregorio.

"*Señor,* there was an extra seat, and this nice *señorita,* she need a ride. No other bus going 'til Friday. And, she very generous." Pogo smiled and shrugged his shoulders.

"I'll be even more generous to make sure she stays here."

"I'll walk if I have to," Lucy said.

"It's a very dangerous road, señor Burleson. I no let my mother or my sister walk this." Pogo shook his head, recognizing a damsel in distress. "She should no walk."

"Michael, may I have a word with you?" Lucy slid out of the van and took his arm. She guided him away from the rest of the group. Grudgingly, he acquiesced, but couldn't have looked more irritated.

"Listen," Lucy began, eyes like blue granite, "you need to accept the fact that I'm going with you."

"I don't have to accept any—"

"No, wait," she continued. "My uncle's murder—yes, murder—ties into what's going on down here. He was everything to me, and *I have to know* what happened. Don't you understand?"

"Anything could go wrong here, Lucy. I can't be responsible."

"Don't give me the war-zone speech again."

"I wouldn't dream of it."

"Good, because I'm in this for the duration. So, I'm asking you, please, can we call a truce?"

Michael scrubbed his hands through his hair then brought them down over his face for a moment. He was not getting away from her and he knew it. Sighing, his eyes met Lucy's. "I lost this battle at the restaurant in Santa Monica, didn't I?"

Lucy nodded, a thin smile on her lips.

"There is more to this than you think," he said.

"And I am more aware of that than you know," Lucy replied.

They stood in silence. "Okay. Get in," he finally said.

Lucy offered a little bow. "Thank you. You won't regret this."

"I already do."

She turned quickly toward the van and jumped in before Burleson could change his mind.

"I thought you were friends," Gregorio whispered as she adjusted her seatbelt.

"We are. He just doesn't always realize it."

At that moment, a fork of lightning ripped across the sky. Thunder sounded in the distance and rain began to sprinkle from the heavens.

"We must get going," Pogo said. "The road is very difficult when too much rain comes."

Burleson caught Lucy's reflection in the rearview mirror and shook his head.

✳

The passengers were quiet as they bounced along the rutted pavement of the Guerrero Alta highway. Several miles outside of town, the jungle grew thicker, and the two-lane pavement gave way to nothing more than a wide dirt road. As the rain intensified, Gonzalo slowed down to avoid the increasing number of deep, muddy potholes and rocky washes. Above the rain, the *slap, slap* of the windshield wipers was the predominant sound. Lucy found it oddly relaxing, and was grateful for the relative silence.

"At this rate, I think we'll be lucky if we reach Pitacallpa by dinner time," Gregorio said, about two hours into the hundred-mile trip.

It was just then that they felt the vehicle skid and

sink. Pogo stepped on the accelerator but the rear wheels just whined and spun, digging in even deeper. Gregorio was the first one out with Michael following.

"Holy shit. We're in up to our bumpers," Gregorio said, frowning.

The rain had abated into a light mist, but the temperature was high, and the insects were starting to swarm.

"Everybody out," Michael said. "Time to push."

Lucy grimaced as she sunk into mud up to her shins. Everyone helped stuff branches and rocks under the wheels in an attempt to give the van some traction. With Pogo at the helm, they managed to get the vehicle rocking back and forth until finally, he gunned it. The van lurched out of the bog. The travelers hopped back into the vehicle, only to go about six feet before it was stuck again. By noon, and sixteen ruts later, they were all exhausted and filthy.

"We could crawl to Pitacallpa faster than this." Lucy sighed and rubbed her neck.

"Feel free to try it," Michael said, refusing to look at her.

"Are we almost there yet?" Gregorio interjected, sounding like a grumpy child on a long summer vacation drive. "Just kidding, just kidding!" he laughed as the others groaned in response.

"We've got about sixty kilometers, or a little more," Pogo said. "We doing good. You good pushers." His wide grin was becoming annoying. "Soon we'll be at the intersection where we go north toward *la selva,* the eyebrow of the jungle that takes us to the highlands. Very soon."

The van seemed to be making relatively good time—fifteen miles an hour with no stops or stall-outs for almost thirty minutes. But then it happened again. The sound of the engine revving and the wheels digging deeper into the mire was becoming all too familiar, and as welcome as the sound of a dentist's drill.

Pogo informed them that at least they had stalled at the intersection in the forest he had been looking for. Unfortunately, the road they were to turn onto looked worse than the one they were leaving.

Lucy's heart sank. But, she reminded herself, she was lucky to be along at all. Damn lucky. "My turn, I'll check it out," she said.

Everyone else appeared too tired to move and remained in the van passing around a bag of energy bars.

Lucy slid open the side door and stepped out into the river of mud. She took several murky steps and froze.

Decapitated human heads on stakes—horrific faces, like the undead from a bad horror movie, looked down at her with milky eyes. But it was real, not a hallucination. Lucy was so stunned she couldn't utter a sound.

"So, do you want us all out to push, or what?" Michael called.

There was a long silence. "Lucy, speak to us," Gregorio said, annoyance in his voice.

Lucy could only stare. Five men's heads were impaled on high spikes next to the roadway. By the looks of them, they were fresh kills. The eyes were open and the faces were grotesquely white and bloodless, like the bluish underbelly of a trout. Dark red coagulated syrup oozed down the pikes amid buzzing insects. The necks of the men had been hacked raggedly. A distended jugular swung slowly in the breeze like a bloody paper streamer. Lucy spotted crumpled bodies tossed into the bushes reminding her of deflated blow-up dolls. The next thing she knew, everyone was out of the van staring up at the tortured faces.

"Oh my God," Gregorio croaked. The two cousins, Jupe and Augusto, mumbled prayers and crossed themselves.

Pogo came around to get a closer look at the atrocity. Although not unmoved, he seemed to take the hideous demonstration in stride. "They were probably *guerillas* or *narcos,*" he said. "Bad men. The police do this to send a warning."

"Very effective," Michael replied.

"PAGA?" Lucy whispered to Gregorio. He could only shrug.

Desperate to escape the scrutiny of the bodiless heads, Lucy, and her traveling companions worked rapidly to free the van. In less than ten minutes they were heading east through the heart of the jungle toward the foothills of the southern Sierra Madre. As the Spanish love song on Pogo's radio faded in and out, the forest road swallowed them deep into its narrow black gullet. The rains began again and they traveled forward blindly. Lucy wiped perspiration from her forehead. Her heart raced with an overwhelming feeling of dread, and the knowledge that, for better or for worse, this was a trip she had chosen and fought for.

CHAPTER 39

After almost an hour of slow but steady progress along the road, with only one stop to push the VW van out of a sandy ditch, Lucy sensed their spirits begin to rise. Closing in on ten miles to Pitacallpa, they were less than an hour from their destination.

The light filtering through the high trees turned dusky purple as the day closed down. The rain had stopped. That was when the faint sound of another vehicle stirred Lucy's attention. She turned away from Augusto and Jupe, who had spent the last fifty miles trying to teach them all a popular drinking tune—the Mexican version of "99 Bottles of Beer."

"A Jeep's coming up behind us," Lucy said. "Looks like police."

In moments, a camouflage-marked vehicle flashed its lights and let loose a percussive wail of its siren, as if they could somehow not be noticed.

"Couldn't be for speeding," Gregorio said.

Pogo pulled to the side of the road and stopped. Michael rolled down the window, his face grim. The police vehicle disgorged four officers brandishing AK-47s. The biggest of the men, barrel gut hanging over his belt and underarms stained dark with sweat, sauntered up to the van.

Gregorio slid open the side door, and smiling pleasantly, spoke to the man in Spanish.

The ominous looking bull of a policeman barely acknowledged the communication. The other three officers surrounded the van, their automatic rifles held high, ready to blast.

The big officer growled at everyone. "Outta the van motherfuckers. Hands in the air." Yellow teeth flashed between his thick, caterpillar-like lips.

"What's happening?" Lucy asked Gregorio, her voice barely audible.

"Just be cool," he whispered, "they're PAGA. Follow my lead." The passengers lined up in front of the van as ordered, hands in the air.

After a quick pat-down for weapons, the officers searched the VW, or rather, trashed it. Quickly and systematically, they sliced open every seat and ripped out door panels. Gonzalo Pogo whimpered at each slash. Then the local Gestapo started the next phase of their shakedown.

"They want all of our money," Gregorio said.

"They're goddamned criminals!" Lucy hissed, too loudly.

The big officer glared at her and licked his lips.

"Do everything they ask," Michael whispered. "I know you'll find that difficult, but do it anyway."

"Stop being such a brat, Burleson. I'm not an idiot."

Her irritation turned to abject fear as each passenger was searched, pockets emptied and valuables confiscated, including cell phones. Lucy's backpack got dumped on the ground. An officer picked through her belongings, leaving everything but her pesos and digital camera. A lump rose in her throat as her camera disappeared into a bag that swung from the big cop's massive fist. Pesos could be replaced, but all her photos from the Tingo Tia slum—gone.

Next, he proceeded to search her personally. Sausage-like fingers lingered along the inner seams of her shorts. Lucy shot a glance at Michael. His fists clenched and he stepped toward the big officer, but the clicking sounds of PAGA firearms engaging, stopped him cold.

Pressed even closer to her now, she could clearly make out the name inscribed on the big cop's badge. Sgt. Cero's breath smelled like old tennis socks and tequila. Should she make a move for his gun? Unwise. She'd be killed.

He licked his lips again and at last turned his attention to the next target, Pogo's cousins.

The men had little money, but surprisingly, both had guns tucked into the back of their jeans. Cero was pleased with the find. One of the younger PAGA officers demanded they hold out their hands. He examined their fingers and then ordered them arrested.

Jupe protested loudly and was silenced with the butt of a gun to his mouth. Lucy gasped. Barely conscious, his teeth on the ground, they pushed him over next to their

Jeep along with Augusto, who was white with terror.

"Why did he check their hands?" Lucy whispered to Gregorio. "Why is he arresting them?"

"People who work in the coca pits often have yellow sulfuric acid stains on their fingers. These guys do."

"You mean they're drug traffickers?"

"Who knows. The police want them to be."

"What the fuck you talking about?" Sgt. Cero growled and moved back toward the van.

"*Nada, nada,*" Gregorio replied.

"Stuff on top." He pointed a big finger at the luggage rack. "I wanna see it."

Two of his henchmen began pulling the cords and ropes that secured the plastic tarp.

"It's just our camera equipment," Michael said. "We're American journalists. We're doing a documentary film in Pitacallpa. We have the required permits."

"Shut up. Lemme see what's in those boxes."

"We're working with Father Juan Jesus de Anza," Michael added.

The mention of de Anza's name definitely slowed the PAGA cops down. For a moment, Cero returned to the Jeep to confer with his men. Then he turned back to Michael.

"Open the fucking boxes."

Lucy glanced over at Pogo. Eyes bulging, he pulled something from under the driver's seat. With a guttural shriek, he came out shooting.

One of the PAGA men was killed immediately. His chest dissolved convulsively before their eyes. Another collapsed to his knees, gun dropping from his hand.

Lucy dove beneath the van. Burleson hurled himself

alongside her. The SAT phone was in his hand.

"No transmission," he said, "but I can't let those motherfuckers find it."

Bullets exploded into the dirt inches away. Wet, stinging, earthen shrapnel kicked into their faces. Cursing and screaming ripped the air. In what seemed like an eternity, but was probably less than a few seconds, it was over. In a cloud of acrid exhaust, the PAGA Jeep sped away.

Michael and Lucy crawled out from beneath the bullet-ridden VW.

"Oh my God," Lucy said, trying to stand on rubbery legs. Gonzalo Pogo and his two cousins were dead, their bodies sprawled across the blood-soaked road. PAGA had taken their own with them. Lucy couldn't suppress a sob. Michael put his arm around her shoulders.

"Are you all right?" he asked.

Lucy nodded her head. "You?"

"I'm okay." His eyes flitted over the mangled carnage. "Where's Gregorio?"

Lucy looked around, anxiety twisted in her stomach again. Could they have taken him? "Gregorio!"

A rustle sounded from the nearby brush. "I'm here." He emerged from behind a tree. His face was scratched and leaves stuck out of his hair. Lucy rushed over and enveloped him in a hug. His body was rigid.

She let him go and stepped back. Some people hated being hugged. "Thank God you're okay." Tears formed in Lucy's eyes. Pogo and his cousins are dead."

Gregorio nodded and mopped his face with the bottom of this T-shirt. He followed Michael around the van assessing the damage. There were so many holes in the vehicle that it looked like a colander ready to drain pasta.

"What in holy hell was that all about?" Lucy asked. She slumped against what was left of the hood. Gasoline and hot pink transmission fluid spilled onto the ground. The van smelled like burned hair and motor oil.

"I'm not sure," Michael said. "Maybe they thought we were drug traffickers." He slipped into what was left of the driver's seat and tried to start the engine. A high keen, then nothing. "Damn."

"Let's check and see what's in those wooden boxes," Burleson said. Then maybe we'll know how fast we've got to get the hell out of here,"

Thunder rumbled again in the distance. Daylight faded fast as the three pulled the bullet-ridden luggage and wooden boxes from on top of the van. Michael grabbed a tire iron and began to pry a box open. With a loud pop and the sound of shattering wood, the top was dislodged. Lucy brushed away shredded cardboard used as packing material. A dozen Israeli-made Uzis, highly portable automatic rifles, was the booty Sgt. Cero had been after.

"My God. Pogo's a gunrunner," Lucy said.

"I'd say we'd better hit the road real fast because they'll be back," Gregorio said, chewing at his lip.

"Couldn't agree more," Michael said. "Let's carry what we can and split. It's going to be dark in an hour, and this won't be an easy hike." He punched numbers into the wet, muddy SAT phone. The uplink was dead.

"Can't get through to de Anza to tell him what's going on?" Gregorio asked.

Burleson shook his head.

"Oh look, my camera!" Lucy said.

The 35mm camera lay on the ground, lens shattered, but she was able to slip the memory card out of the slot. The card appeared intact. Maybe her photos would survive. Lucy pulled her video camera case from the roof and was relieved to see it had only a few nicks. Inside, the camera looked functional. She stuffed the Sony mini-cam and battery charger into her pack along with a bag of trail mix she'd found strewn on the floor of the van. There wasn't room for anything else but a few toiletries, a change of underwear and a couple T-shirts. Even traveling with only the basics, her pack was heavier than she'd anticipated.

The rain began again, this time in an unrelenting torrent. They struggled into plastic rain ponchos and then laid out the remains of Gonzalo Pogo, Augusto, and Jupe. The bodies were covered with a canvas tarp weighted down with stones. Gregorio murmured a prayer. Then Lucy, Michael, and Gregorio left the wreck behind and started back up the endless road to Pitacallpa.

CHAPTER 40

Bea tapped the steering wheel impatiently as she wound through back streets below a freeway overpass in an industrial park near the airport. The night was cold and blustery. Fat raindrops splattered against the windshield. She had promised to take Truckee to pick up his "good car" at his mechanic's shop on her way home but hadn't realized that it was in such a sketchy area.

"People, besides you, actually bring their Beemers down to this joint?" Bea asked. The sidewalks were deserted. They seemed to be the lone car on the road.

"Sure, why not?" Truckee seemed oblivious to their surroundings.

"Not exactly upscale. I thought you BMW owners liked comfortable waiting rooms with wine and pâté."

Truckee laughed. "Beemers may be wine and pâté, but I'm Schnapps and Braunschweiger. I like my German cars. The one and only thing I've trained my kids to do is not touch it—ever," Truckee said. His voice became more serious. "Hey, are you really nervous driving here, or are you just worried about Lucy?"

Bea sighed. "We never should have let her go down there alone."

"Yeah. Well, if it's any consolation, I sweet-talked one of the production secretaries over at PBS for Burleson's itinerary."

Her face lit up. "Oh, you're smooth. Did they tell him Lucy was on her way?"

"Naw, I thought ol' blue eyes could find that little surprise out all by himself." Truckee grinned. "And I got the number of a guy in Tingo Tia who can reach them by radio in that Pita whatchamacallit place."

"Bless your big ol' bad boy heart," Bea said, already feeling more at ease.

"Hey, baby, you know I always try to take care of my women."

"If you didn't already have a gorgeous wife and four darling kids, I'd marry you, big fellah."

"Next life," Truckee said. "I'll be looking for you."

Bea knew that at one level they both really meant it. They would never be lovers, but they had a friendship that was rare.

"You think Lucy's talked Burleson into taking her on as a crew member yet?" Truckee continued.

"You kidding? She gets something in her head and it's a done deal." Bea eased up to a traffic light that swung wildly on an overhead wire in the bitter wind. "She's probably riding through the jungle right now in a Land Rover, drinking margaritas served by a fawning production assistant."

"Yeah, she's a bloodhound on a scent. I've seen that look in her eyes before. Makes me real jumpy." Truckee bounced his knee annoyingly.

As Bea began to accelerate away from the stoplight, a dirty gray paneled truck screeched to a stop in front of them and blocked their way.

"Sweet Jesus!" She jammed on the brakes and was forced up into a curbside mailbox. Her front bumper ground against the metal receptacle with the grating of a big rusty hinge. "What the—"

The windshield shattered into a crumbling puzzle of tempered glass. A man in a dark ski mask jumped out of the truck, baseball bat in hand. Three others followed right behind. What was left of the windshield blew apart; pieces of flying glass stung Bea's face.

Truckee kicked open the car door, smashing it into one of the approaching men who groaned and fell hard onto his back. He jumped out and ripped a crowbar from the stunned guy's hand.

Pop.

Bea slumped forward onto the steering wheel.

"Motherfuckers!" she heard Truckee roar.

Bea's eyes struggled to open. Had she been shot? She pressed her fingers to her shoulder and felt warm liquid. The smell of gunpowder and blood permeated the car.

She saw Truckee battling three men. The big guy could give Mike Tyson a run for his money any day. He clubbed the men with his crowbar, then another *pop* sounded and Truckee crumpled. As he fell to the street his weapon clanged onto the sidewalk.

The sickening sound of something hard brutally

pounding something softer was horrifying. Bea saw a bat rising and falling, again and again.

"Truckee," Her voice was a scratchy whisper.

In an instant, Bea's rear window shattered, then her side window met the same fate.

Her car shuddered as its headlights were bashed out. Lurching drunkenly for the glove compartment, Bea found it locked. Ripping the keys from the ignition, she stabbed at the keyhole with a spastic hand. Finally, she twisted the key and the door sprang open.

As the bat rose again to deliver another blow, now to the hood of her car rather than to Truckee's head, Bea's Smith & Wesson delivered its own message. The bat exploded into the air along with the hand holding it.

"Fucking bitch!" the man cursed. His voice was familiar. Where had she heard it?

"Get out of here you sonofabitch or I'll take your head off," she screamed. A bullet buried itself in the doorframe inches from her head. How many more rounds did she have?

The men scattered. She kept firing until she heard the doors to the truck slam and the engine rev up. In seconds, they were careening away.

Bea collapsed against the steering wheel, bleeding and exhausted. The sound of gunshots and breaking glass still rang in her ears. Darkness began to close in on her, but her iron will held. Rummaging in her purse, she found her cell. She fumbled with the tiny numbers on her phone but finally managed to dial 9–1–1. After talking to the dispatcher, she crawled out of the car on her hands and knees and made her way to Truckee.

He was unconscious, lying on the sidewalk in a

growing pool of blood. She put her head on Truckee's chest. He was still breathing, barely. His face looked like chunks of pulpy red jam spread on bread.

"Big guy, you die on me and I'll beat the shit out of you." She turned to vomit into the gutter.

The last thing she could remember was the distant sound of an approaching siren.

CHAPTER 41

Lucy checked the time on her blue plastic watch. The PAGA gangsters had not wanted it for their bag of loot. Similar styles were sold on the streets of Tingo Tia for about three dollars American.

She'd been walking alongside Burleson and Gregorio for more than an hour. The jungle wrapped them up like dark bat wings as they came to a fork in the road.

"We can't be more than a few miles from Pitacallpa," Gregorio said. He took a long swig from a water bottle then passed it to Lucy and Burleson. "But I don't know which way to turn. It's been too long."

"Damn." Michael shined his flashlight up the road. "Looks like the most traveled part veers off to the left. I'd say the choices are, go left and hope for the best, or camp here 'til dawn."

"No camping," Lucy said. "Snakes, weird bugs, big

spiders, more PAGA—forget it."

Michael laughed. "Lucy, our etymologist, votes to continue on. Gregorio, you game?"

"Sure. I think you're right, about the road. Yeah, has to be left. Any luck with that SAT phone?"

Michael shook his head and pretended to hurl it into the woods. "Got soaked in a mud puddle. I don't think this is the deluxe model."

Lucy heard the sound of a motor rumbling in their direction. Her heartbeat pounded in her ears. A bird squawked and took flight from a tree overhead. Dead leaves floated down from the disrupted branches like moths in the gloom.

"In there." Michael pointed to a swampy ditch filled with high grass along the roadside.

Gregorio pulled an Uzi from his backpack and crouched low in the weeds. Lucy hunkered down beside him.

"Where did that come from?" she asked, ambivalent at seeing the gun. There'd been way too many weapons used in the last few hours.

"Thought it might be a good idea to grab a souvenir from the arms cache, just in case."

"Did you find ammo, too?" Lucy asked.

"Yeah, a clip." He immediately engaged it.

"Keep your finger off that trigger," Michael ordered. "We can't afford any accidents."

"I know how to use this motherfucker." Gregorio's mouth drew into a deep frown. "Any shooting'll be no accident."

Gregorio's response to Burleson made Lucy's skin prick. Where and when did he learn to use an assault rifle?

The vehicle drew nearer, its headlight beams bounced along the road. She could see the shadowy form of a pickup truck heading slowly their way.

"I think it's de Anza," Michael whispered. "Looks like the same piece of shit truck he had twenty years ago."

In seconds, Michael was in the road, waving down the driver. Gregorio leaped out of the ditch and joined him.

Lucy remained crouched on the ground, unwilling to move until she knew exactly who was in that vehicle.

It slowed to a stop and the window rolled down revealing a moon-faced Hispanic man in his mid-sixties.

"Juan!" Michael exclaimed, jogging toward the truck. "I can't tell you how happy we are to see you."

"*Padre!*" Gregorio followed Michael. The former priest jumped out and embraced the men. They enthusiastically thumped each other's backs.

"Two people I haven't seen in more years than I can count! *Bienvenidos, mis amigos!*"

Lucy slowly rose from her hiding place. Burleson had spoken so highly of the priest and he'd come to their rescue. She didn't realize that Gregorio knew him too.

Weak with relief, she approached the men. De Anza's face registered confusion at seeing her.

"Ah, we have another guest? And what is your name, *señorita?*"

"Sorry," Burleson said, "this is Lucy Vega. Lucy, Father Juan Jesus de Anza." He shifted his pack to the opposite shoulder.

"Welcome to Pitacallpa." He was a hugger. Short in stature with strong arms, he smelled like eucalyptus soap.

"So happy to meet you, Padre," Lucy said, breathing with relief.

"We decided to invite her along at the, uh, last minute. She's our photographer, from a TV station in L.A. Gonna help us think through the visuals."

Lucy knew it choked Burleson to say these words. He was committing to keeping her.

"What a good idea," de Anza said. "And a lovely addition to your crew. Now climb in and let's get you some dry clothes, some food, and a bed."

"Fantastic," Michael said. He crawled into the passenger seat of the two-person cab. Lucy and Gregorio climbed into the back.

After thirty uneventful minutes, they pulled in front of de Anza's small, modest house near the center of town. It was almost midnight. Despite the late hour, his quiet, nun-like wife, Rosa, set up supper for them in the courtyard. The fabulous smell of spices was enough to bring tears of joy to Lucy's eyes. The three travelers were wet and dirty, but no one seemed to care. All enjoyed a delicious meal of chicken, tortillas, black beans, and rice.

De Anza sipped a glass of red wine. "We are deeply sorry you had such a bad experience in getting here. Anything you need, let us know and we'll try to provide it."

"Thanks. This is great." Burleson said. He seemed to have gained some energy back after consuming the excellent supper. "I still can't believe this reunion! It's been eons since we first met each other in Chiapas."

"Yes, indeed. You were a brash young journalist

cutting your teeth on a difficult story, looking for stardom."

"And you were an idealistic young priest who thought you could save the world."

"We were both delusional, eh?" de Anza said, a burdened smile on his lips. "Soon we will have to fill each other in on those years, but for tonight, I am sure you all are ready to be shown to your accommodations. Tomorrow, we'll send some people back to where your van was ambushed to recover the bodies and your belongings. Acceptable?"

They all nodded in agreement, finished up their meal, and were soon following de Anza through the sleeping town. The scent of night-blooming jasmine helped to calm Lucy's jangled nerves.

De Anza's austere, stucco house was several blocks away from a church and school complex adjacent to a garden-like center square. He explained in a tour guide voice that hundreds of locals also farmed the remote fields surrounding Pitacallpa in a shallow valley where the jungle met the lower Sierra highlands. He described the weather as moderate year round with soil that was decent for growing.

They approached a whitewashed building attached to what appeared to be a small chapel next to the main cathedral. De Anza pushed through a heavy wooden door. It looked rich and ancient.

"At one time," he said, "this was a convent where the teaching nuns resided, but it's been mostly vacant for years. We occasionally use it as a guesthouse for special visitors, like yourselves. The few schoolteachers in town are now secular. One still lives in the convent wing and will tend to your needs. Her name is Sister Ramona. Here she comes now."

Father de Anza bid them goodnight, and arrangements were made for a late morning breakfast. Lucy, Gregorio, and Michael all offered thanks to their host and were then ushered to their lodgings by the dark, waif-like teacher-in-residence.

Lucy was relieved to be shown to her small room. It contained a comfortable-looking single bed and a dresser, along with a mirror and sink. Shared bathrooms were at the end of the hall. Sister Ramona, a humble woman in her late fifties, placed a carafe of drinking water on the pine bed stand. The lamp on the stand had been fashioned from a blue and white Talavera pottery jar. A hand-woven Mexican rug covered the wood plank floor and a simple crucifix hung on the wall over the bed. It was the only decoration.

Lucy bid her *buenos noches* and then went to her screened window, which overlooked the central town square. De Anza, Michael, and Gregorio's footsteps receded down the hallway. Doors opened and closed as they retreated to their quarters.

Her room was dark, but the stars were brilliant and offered muted ambient light. The town below rested peacefully.

The stormy weather front had withdrawn to the tops of the mountains far on the horizon. Lightning still flashed inside the pale, cottony clouds like luminaria flaring in the wind. Thunder was barely audible in the distance.

Before she closed her shutters, she saw Gregorio leave the convent and head toward the far end of the square. He was joined by another man, and together, they disappeared into the darkness. She knew he must still have old friends in the area. Perhaps that was one of them?

The clear air made the edges of the buildings and their long shadows clean and precise. But even so, Lucy's sleep-deprived eyes began to lose focus. She dropped her clothes where they fell, stumbled to her bed, and was immediately claimed by the comfort of the clean, soap-scented coverlet.

Before she could sink into oblivion, a knock sounded at her door.

"Yes?" Probably Ramona checking on her.

"It's Michael."

The door opened, and he stood in the dark hallway. A faint glow outlined the shape of his body. Shirtless, with cotton drawstring sweatpants that hung low on his hips, he leaned against the doorjamb.

Lucy swallowed a soft gasp. He was one fine-looking man. She pulled herself up onto her elbow and pressed the sheet against her bosom. Exhaustion gave way to a flush of arousal.

"Sorry to bother you," he said, "but I wanted to check and make sure you were okay. And I'm not being patronizing. I just, well, it was a tough day for everybody. I know it was for me."

She recognized his sincerity and could feel his need to connect, to be among the living. "I'm thankful we're finally here and safe," Lucy said.

"Yeah, you never get used to being shot at," he said. "And today I realized that I'm really, really sick of it—sick of conflict, sick of bad people. I think I'm on the verge of a mid-life crisis or something. Gotta find something else to do."

"Well, when we get back, buy a red Porsche, get yourself a twenty-something girlfriend and go wild for a few years." Lucy smiled at him. He didn't smile back.

"Been there, done that. It's pathetic." He sighed and stepped back from the doorway. "Sorry to get so, I dunno . . ."

"Hey, near death experiences make all of us think about what the hell we're doing with our lives." Lucy clutched the sheet tighter against her body and shivered at the recollection of Cero and his goons.

"Yeah, you're right," Michael said. "By the way, have you seen Gregorio? He's not in his room."

"He left with someone a little bit ago. Maybe the *padre.* Gregorio could probably use a priest right now."

"He seemed very quiet tonight," Burleson said, shifting his weight against the doorjamb again.

"He's got major baggage, Michael. His father was murdered in front of him by *guerillas,* and he's repressed the whole thing. I think coming back here is causing some serious distress. I recognize a bit of myself in Gregorio. I know what the anger can do. It can kill you."

Michael nodded.

"And, hey, I'm sorry about the red Porsche comment. I have a tendency to say stupid things like that to push people away that I like. I have this thing about getting close. I know it's such a cliché, but at some level, I'm convinced that everyone I care about will die."

"You're right, they will. They'll drop stone cold dead. But probably not any sooner or later because of knowing you."

Lucy fell back into her pillow. "The three of us have some pretty gnarly stuff we deal with, don't we?"

"Go to sleep, Vega. This is all too heavy for my immature intentions tonight. I just wanted to see what you looked like in bed."

Lucy felt the chemistry between them hum big time, but there was nothing like sex to send one veering off in a distinctly wrong direction. For this trip, everything had to be about finding her uncle's killer and stopping him before any more lives were destroyed.

"Goodnight, Burleson." Lucy pulled at the sheet.

"Glad to hear you kinda like me."

"It's the exhaustion speaking. I won't remember any of it in the morning."

"In that case . . ."

"Get the hell out of here."

He chuckled and shrugged his shoulders. There was a long pause before the door closed and his bare feet padded away. After a harrowing day, she imagined curling into Burleson's arms, feeling the warmth of his body against hers.

Sleep, however, a rung up on the hierarchy of needs, had its way with her before she could issue a breath of protest.

❄

Burleson returned to his tiny apartment, exhausted, but now too aroused to sleep. Pale light from the open door to his room provided a watery blue path in the darkness. Booze, painkillers, sex, war—all kinds of intensity, all kinds of escape. And now, all he wanted in his life was the truth—the scariest experience of all. The truth was that he had spun out of control on the axis of his own ego, doing massive damage, hurling everyone around him off into distant emotional places where they would never come back to him. Would never want to.

He sat down on his bed in the darkness and squeezed back the tears that ached in his eyes. His dad had been military—rigid, angry, violent, intensely unhappy. Once the Burbank High School prom queen, his mother had become addicted to prescription drugs. His father disdained her for her weakness. She self-medicated to ease the pain of his hatred and the disappointment of what her life had become.

Michael's older brother rose above it—Michael sank beneath it. He became the best, the boldest, and the hardest-drinking journalist on the planet. But it was a house of cards. Only now, in recovery, working *gratis* in a region devoid of any high-profile notoriety, with a crew of one inexperienced graduate student and a woman who, whether she knew it or not, was already pushing him to be a better man. He feared he could never be that person for himself, for her, or for anyone.

CHAPTER 42

Lucy greeted *the padre* with a warm good morning handshake. His face was bright with intelligent eyes, high cheekbones, and skin burnished the color of red clay. Well into his sixties and almost bald, he appeared to have the fitness and strength of a far younger man. He wore a clean, white short-sleeved shirt, dark pants, and sandals. A gold crucifix hung around his neck.

A knock sounded. De Anza's wife, Rosa, a demure woman who spoke little English, escorted Michael and Gregorio into the sunny dining area. The large open windows, overlooking a fragrant herb garden, made the room feel spacious.

The men both looked flushed and healthy from an early run and shower. His skin still slightly damp, Burleson combed his hair with his fingers and ran his hands down the front of a wrinkled black polo shirt in an attempt to iron it the guy way. Against her better judgment, Lucy found this unassuming slovenliness marginally endearing.

"*Buenos días,* Father, Lucia," Michael said. He eyed the coffee pot. De Anza poured both men a cup and refilled his and Lucy's.

"Hey, Lucy," Gregorio chimed in and reached for the cream. Unlike the snow white American variety, it was the color of pale buttermilk.

"Hey, Gregorio." Relaxed and open, he seemed a different person than the day before.

"Gracias, Rosa," the *padre* said, as his wife served up burritos stuffed with eggs, bacon, and salsa.

To Lucy, she seemed more like a servant than a spouse.

The woman smiled faintly and then disappeared into the kitchen. De Anza blessed the food and thanked God for their safe arrival. After an enthusiastic "Amen" all around, they dug in, making appreciative sounds as the steaming breakfast was obliterated.

"This is wonderful. And I can't tell you how relieved we are to be here." Lucy spooned more salsa onto her eggs. The cilantro was fresh and the tomatoes had a vivid earthy taste that was long gone from any store-bought variety.

"Food's awesome," Gregorio said, mouth full.

"Praise the Lord," de Anza said. He raised his hand, with full fork, to the heavens. "When the rains started last night and you still weren't here, we got extremely concerned, to say the least. There's been a recent outbreak of *guerilla* activity in the area, and you just never know."

"We didn't have any trouble with *guerillas,*" Lucy said, "just the police." Vivid images of the carnage played like a movie trailer in her brain. Where the hell was the off switch?

"In these hills, it's sometimes very hard to tell the difference." Father de Anza gave a sad smile. "Our chief of police will be over in about a half hour to take your statements. He is a good man. I hope we can catch these rogue PAGA officers. In the meantime, stay safe within the village and don't venture beyond."

"We'll heed your advice," Michael said.

"Do you have cell phone service here in town?" Lucy felt incredibly vulnerable without access to any communication beyond the temperamental SAT phone.

"No, we're not on the network, yet. Several of our people are in the process of building a tower on the mountainside to tap into reception through a small company in Oaxaca." De Anza raised his hands in surrender. "We're not there yet, though."

"It'll get better here when we can bring more economic development money into our rural areas," Gregorio said.

The *padre* nodded and switched from breakfast host to preacher. "Replacing drugs with viable alternative crops or products is the only answer. The people are poor and hungry. They'll produce whatever they get paid for." De Anza gestured to the heavens again, fork empty this time. "Lord knows, chocolate is an entity that should bring peace and happiness to our region."

"If chocolate can't do it, we're in pretty bad shape," Lucy said.

Despite her attempt to be upbeat, a heaviness filled

Lucy's chest. She had to find out what de Anza knew about her uncle. Feigning nonchalance, she took a hearty bite of another warm tortilla.

"Were you, by any chance, acquainted with Henry Vega?" she asked. "He was working with the Californian government to raise and disperse economic development funds to Mexico, much like the funding behind your chocolate business."

A shadow flitted behind Father de Anza's eyes then vanished.

He reached for a bowl of *pico de gallo* salsa and spooned more onto his plate. "Vega? No, I have not met this man, Henry Vega. A friend of yours?"

"My uncle," Lucy replied. Was de Anza telling the truth about not knowing him? She stole a quick glance at Michael. He studied a sprig of cilantro on his plate.

"Ah, in that case, *señorita* Lucia, I am very sorry I didn't meet him. Perhaps he will visit sometime."

Rosa came back into the breakfast room with a fresh pot of coffee in hand. "*¿Mas, señorita?*" she asked.

Lucy nodded. "*Por favor.*" She smiled at Rosa.

A swirl of dark liquid, as brown as melted chocolate, filled her cup.

"Did you know that chocolate was invented right here in Mexico?" Gregorio asked, steering the focus back to economics and food. "Most people think it originated with the Europeans, but they only brought it back with them when they returned from ransacking our culture. The Mixtec Trail Chocolate Company will set the facts straight."

The *padre* smiled at Gregorio with the warmth of a father gazing upon a son. "The cacao bean was used as currency among our Aztec ancestors," he said. "The tree was a symbol of strength and wealth."

Lucy found de Anza's enthusiasm contagious.

"There are so many health benefits from dark chocolate consumption," Burleson said.

"Yeah, like flavanols." Gregorio mopped a tortilla across his plate and wiped it clean. "Improves blood flow and decreases blood pressure—all sorts of good stuff. Also, prevents clogging of the arteries."

"I'm taking notes to justify any future indulgence," Lucy said and smiled. For the first time since leaving Tingo Tia, Gregorio smiled back.

"De Anza chuckled. "And of course, our dark chocolate is especially rich in antioxidants, essential to cell repair. Dark chocolate has a higher concentration of antioxidants than blueberries, pecans, or cranberries."

Lucy smiled again and shook her head. "Now I can look at a blueberry and a chocolate truffle, and know I'm making the right decision. Couldn't tell you what a cacao bean on the tree looks like, though. It's one of the few foods I've never seen actually growing."

"I'll do better than tell you about it," Father de Anza said. "We'll ride into the hills and I'll show you the real thing!"

"Gentlemen," Lucy said. She nodded at Gregorio and Burleson. "I hope you had a great run this morning because the rest of the day will be dedicated to the pursuit of chocolate."

CHAPTER 43

It was a chocolate lovers dream. To go to the source, to hold pale green, acorn squash-like pods in her hands, was a tantalizing treat. She climbed into an open-topped Jeep along with Gregorio and Burleson. De Anza, pistol in a holster around his waist, was taking them to an area where the rugged cacao trees grew their beloved fruit. The morning was bright and spirits high. Lucy stuffed the horrors of the day before into a mental drawer and slammed it shut.

With de Anza at the wheel and Michael as the priest's wingman, Lucy and Gregorio commandeered the rear. An armed guard named Colombo, stood on the sideboard, hanging onto the roll bar. Lucy checked out the Uzi the man was carrying. Another one—must be the weapon of choice in this area. Seems like everybody had one. She noticed brown stain marks on Columbo's fingers. She glanced over at Gregorio. He raised his eyebrows.

The little excursion had driven barely a mile beyond the village when a PAGA Hummer lumbered around the bend and pulled to a stop. Lucy grabbed Gregorio's arm. Three officers got out and greeted *Padre* de Anza. Thankfully, Cero and his minions were not among them. The men surrounded the vehicle.

"*Buenos días, Padre,* and American friends." A stocky, mustachioed officer with a spurious grin and protruding ears offered an informal salute. "*Bienvenidos.* We are so happy to have you filming in our beautiful region."

"I am Captain Ramon Carbajal, and these are my men, Officers Eduardo and Enriquez Cruz." The identical twin brothers, with beady eyes and big round heads balanced on stalk-like necks, nodded in unison.

De Anza reciprocated and introduced his guests.

Lucy, Michael, and Gregorio responded cordially. Lucy tried not to grimace as Carbajal's flaccid, wet hand shook hers. He held the grip an annoying moment too long.

Carbajal stepped back and rocked on the soles of his feet, hands behind his back. He looked Gregorio up and down. "There are Hidalgos in this area. You have any relations here, *señor?*"

"*Sí,*" Gregorio responded. His friendly smile faded and eyes narrowed. "My parents were Maria and Amedeo Hidalgo from Julca. You know them?"

"Ah, yes," Carbajal responded, looking smug. "A few of your people are left. I knew your father many years ago. A shame when he got himself killed."

Lucy could feel Gregorio's body grow rigid. He pulled his arm from her grasp.

"Got himself killed?" Gregorio sneered. Slowly, he opened the Jeep door. "He was murdered."

Carbajal seemed to enjoy Gregorio's reaction. "He was too nosy for his own good, could never mind his own business."

"What did you say about my father?" Gregorio's voice turned murderously calm.

An alarm blared in Lucy's head.

"Now, now, gentlemen," de Anza warned. He slid out of the vehicle and Michael followed.

"I said he was asking for it." Carbajal glanced over at the twins and smiled.

"That's what I thought you said," Gregorio whispered.

He leaped out of the vehicle like a panther attacking its prey. Before anyone knew what was happening, he knocked Captain Carbajal to the ground and began banging his head against a rock.

Michael tore after Gregorio. The twin officers pulled their guns from their holsters while de Anza and Burleson peeled Gregorio off the bleeding captain. The officers aimed their guns at Gregorio's head.

"Don't you dare shoot!" Lucy threw herself in front of Gregorio and held out her hands to stop Carbajal's men. There was another skirmish and one of the twins smashed Gregorio under the chin with the butt of his pistol. Blood sprayed over both Michael and the PAGA captain.

Carbajal struggled to his feet. Shaking with rage, his face already purple and bruised, he aimed his pistol at Gregorio.

De Anza boomed in an authoritative voice above the commotion. "Please! Enough. *Por favor, mis amigos.*"

"I want this bastard," Carbajal snarled to de Anza.

De Anza's face turned stony. "Unfortunately, Captain, you brought this on yourself. One does not speak of a child's deceased father so disrespectfully. Where was your civility? Your Christian sense of compassion?"

Then the priest turned to Gregorio who slumped against the bumper, blood trickling down his neck. "And you, Mr. Hidalgo—assaulting a police officer, under any conditions, is reprehensible. It is a criminal act."

Lucy could see the effort it took for Gregorio to pull himself together. He wiped blood from his nose, shut his eyes for a moment, then took a deep breath. "Please, accept my apologies to everyone involved." He stood up, legs unsteady. "I sincerely regret my actions."

"I want him, de Anza." Carbajal's gun still pointed at Gregorio's head.

De Anza and Burleson guided Gregorio back to the Jeep. "Captain Carbajal," de Anza said, "I think it would be better for all to accept Mr. Hidalgo's apology. We do not want to blow this one small incident into something more difficult to deal with, do we?"

The captain shifted his glare from Hidalgo to de Anza. He finally lowered his weapon. An ominous smile slit his face.

"Of course not, *Padre.*" He tucked the firearm into its holster. "We will try to forget this little altercation. Good day *señors,* and *señorita.* Enjoy your stay in Pitacallpa. And do be careful out beyond the village."

The PAGA officers climbed back into their Hummer and roared away down the road. It was clear to Lucy that de Anza had saved Gregorio's life.

✳

When they arrived at the cocoa plantation, Lucy could not turn her thoughts away from the incident with Captain Carbajal and the PAGA twins, Humpty and Dumpty. But this morning, her job was not to stumble around distracted—it was to move through the forest of scrubby cacao evergreens, their black, lichen-mottled branches heavy with ripening fruit, and find the visual story. She wanted to capture fresh, intriguing digital images Michael would find useful.

Lucy photographed close-ups of the workers and their machetes as they chopped pods from branches. She recorded a huge praying mantis as it leaped out of blade range in the nick of time, and baskets of cacao pods the color of lime juice and luna moths. Trying to concentrate on the job at hand, Lucy's mind kept wandering to Gregorio and his unnervingly close call with PAGA. Seemed like their whole force was just a collection of loose cannons ready to spew violence.

It was clear, however, that de Anza was an incredibly powerful man. Captain Carbajal had wanted Gregorio with homicidal intensity but backed off at de Anza's appeal.

When the workers broke for lunch, Lucy searched for Gregorio. She finally found him sitting by himself on a rock next to a tiny stream. He sipped a steaming drink from a battered tin cup; his chin was taped with butterfly bandages, compliments of de Anza's first aid kit.

"Tastes like a hot Hershey bar with a hint of bitterness," he said.

She looked down at the thick, reddish-brown liquid. "Where do I get some?"

"Here," he said, "take mine." He offered her his cup. "I'm really not hungry."

Lucy obliged and swooned at the delicious semi-sweet taste. But she couldn't take her eyes off of Gregorio. "Are you okay?" She was sure he wasn't. "What happened this morning was terrifying." She gave his shoulder a warm squeeze.

He lowered his head onto his knees.

Lucy sipped her chocolate and studied him. His shiny black ponytail fanned out across his slumped shoulders.

Ever so slightly, his body quivered. "You must swear that what I am going to tell you remains between us. You cannot tell a soul. Not a soul," he said, his voice muffled.

"I promise. It's between you and me." Lucy sat down on the ground next to him.

Gregorio's glassy, dark eyes caught hers. He nodded.

"The night my father died has always been a complete blank. I couldn't recall anything but the screaming and the terror. When I left all those years ago, I swore that I'd never come back, but circumstances led me here again. Now I know why. I've been having dreams ever since I arrived, at night and in the daytime, too."

"What kind of dreams?"

"About my father's murder. And the murderers are beginning to materialize." He rubbed the long scar on his arm.

"What do you mean?" She put the cup down and it tipped over. Chocolate bled into the earth.

"This darkness I always remembered is congealing into faces." An anguished sob escaped from a place deep inside him. "Carbajal was there when my father was murdered."

Lucy could feel her skin tingle with goosebumps. "Are you sure? It's been a long time."

"Absolutely certain." He sat up straight. "If Burleson and Father de Anza had not stopped me, I would have murdered him. De Anza saved my life. Carbajal wanted my head on a pike."

Lucy thought about how she would react if she ever came face to face with Uncle Henry's killer. Rather, *when* she came face to face with him.

"But I still can't see the one who actually pulled the trigger."

Gregorio rested his head on his knees again. He appeared tired and drained. "I want to kill them, make them suffer," he whispered.

"I'll bet you do. But thinking it, and doing it are two different things, my friend. Would be suicidal to kill a PAGA officer. You know that, don't you?"

"Part of me doesn't care."

"Stay with the part that does care."

"It's small, weak."

Lucy reached out to touch his hand. "You're a very strong person, Gregorio, just off balance right now."

Gregorio raised his head and gazed into the clear stream. A golden dragonfly hovered at the surface.

Lucy felt him drift away. "Any time you want to talk, day or night, I'm here. I mean it."

"I appreciate that." Gregorio looked at her and forced a feeble smile. "How do you like our hot cocoa? Think it'll sell in the States?"

"It'll be a hit." Lucy picked up the empty cup and

returned it to Gregorio. "I've got to get back to work now. I think we're leaving in about an hour. You gonna be all right, kiddo?"

"Of course. I'm a survivor."

But at what price, Lucy wondered? With a heavy heart, she disappeared among the evergreens, her camera alive again in her hands.

CHAPTER 44

That evening, the annual fiesta to honor the patron saint of the village, Saint Sebastian the Martyr, reached its high point. The rain had cleared, and the sky, still roiling with cumulus clouds to the west, promised an exquisite sunset. It appeared to Lucy that the entire village of five hundred residents had gathered on the community soccer field. The people congregated around picnic tables and danced to the tunes of a local mariachi group. A pile of logs, five feet high and growing, promised to provide a joyous bonfire. All manner of benches, chairs, and blankets ringed the great pit. On the far end of the field, men set up fireworks for later in the evening. Fiestas and fireworks were always simultaneous occurrences in Mexico.

Lucy glanced around the field, hoping to find a familiar face. Michael was with *Padre* de Anza and his men. They'd headed back to where he, Gregorio, and Lucy had collided with Sgt. Cero and his band of PAGA thugs. They hoped to retrieve any personal belongings, and most importantly, bring the bodies back for burial. The black-market cache of guns would doubtlessly be long gone.

With cell phones absent and the SAT phone intermittently functional, Lucy was desperate to contact Bea. She'd promised to let her know that they'd arrived safely in the village but communication to California was not possible right now.

Lucy resolved to put away her anxious thoughts and enjoy the party. It was good to be alive. A group of teenagers dressed in native costumes ran by her. They laughed and teased one another. The boys wore white shirts and trousers, topped off with wide-brimmed sombreros. The girls dressed in embroidered blouses and colorful skirts that swished and swirled around their sandaled feet. They held hands and practiced their dance steps as they went. Younger children, clothed in brilliant hues, ran through the gathering like flocks of parrots.

For an instant, Lucy could feel her mother's happy abandon sweep through her and disappear up the cobblestone street in the wake of the youngsters' high spirits.

These were her mother's people. Her chest swelled with common connection. Visceral memory, almost at the cellular level, tumbled forth. *Déjà vu*. Somehow, she had been here before. Another life?

As Lucy drew closer to the field, a new group of musicians, in black vests, white shirts, and blue jeans, began to play. She smiled as a familiar face appeared. Gregorio had picked up a guitar, offered by someone in the audience, and joined the band. His strong tenor voice with a scratchy hint of Joe Cocker or Janis Joplin was impressive. He played background on a few more tunes then joined Lucy in line for tamales with chocolate *mole,* rice, beans, and flan. Holding a beer in each fist, he handed her one.

"*Muchas gracias, señor,*" Lucy said, with a little curtsey. "You sounded so good up there! How long have you been singing and playing?"

"Since I was born, I think." He smiled. "I sometimes fill in with a couple mariachi bands up in L.A. when I need a little extra cash. We do weddings, family celebrations, stuff like that. It's fun. Worries just fade away, and *la música* takes over."

"I have a friend in L.A. who I just found out is a mariachi, too. You know Ernie Vargas, by any chance?"

"Can't say that I do, but I might recognize him if we met."

"I'll introduce you when we get back home." Lucy offered a silent prayer for their safe return.

Gregorio and Lucy finally got their food and sat down on a patch of grass near the stage. The next musician was Tlaloc, a Mixtec artist from Oaxaca, one of Gregorio's favorites but new to Lucy. She couldn't understand much, but his songs had a haunting yearning that brought tears to her eyes.

"What a talent," she said to Gregorio, "and hidden away here in the foothills. He could knock the socks off similar bands in L.A."

"The marketing machine that drives Western culture

makes us think we have the best of everything in the States. Then you find someone in an obscure corner of the world who makes you realize that there must be millions of brilliant people in places like this."

"More people should travel when they have the opportunity," Lucy said.

Gregorio raised his bottle at that. "So, what do you think?" His eyes scanned across the throng of villagers, all enjoying the festivities.

"It's awesome." Lucy took a big bite of a stuffed pepper. "And the food is so good."

"I've missed this." Gregorio finished off his beer and wiped his mouth with the back of his hand. "You like the chocolate *mole?* It's an Oaxacan recipe."

"It's an unusual flavor, but I'd definitely have it again." Lucy helped herself to another generous forkful. "Yeah, I would."

"When you finish, let's walk closer to the soccer field. I hear the local team is excellent. Our Saint Sebastian is the patron of athletes, so the players are giving a demonstration for the kids to honor the saint. One of the guys was actually on the Mexican Olympic team. Blew his knee out so couldn't go pro, but still's pretty damn good."

"I love soccer players—they always have those gorgeous thighs and flying hair," a woman said. Lucy turned around to find the source of the voice. "Food, a bonfire, music, dancing—just like old times, eh, Gregorio?"

Gregorio looked intently at the woman and appeared to mine his brain for the connection.

"It's me, Greg-o. Hilda!"

He jumped up. "*¡Dios mío!*" he exclaimed.

The round-faced woman with a long, black braid tossed over her plump shoulder, had an infectious smile. She threw her arms around Gregorio in an enthusiastic embrace.

He picked her up and spun her around. "Hey there, Hildacita! It's been a while, huh?"

When he put her down she stepped back to take a good look. Then she hugged him again and crushed him against her substantial bosom.

"And what's all this talk about dancing and great thighs?" he said. "Where is the modest maiden I left here all those years ago? All grown up and pretty as can be."

"You're not looking too bad yourself, *mijo*," she said and threw herself at Gregorio again.

Lucy rolled her eyes. *Get a room.*

"You used to be so shy and proper. My, my." He peeled her arms from around his neck. "Lucy, I'd like you to meet Hilda Piñon, a friend and schoolmate from my childhood."

Lucy rose to meet Hilda. The woman maintained her hold on Gregorio's arm, her face a question mark as she checked out the competition.

"Hi, Hilda. A pleasure to meet you. I'm Lucy Vega, Gregorio's colleague from Los Angeles. We're working on a documentary project here." Lucy held out her hand and Hilda shook it without much enthusiasm.

"You're colleagues?" she asked.

"Yep, just colleagues."

"Ah, a pleasure to meet you, too." Hilda's smile was back full force.

"And what are you doing here in Pitacallpa?"

Gregorio asked.

"I left like you did. Father de Anza helped me get a scholarship to school in Mexico City and then I came back here to teach. Oh, and I spent a semester at Arizona State to work on my English. Father de Anza thinks every educated person should be bilingual. I have a three-year contract here that pays off all my student loans."

"You're a public school teacher? Corrupting all of these innocents?"

"*The* public school teacher. I'm the only one at the elementary level. I love *los niños*. But you, I wouldn't mind corrupting you, Gregorio Hidalgo!"

"Who is this woman?" Gregorio asked, laughing.

"Sometime this week I'd love to visit your school," Lucy said. "I teach ninth and tenth-grade video production in an after-school program but I adore the munchkins."

"Please, I'd be honored to have you come by. Any time at all. Bring your camera, too. We'd love to be in the movies." Hilda flashed her engaging smile again.

"Shall we head on up to the soccer match?" Gregorio asked the women.

"You two, go on," Lucy said. "I have to find Michael. I need to make a phone call. Join you later?"

Gregorio looked imploringly at Lucy. He seemed undoubtedly pleased to see his friend but didn't look confident that he could handle her amorous aggression.

Lucy winked at him. "Switch to coffee and things might go better for you," she whispered.

"More *cerveza!*" Hilda shouted. "*Adiós,* Lucia," she called and happily dragged Gregorio off to the field.

"Rescue me. Soon," Gregorio mouthed over his

shoulder.

"Good luck, Greg-o," Lucy mouthed back and smiled.

✳

The sun dropped below the horizon and the sky was transformed to a fiery palette of orange and pink, indigo and purple. A slim wafer moon rose. The humidity of the day was replaced by cool eddies of air that exhaled down from the mountains above. At the end of the soccer field, the bonfire was lit. A thread of smoke rose; the wood crackled and threw a bright confetti of sparks.

Lucy turned back toward the village. For an instant, in her peripheral vision, she thought she spotted Sgt. Carbajal dressed in civvies, but when she turned to look—nothing.

Enough with the paranoia.

When she finally returned to her room in the old convent, she was pleased to see a pile of clothes, toiletries, and other belongings neatly stacked in the center of her bed.

"Thank you, Juan Jesus. Thank you, Michael," she said out loud. The SAT phone was next to her socks with a note from Burleson to return it when she completed her calls.

Grabbing the phone, she headed down the hall, past the bathroom and up a circular staircase that led to the roof. It was a flat terrace with a spectacular view of the village and surrounding area. In the distance, the bonfire blazed and muffled strains of a flamenco tune and cheering for the soccer players drifted across the town.

She punched in Bea's cell number. The phone rang

and rang. She left a voicemail then tried her landline. After a few rings, Dexter picked up.

"Middleton residence," he said.

"Dexter, it's Lucy, down in Mexico."

There was a long pause at the other end of the line. *What was going on?*

"Are you all right, honey? Everything okay? I thought you'd be at your dad's this week."

"Lucy," he said, voice shaky, "my mom's in the hospital. She's been shot, and Truckee's in a coma." He broke down in tears.

Ernie came on the phone.

The taste of chocolate *mole* and beer rose in her throat as he described what had happened. Lucy sank to the rooftop and tried to process what she was hearing.

"Bea thinks she managed to shoot a couple fingers off one of the attackers," Ernie said. "But no local hospitals reported treatment of such a wound. Gunshot injuries have to be booked with the cops. Right now, it looks like the assholes are gonna get away with this. They're gone. Vapor." Ernie sighed.

"No leads? Nothing at all?" Lucy scrubbed at her forehead.

"Maybe some blood spatter on the sidewalk, but it was raining hard by the time crime scene folks showed up. The M.E. said it didn't look hopeful."

When she and Ernie ended their conversation, the color of the sunset had faded from an impressionistic palette to the color of a purple bruise. Lucy returned to her room, shut the door, crawled onto her bed, and leaned back against the wall in the gloom. Up on the hillside, the fireworks began. The blasts were unnerving.

She began to rock back and forth. Tears dripped down her cheeks as she struggled to control her growing panic. Too much loss, too many people hurt to begin to cope with.

Several minutes later, there was a knock on the door.

"Lucy?" Burleson asked. "You find the phone?"

She couldn't answer. A pitiful cry escaped her lips.

"Lucy? What is it?" The door opened.

She mopped tears from her eyes. "Bea's been shot and Truckee's in a coma."

"What?" He paused for a moment then entered the room and closed the door. Firecrackers popped in the streets below. Dogs howled and people screamed.

Lucy couldn't hold back a sob. Michael sat down beside her and took her in his arms. She fell against him. He held her tightly as she wept.

When the tears had finally run their course, Michael looked at her, questioningly.

Lucy took a deep breath. "I just spoke with Ernie. Bea and Truckee were attacked in their car by a group of men with baseball bats, tire irons, and guns."

Burleson's eyes widened. "When did this happen?"

"The night before last. Bea was hit in the shoulder with a 9mm slug. They beat Truckee senseless. Bea keeps a gun in her glove compartment and shot one of the guys in the hand. When they realized she was armed, they split."

Lucy looked at Michael. His face was grim.

"Bea thinks Gary Mercer, the guy who smacked me with his camera in the helicopter, and Tom Rubio, the asshole fake cameraman, were in the group." Lucy shivered.

"Why does she think that?" Michael rubbed warmth into her cold arms.

"They wore ski masks but she could hear them shouting. She thinks she recognized the voices."

"Is she, are they, going to be all right?" He took Lucy's hand.

"Bea's in fair condition at Santa Monica Hospital, and Truckee's at Cedars-Sinai on a respirator. Brainwave activity looks bad. Michael, he has four children!"

Lucy's tears began to spill again. Michael pulled her close and stroked her soft, damp hair.

"Listen, Lucy," he said, "I think it's time to fill you in on some things."

"We need to work together," she said, hiccoughing. "I keep telling you that."

"I know. You're right, okay? I'm sorry. Sometimes it takes me a while to see things, but the situation's clearer now. We're in big trouble here, Lucia. Our radio contact in Tingo Tia may work for the wrong people, and the CIA operatives who were supposed to be shadowing us, they're dead."

Lucy's eyes widened in the darkness. "You mean our driver, Pogo, the gunrunner? Is CIA?"

"And his dead, so-called cousins, too. Governor Scanlon has an old friend in the Agency who made big promises about people to back us up, but obviously, he didn't come through."

Lucy felt the muscles in her chest painfully constrict. Her stomach was seized with nausea and she felt a panic attack ready to pop. But she had to ask Michael the question. Would he know the answer? Or even tell her the truth? She gritted her teeth and blurted, "I heard there's an American involved with Alvarez. I have this terrible fear that it could be my uncle. What can you tell me? This horrible suspicion is killing me. I keep trying to put it out of my mind, but I can't."

"Lucy, Lucy." Burleson took her by the shoulders; his eyes drilled into hers. "Your uncle was about to expose the cartel operation to Governor Scanlon and the feds. Alvarez has been using millions and millions in economic development money for years to help fund his drug cartel. Your uncle figured it out. That's why he was killed."

Lucy felt a rush of both relief and fury. She shivered with pent-up emotions.

"Can de Anza help us?" Lucy asked.

"Michael took a deep breath and slowly let out the air. "He's a good man, was a good man, but it looks like our Robin Hood may have gone over to the dark side. There comes a point when too much compromise goes bad. I don't have evidence, just a gut feeling, that he may have crossed the line. I don't trust anybody right now."

"What're we going to do?" Lucy said.

"We're going to get the hell out of here, tomorrow or the next day, at the latest."

"I can't leave without some proof, something," Lucy said. "Too much shit's gone down for me to walk away and let it be. I have to find something on Alvarez. He has to pay."

"I was afraid you'd say that."

She pulled back to look at him. His eyes were brooding and his shirt was wet from her tears. He took her head in his hands, tangled his fingers in her hair and kissed her, slowly, tentatively.

She pressed her lips to his neck. The feel of his skin against hers was electric. They lay side by side on the bed, exquisitely exploring, their clothing soon forgotten on the floor.

"What happened here?" he whispered. He ran his hand across the jagged scars on her gently rounded stomach.

"My accident, when I was a kid."

He moaned softly as she moved on top of him, all silvery velvet in the moonlight. Her body opened to him like a honeyed flower. Possessively, they consumed each other, and, for a few blessed moments, nothing else mattered.

CHAPTER 45

A doper running a little late on his next fix, Gary Mercer was just a wee bit strung out. Rain beat against the corrugated metal roof of the big porch. The air in the PAGA headquarters outbuilding was cloyingly humid and smelled of pork grease and gun oil. He rubbed at his nose and glared at Gregorio Hidalgo with open disdain. The kid was behaving inconveniently, and he detested inconvenience.

Mercer scratched at his gold watch and twisted it around and around on his wrist. He rolled up the sleeves of his starched pale blue shirt to make sure the rattlesnake tattoo that crawled down his arm was on full display.

"What the fuck keeps happening, Hidalgo? You've had every opportunity to bring her to me and you just keep fucking up. It's just gonna get harder." Mercer crossed his arms on his chest and studied Gregorio as if he were an odd, curious bug on a sidewalk.

Gregorio looked away. He chewed at his lip.

"Personally, I don't think you have it in you, but Alvarez says you do. You have one last chance. You owe de Anza your life. Never forget that fact. You knew that payback would come due someday. That day is now."

"I'm not a killer. I told you that from the beginning. You said the people in that van would simply be taken prisoner."

"They got shot instead. Things change, don't they? Life's like that. But fine, we'll make it easy for you. Forget apprehending Burleson, just bring the bitch to me—she's mine. We'll put someone else on her boyfriend, eh, Cero?"

The big PAGA officer grunted, distracted by the plate of beef tacos he was obliterating. Other guards played cards on a rickety folding table. Their rifles rested against the wall nearby.

"What about Carbajal?" Gregorio asked.

"De Anza's gonna let him fucking pull the trigger next time. Stupid move, Greggie, really stupid."

Gregorio's eyes grew hot and narrow. "He was one of the motherfuckers who tortured and killed my father! You need to arrest him!"

"Ancient history," Mercer said. "How old are you, dog? Time to stop sniveling and move the fuck on."

Gregorio clenched his fists and stepped toward Mercer. The guards at the card table stopped mid-deal and reached for their weapons. Gregorio pulled back, face flushed with anger. "Find somebody else to do your shit. De Anza can't have any idea what you assholes are up to."

"Don't delude yourself, choirboy. De Anza's all chocolates and community spirit on the surface, but how do you think he can make that happen? How can a little hole of a village be so candy-bright and prosperous? Ask yourself that. We gotta work with reality somewhere along the line, Greggie. And so do you, or you can kiss that Ph.D. goodbye. You'll be back sucking dick in the jungle."

"Fuck you, Mercer." Gregorio up-ended the card table, stomped across the stained cement floor and banged through the screen door.

The guards started after him but Mercer signaled for them to stand down. As Cero finished his last taco he said, "asshole needs a lesson." He wiped his mouth on his shirtsleeve.

"Agreed. Teach him good," Mercer said. He pulled a baggie and pipe from his desk drawer. "Do what we talked about."

Cero licked his lips and laughed out loud.

✳

It was dusk by the time Gregorio made it back to Pitacallpa. He had trekked into the hills and pushed himself physically until he was exhausted and drained of rage. Back at the old convent, he took a warm shower and bought dinner at a nearby *tienda,* before returning with it to his room. He couldn't face de Anza, Lucy, and Burleson. Thankfully, they weren't around.

He sat cross-legged on the bed and ate, but the food tasted sour in his mouth. Could *Padre* de Anza actually be involved with Alvarez and the hideous American,

Mercer? No way.

Gregorio knew de Anza loved him, unconditionally. He had saved him from being among the doomed orphans in Tingo Tia, had given him an opportunity to live a real life in L.A. Gregorio owed de Anza everything—that was true. But the *padre* would never ask him to do this bad thing. Never.

He choked down the remains of his meal. Mercer was getting to him, twisting his mind, making him begin to question things that were unquestionable.

Gregorio sighed in frustration and dropped a half-eaten tortilla onto the paper plate.

For now, he was exhausted and wanted only to sleep, to shut out the anguish for even a few merciful hours. Lucy's door opened and closed down the hall. Gregorio wouldn't let Cero or Mercer touch her. They were evil. She was kind, good.

He undressed to his undershorts and crawled between the cool sheets. Never a person who could get by on little rest—he'd been up for too many stressful hours. Stretching his legs out to the very end of the narrow bed, he groaned with relief at the prospect of oblivion. He prayed that in the morning, he would think more clearly, see options, and it would be less terrible.

Seconds later, hot stings burned up and down his legs and feet.

"Shit!" he cried out. Fire ants? A scorpion or some nasty big bug? Then the bites came fast, one after another, in excruciating succession.

Gregorio leaped out of bed. The covers fell to the floor and disgorged a slithering frenzy of baby rattlesnakes—a nest of a dozen, maybe more. The snakes, each about eight inches long, seemed to be everywhere.

He shrieked, staggered toward the bedroom door and ripped it open. His vision blurred as his body seized in shock and began to shut down.

Three steps, four—the room began to spin and dissolve around him. Gregorio could hardly breathe.

Five steps. He dropped like a deer who'd taken a lethal shot by an expert hunter.

✳

The frantic rush to save Gregorio Hidalgo's life lasted through the night. By mid-morning, the crisis was over. Gregorio had survived. Barely.

Lucy stood in the doorway. Gregorio was the only patient being cared for in the local clinic's six-bed hospital ward. A young, blue-uniformed nurse, stripped the bed next to him of bloody sheets, stuffed them into a plastic bag and disappeared with a muttered apology.

"Come in, Lucia," Gregorio said, his voice thin and scratchy. An I.V. was attached to his arm.

She entered the room and sat carefully on the end of the bed.

The *curandera,* or local healer, from the previous evening, sat in the chair next to Gregorio. Heavy, pungent herbs burned in a bowl on the bed stand next to a Bible and rosary. The herbs almost managed to overpower the smell of the ward's medicinal disinfectant.

Gregorio wore an oversized white T-shirt and basketball shorts. His legs, covered in thick ointment, were purplish-red balloons. Dark circles rimmed his eyes. There was a fearfulness about him that was almost palpable, like a small, beaten dog.

"This is Sister Catherine Lucia," Gregorio said slowly. His face looked drawn and haunted. "She was with me through the night." He raised his hand and gestured at Lucy, then he dropped it back to the bed as if the move exhausted him. "This is Lucy Vega, Sister. She's a Lucia, too."

"Lucia—two light-bringers." Warmth glowed in Sister Catherine Lucia's bright brown eyes. "We met briefly last evening, but all was so chaotic."

Lucy nodded and shook hands with the older woman. She had a strong, comforting handshake, like the touch of a dear old friend.

"A pleasure to meet you officially, Sister. Thank you so much for helping to save him."

The woman nodded then spoke in heavily accented English. "Those baby rattlesnakes actually have more concentrated poison than the adults. He was in full shock. Has lots of swelling in his legs, maybe a bit of permanent nerve damage. Time will tell. But overall, he will be *muy bueno* soon." She patted his arm.

"I am so glad to hear that." Lucy gave Sister Catherine Lucia a relieved smile. She felt an instant and easy connection to the woman. "For a while last night things looked pretty bad."

"Yes, but that time has passed. The Lord was looking down upon Gregorio."

He winced as if she'd said something he didn't want to hear. Lucy didn't pursue it. She turned her attention to the nun.

"How did you become a *curandera?*" Lucy asked. The woman didn't seem like just a local healer. She seemed more sophisticated and worldly.

"I was once the nurse at the convent you are staying at," Catherine Lucia said. "I studied for my degree at a Catholic hospital in Guadalajara, but I also learned the ways of the indigenous healers. I read the Brother Cadfael books by Ellis Peters a long time ago and decided I wanted to be an herbalist as well as a more traditional healing nun. I studied very hard."

"Cadfael was the soldier who withdrew from the secular world to become a Benedictine monk and make his own medicines," Lucy said.

"Yes, twelfth-century England. Still feels much like that in these parts."

"And he was a super sleuth, too," Lucy said. "I own every book in the series."

Catherine Lucia smiled, delighted. "A girl after my own heart, as they say." She looked carefully at the young woman with quizzical eyes, then over at Gregorio. Her smile faded.

"You are the one who found Gregorio last night, *señorita?*" the sister asked.

"He'd collapsed and his legs were already swelling. The floor of his room was full of little rattlesnakes." Lucy grimaced. "I slammed his bedroom door shut then dragged him farther down the hall. A guy came later with a machete and killed those he could find. Who knows where the others escaped to."

The woman nodded and studied Gregorio's bloated feet and legs. "You know who did this cruelty to you?"

He shook his head. "No, no idea."

What kind of person would do such a thing?" the sister asked.

Gregorio avoided eye contact. Instead, his gaze

turned to the empty bed where the bloody sheets had been removed.

Lucy wondered if Gregorio knew more than he was telling. Something was off-key. "What enemies could you have?" she asked him. "Think Carbajal was involved? Seems like he could be a vengeful sonofabitch." Lucy flushed. "Woops—sorry for my language, Sister."

Catherine Lucia's brows drew together. "He *is* a vengeful sonofabitch, my dear."

Gregorio twitched, agitated. "No, no, there's no one. Carbajal wouldn't do anything to upset the *padre*. And this upset the heck out of him."

"The perpetrators must be punished." The sister studied Gregorio's bloated legs again. Like overcooked yams, they looked ready to split open.

"Has been a difficult few days," Lucy said. "We've not had an easy time of it here. Some people are obviously not happy to see us."

"Such fools." Sister Catherine Lucia rose from her chair. She pressed a hand against her lower back and stretched. "Well, I hope you can excuse me for now. I don't have the stamina I used to." She smiled at both of them then picked up a colorful carpet bag that was next to her chair. "I'll be back to check you soon, Gregorio. You have friends here who will help you if you let them." The old woman patted Lucy's shoulder.

Gregorio's eyes followed her as she left the room. "the sister is a woman of wisdom," he said, voice low.

"She feels so familiar, it's strange. But speaking of strange, you look remarkably decent for a guy so totally trashed."

"Flattery will get you *nada*." He gave her a half-hearted smile.

"Flattery aside, it's so great to see you alive and a little sassy. How do you feel?"

He reached for a glass of water, and Lucy helped him with the straw. He finished the drink then rolled his eyes. "Throbs like a sonofabitch, but believe me, it's better than last night. I've never felt such pain. It was beyond pain. I guess I just flipped out through part of it. The brain must go on overload at some point, and the circuit breakers pop."

"It's called shock. The morphine drip'll help with that. Putting those poppies to legitimate medical use, right?"

The haunted look filled Gregorio's eyes again. "This must be what torture is like. And punishment." He reached for the rosary the sister had left behind. Beads began to click in his fingers.

"Ah, such moroseness," she said. "You're alive, the sun is shining, and like Sister Catherine Lucia said, you're among friends."

Lucy gently squeezed his hand. Gregorio looked away.

Their convent innkeeper, Ramona, arrived with a bowl of broth and a slice of fresh mango. Gregorio thanked her. He appeared only vaguely interested in the food but ate a few bites anyway. He seemed to have turned the corner toward recovery, at least physically.

Psychically, Lucy had no idea where he was—but the place was not a good one.

CHAPTER 46

L uis Alvarez sat in his office chair, pants around his knees. The girl had become a whiny pain in the ass. They all came to that point once they got hooked. Fortunately, they were completely disposable.

This one was maybe thirteen but could've been a couple years younger. Even the cherry red lipstick, bleached blonde hair, and white silk lingerie couldn't hide the fact that he liked child-women. All the budding physical attributes of the real thing, with an ego so unformed it was as malleable as hot wax. The area held hundreds of missing women and girls. Nobody cared, or nobody cared enough to do anything about it. Alvarez acknowledged that his abundance of prepubescent female riches was a wet dream few could imagine.

The girl sniffed a couple lines of pale brown powder from the blotter on Alvarez's desktop and followed it with a tequila chaser. In less than a minute her irises constricted to pinpricks, and she began to drool. Slowly, she exhaled. Too many seconds passed before she inhaled again. She wiped her hand across her mouth. Red lipstick smeared her face like blood. Alvarez stood and zipped up his blue military trousers.

"That shit is only for stupid *putas* like you."

The girl smiled and began to dance in slow, sleepy twirls, until she fell down. She crawled pathetically toward Alvarez.

"We're done, slut. Get out of here." He adjusted his balls then sat down and logged into his computer.

She sat back on her heels and seductively rubbed her breasts with sad, nail-bitten hands. Her eyes closed as if she were acting out a dream.

It was about to change into a nightmare.

"Are you fucking deaf?" he shouted. "Out of here, you little bitch, or candyland will be history."

A look of panic filled the child-woman's now fully-open eyes. She stood, grabbed a half-full envelope from his desk, staggered dizzily to the door and slammed it behind her.

Alvarez sighed with relief. It was definitely time for a new batch of diversions.

Angry voices drew near the office. One was particularly familiar. A crash sounded in the outer hallway. Then another crash. Something hit the wall. His copper vase of calla lilies? He should have guessed that Mercer's rattlesnake thing would bring the *padre* in screaming like a howler monkey.

Alvarez rose from his desk, crossed the room, and opened the door to the outer office. His skinny, seventy-something aunt who was his secretary, cowered in the corner. Calla lilies littered the floor. Damn de Anza.

"Father, you seem upset." Alvarez kept his voice soothing and controlled, in counterpoint to de Anza's rage. "Please, join me."

De Anza stormed into the inner office and almost knocked Alvarez over. They exchanged murderous glares.

The two men went back decades, needing each other in ways that kept one from killing the other. Juan Jesus needed Alvarez's resources to build the society he envisioned for his people, and Luis Alvarez used de Anza's surface respectability as a foil for his operations. It was a shared relationship of profound utility. They respected each other's limits, but Luis knew he'd stepped over the line.

He poured a finger of tequila from the bottle on his desk and offered it to de Anza, who refused. Alvarez added another splash then drained the clear liquid in a gulp. He would atone for this little mistake. The priest would forgive him as usual. Life would go on.

"You almost killed my boy." De Anza's hands fisted in fury. "How dare you even touch my children?"

"He's not one of your prick kissers anymore, Jesus. He's a grown man, who made a contract that he failed to fulfill. We can't let him just walk away from his responsibilities."

"Don't compare the compassion I have for my boys to your exploits with those doped-up baby whores. Gregorio Hidalgo may be grown, but he is still mine. You do not do business with him. Ever. No contracts, no deals, nothing. I gave him what he needed—love during his darkest days, an education, and independence. When have you ever given anyone anything that was good? Whom have you ever cared for?"

Alvarez stifled a laugh and sat down heavily behind his desk. He couldn't count how many times he'd heard this lecture. It was part of their dance.

He poured out another shot of tequila and contemplated it. "You and me, we're two sides of the same coin, Juan Jesus. The same dirty coin, but you refuse to see it." He downed the clear liquid and gritted his teeth. Set the empty glass on his desk. "Mercer did this deed you are so upset about. I had no idea what he was planning until it was too late."

"He is completely out of control, Luis." De Anza's voice shook with anger.

"I will rein him in, I promise. I am truly sorry. But you have to understand, he is very frustrated with how these American spies are pushing their noses into our business. He really must have Gregorio's help to end it. Just a bit of cooperation. Perhaps, when Hidalgo is feeling better, you could talk to him."

"He is not doing well. Hidalgo must be left out of all of this."

"The new tractor that you wanted? We'll see about getting it. I have a connection in Tucson. All we need is a little help from your boy. Nobody gets hurt. The Americans get spooked and run off to *el Norte*. We let the girl find out that Mercer killed her uncle. That's for the two of them to settle. And then it's over. Just like that."

De Anza's fists began to relax. Alvarez knew the priest hated him, but they'd always separated with a compromise they could each abide. He also knew there would come a time when one of them would pull the trigger. The time was drawing closer. And they both knew it.

❋

The sky bled gray mist and threatened more rain as Lucy and Michael jogged the rutted, quarter-mile track around the soccer field. After two miles, Lucy stopped and stretched tight muscles against a goal post while Michael continued to run. She enjoyed watching his loose, easy gait. She enjoyed watching him do anything at all.

What was she getting into? Lucy pressed her fingers to her temples.

Bea would say, just have fun—the guy's a disaster, but a pretty one. Lucy reminded herself that there was only one reason she was in Pitacallpa, and it was not to have an affair with Michael Burleson. But he sure was one hell of a pretty one.

Lucy glanced around the area. Charred remains from the bonfire still smoldered. She could smell ashes from the fireworks, too. Villagers were about, but no one paid them any attention.

At the far end of the field, Lucy noticed a young mother and her two lively children. They skipped down through an opening in the trees to what appeared to be a trail into the hills. When the little family came to the soccer field, the boy and girl, perhaps three and five years old, began to run and tumble like happy puppies. An old man riding a bony donkey emerged seconds later.

With nothing more to occupy their time until they were sure Gregorio was going to remain stable, Lucy decided to see if Michael would come with her to follow the pathway a short distance. It was probably a beautiful hike up into the rocks, much like at home in the Santa Monica Mountains.

She loped over and joined Burleson as he rounded the track by the soccer net. "Hey, join me for a ramble up that trail? I bet there's a great view of the town. I hate track running; it's so boring."

"Well, I happen to like knowing exactly how far I've gone. And you know what de Anza said about leaving the village."

"Come on, it's practically in the village. Kids, moms, old guys like yourself, all going up and down there."

"Did you really say 'old guys'?" Michael stopped, hands on his slim hips, a smirk on his lips. "Old guys rule. Didn't last night prove anything?"

"Hey, I'm not saying you're not one hell of an old guy but the steep terrain's probably a little intimidating." Lucy checked him out, then shrugged and sighed. "I understand. You have a little arthritis in those knees, gotta take it easy."

Michael laughed out loud. "Okay. Let's see what you're made of, *chica*." He peeled off the track and streaked toward the trailhead.

The path was steeper than Lucy had bargained for, consisting of switchback after switchback. She was well behind Burleson but kept pushing until her lungs were about to explode and the stitch in her side became unbearable.

"Slow down!" Lucy shouted out. "I give!" The effort reduced her to gasps.

The sound of Michael's footfalls on the gravelly

ground ahead stopped receding and pattered back her way.

When Burleson reappeared, she was doubled over on the path, hands clutched to her side.

He laughed out loud at her humiliating bail-out. "Well, at least last night proved you have other redeeming skills besides distance running."

Lucy's narrowed her eyes. "It's just a random cramp. Even people of many talents get them. We're gonna need a rematch."

Your place or mine?" Burleson smiled and wrapped his arms around her. She pressed hard against his body, took a deep breath, and savored the fabulous feel of him. But she couldn't let herself get lost in this. A weird vibe hovered about the trail, and she needed to pay attention.

Lucy pulled away. "Something's hinky out here." She tugged the ponytail holder out of her hair, then retied it. "You sense it?"

Burleson nodded. "There's a building up ahead. We should take a quick look. Probably nothing, but since we're almost there . . . You okay with that? Can you make it another hundred yards?" His smile was wicked.

"Let's go." Lucy smirked and took off up the path, re-energized.

A few minutes later, they came upon a garage-like structure built of mossy cinder blocks and topped with a rusted, corrugated roof. Bars covered both windows and a heavy padlock hung on the hefty wooden door. Hummingbird-sized mosquitoes grew in number and began to swarm as the two approached the building. The word was out in seconds—fresh blood in the forest.

"What is this place?" Lucy peered through a window

at rows of white fifty-pound bags. She thought of Dyna-Cide. More poison?

Michael reached his arm through the bars and pinched a sample of the gray dust from a partially torn bag. He smelled it first, then touched his tongue to the powdery substance.

"What is it?"

He wiped his fingers on his T-shirt. "Calcium carbonate. Limestone, like in cement mix."

"Lime—isn't that what murderers use to make dead bodies decompose faster?" Lucy asked. She turned away from the window and scanned the forest for any activity.

"Uh-huh, but it's also used in the initial steps of turning sap from opium poppies into black tar. I saw how this is done when I was in Afghanistan." His gaze shifted to the far side of the interior. "The burlap bags over there, plastic barrels, cans of acetone—all part of the process. This is a storage shed for heroin production supplies."

"Whoa! Someone's processing heroin right under de Anza's nose?" Lucy shuddered. "He must know about it."

"How could he not?" Michael scrubbed at his damp hair. "If the folks making this shit find out we're on to them, we're not going to get out of here to talk about it."

CHAPTER 47

Relieved to be back in the relative safety of the convent, Lucy nervously glanced up and down the hallway. All seemed quiet and secure, but she didn't trust it.

She hopped into the shower with visions of the bloody stabbing scene from *Psycho* playing in her head. Surviving the shower, she changed into fresh clothes and walked briskly toward the clinic to see Gregorio. Burleson was scheduled to join Father de Anza and meet with workers in a nearby village to discuss the merits of cocoa farming. Would Michael be all right? Nothing felt safe.

The convent innkeeper, Ramona, sat with Gregorio as he slept. "How is our patient?" Lucy asked.

The woman assured her of his progress and then turned back to the Bible she'd been reading. Rosary beads clicked in her long, thin fingers.

"I'm going over to the school for an hour or so to visit Gregorio's friend, Hilda," Lucy said. "She told me this morning would be a good time to come. I'll be back soon to relieve you."

"*Gracias, señorita Lucia.* No rush." The woman turned her attention back to the Bible. It was open to First Corinthians. Lucy remembered one of its themes was cleansing sin and corruption within the church. Funny the random recollections that stick in your head. Uncle Henry had made sure she'd attended catechism classes despite her Norwegian father's commitment to Lutheranism.

Lucy walked several blocks to the old, red-tile-roofed school building, scanning the area in her peripheral vision, looking for signs of being followed. All seemed clear. She hoped there was something fun she could do to help with the students. An art project, maybe? Anything to take her mind off of drugs, murder, and deceit.

She found the small, neat schoolhouse empty. A sign on the door indicated that the children had gone on a field trip to the botanical garden. Disappointed, Lucy sat on a bench in the school's gaily decorated courtyard. A tiny brown lizard dashed by her feet and disappeared into a clump of shrimp-colored bougainvillea. Finger-painted birds of imaginative varieties were clipped with clothespins onto a line. The paper flapped like wings in the breeze.

In the stillness of the empty playground, she became obliquely aware of a subdued conversation taking place under a tree on the other side of the school's stucco perimeter wall. Something in the tone of the voices caught Lucy's attention. She listened carefully in order to understand the fast-firing Spanish.

Two men discussed a plane that was to arrive just before dusk which would be loaded up with black tar heroin and flown into Southern California.

Lucy stifled a gasp. She hugged her arms around her shoulders as an icy hot stab of adrenaline shook her body. Could they hear her breathing? *Please don't let them find me.* The wall was tall enough that there would be no reason for them to look over the top. Would there? She sat for several interminable minutes. Sweat moistened her skin.

When they finally dispersed, Lucy moved from the shadows of the schoolhouse and cautiously walked back toward the health clinic. She tried to appear unconcerned and normal but her stomach was knotted in fear. Tonight was the night. At dusk, she'd record the activities at the airstrip. Burleson would be back by then to come with her. It was dangerous but was also an opportunity they shouldn't let slip by. These were likely the people her uncle had tried to blow the whistle on. He'd lost his life in the process. She'd finish what he had started. This could be her last chance.

Locating the airstrip might be tough. It sounded remote. Maybe Gregorio could help her find the way. Was it a crazy idea? Doubtless. It didn't matter; she had to go.

Lucy now hustled toward the clinic. She needed to talk with Gregorio, alone. The facility was busy so few seemed to notice as she made her way through the waiting area and down the hall to the hospital ward.

"*¿Cómo está, mi amigo?*" she called at Gregorio's door. She took a deep breath to calm herself.

"Come on in, Lucy." His voice was still weak.

A nurse had just finished changing his bandages as she entered the room. His legs still looked like they belonged to the Michelin tire man. The aromatic smell of the poultice left by the *curandera* was strong.

"You sit up now," the nurse ordered. She pushed extra pillows behind his back and helped him get adjusted. "One of the men will be here in a few minutes to help you with your bath."

Gregorio smiled. "I'd rather have Lucy help me."

Lucy raised an eyebrow. "Think he's recovering a little too fast for his own good?"

"He's all bluster," the plump, middle-aged nurse said, chuckling. "After his bath, he'll be ready to sleep for another twelve hours. I guarantee it."

"I can't wait to return to work," Gregorio said. He appeared exhausted—days or weeks from going back to the job. "Michael and the *padre* can't talk to the indigenous people until I can get out of here to translate the tribal languages. They all must be getting impatient."

"It'll be a while before you can think about going anywhere," said the nurse. "You must continue to rest, but you are recovering *bien*. I'll be back soon." She gathered her equipment and left Lucy and Gregorio together.

Lucy sat in the empty chair next to his bed. He seemed tired, but alert. Lucy told him what she'd overheard at the schoolhouse. His wan face paled even more. It upset her to share bad news in the weak state he was in, but she had no choice. Time was of the essence.

She picked up the rosary beads from the table. They were still warm from use. "The gist of it was that a major shipment is going out from a local airstrip around dusk. Tonight."

"Heroin trafficking. It's everywhere." Gregorio's last bit of energy dissolved before her eyes.

"Do you have any idea what airstrip they might be talking about?"

He paused, then let out a long sigh. "There are three such small airfields in the region, but there's one that is especially hard to get to. Drug runners used it back when I was a kid."

"It's nearby?" Lucy asked.

"About an hour's walk from here. But you can't go if that's what you have in mind."

Lucy stared out the screened window of his room. Birds chattered on a wooden feeder. Biting her lip, she turned to Gregorio. "I'm going. Burleson will come with me. And you have to help us. We need directions."

He shook his head. "Impossible. It's not the kind of place anyone can give directions to. You must know the region and be able to recognize certain landmarks. Only someone familiar with the area could get you there. I'm sure Michael would be most unhappy if he knew you were planning this."

"He's with Father de Anza visiting some cocoa farmers in a neighboring village, not sure which one. I'll talk to him as soon as they get back. He'll understand. We'll take covert photos, I.D. the traffickers and email them to the U.S. authorities—Governor Scanlon, the ATF, DEA, anyone who'll listen."

"The real traffickers will not be there—only the peons."

"We have to start somewhere," Lucy said.

His gaze seemed to blur into a middle distance. "You've seen the TV ad of the kids running into a garage full of chainsaws to hide from a homicidal maniac?"

Lucy nodded.

"That's you." He wiped sweat from his neck. "But you insist on going?"

"Absolutely. And that's not me."

Gregorio's head hung as if from a noose. His face was bleak. "Perhaps Hilda will take you. I'll ask her. She is trustworthy." He lay back on his pillow and closed his eyes.

"I'm sorry, you're exhausted. Rest, Gregorio. And thank you."

✳

Lucy paced back and forth in her room. The stark walls and crucifix over the bed, flaking with ancient red and gold paint, were starting to get to her. Where the hell was Burleson? He said he'd be back early afternoon. Dusk would be falling in no time. She checked her watch.

Then there came a knock. *Finally.*

"Where have you been?" Lucy said as she pulled the door open.

Ramona's brown eyes peeked shyly up at her.

"Oh, I'm sorry, I thought you were *el señor* Burleson. Please, come in." Lucy's shoulders slumped.

"I have a note for you, *señorita.*" She offered a white sheet of folded paper.

Lucy took it and read. "Car trouble. *Padre*'s truck broke down?"

"*Sí, señorita. Padre* de Anza radioed us. He and *el señor* Burleson will stay the night, be back tomorrow."

Disappointment and the tang of fear soured in Lucy's mouth. "Okay. Thank you, Ramona."

The woman bowed slightly and bustled away.

Lucy shut the door and leaned against it. Now what? There was only one option—she would meet Hilda alone. It was now or never. She scribbled a cryptic note on the back of the paper she'd just received and left it on her pillow. Michael would find it when he came to look for her.

With a daypack and camera over her shoulder, Lucy headed out.

CHAPTER 48

Lucy and Hilda met promptly at the agreed-upon location near the soccer field. Listless gray clouds obscured the peaks of the nearby Sierra Madre del Sur.

"Hello, Hilda, and thank you," Lucy said.

The two women clasped hands in greeting and then Lucy pulled Hilda into a quick hug. Stiff and hesitant, Hilda seemed to be a subdued version of the wild woman Lucy'd met a few days ago at the fiesta. She wore a modest cotton shift, leather *huaraches*, and a traditional gold crucifix around her neck. A straw, cross-body purse rested against her ample hip.

"*Buenos tardes, señorita* Lucy. I want to apologize for the miscommunication about your visit to the school this morning. Perhaps you can come tomorrow? I promise we'll be there."

Lucy nodded. "That would be great."

Hilda smiled and patted Lucy's arm.

Although Lucy had missed seeing the children—if she hadn't been alone in the courtyard, she wouldn't have overheard the men discussing this operation.

"I enjoyed the bird paintings. They were so imaginative and fun." Lucy glanced at her watch. The time was moving fast into late afternoon. "We'd better get going."

"*El señor* Burleson no joining us?"

"The *padre*'s truck broke down. Unfortunately, they won't return until tomorrow."

Lucy took a swig of water from her bottle then hooked it back onto her pack. Her mouth was still dry. "We're on our own, Hilda."

The woman raised her eyebrows and nodded.

"Do you think this is crazy?" Lucy asked. "*Por favor,* be straight with me. I know I can occasionally be overly-impulsive and risk too much."

Hilda smiled and tugged at her crucifix. "I know the area even better than Gregorio. This kind of druggie thing goes on around us all the time. Sadly, people barely notice. You and me, we'll be fine. Nobody cares about school teachers walking in the forest. Ready, *señorita* Lucia?"

Lucy nodded and hoped Hilda was right, that all would be well. "Thank you. Gregorio says I should trust your judgment. This means a great deal."

Lucy and Hilda hiked for almost an hour through the jungle without coming upon another person. The two women passed clusters of giant blue agaves, pine, fir, and ancient oaks, their trunks carrying a maze of twisting, parasitic vines, or *lianas,* as Hilda called them.

The light through the leaves was diffuse and restful. The peaceful stillness in the air gave an ominous contrast to the drug transpo deal about to go down.

"We're getting close," Hilda said. She veered off onto a narrow game trail with Lucy at her heels. The path was overgrown and difficult. Branches slapped and tore at the women's skin. Flying insects swarmed, drawn by the warm scents of perspiration and blood. After a good twenty minutes, they seemed to be getting nowhere slowly.

Lucy took another long gulp of water and wiped her mouth. "You're sure we're going in the right direction?" She was getting spooked. It was too quiet. She couldn't help flashing back to Gregorio's quip about her trying to avoid a homicidal maniac by running into a garage full of chainsaws. Right or wrong, these traffickers were directly or indirectly responsible for murdering her uncle. Recording this event and getting it back home would be a big step toward making them pay.

"There's the field, just ahead on your right," Hilda said, pointing.

Lucy caught sight of a pallid slice of overcast sky above a clearing. At last, the airstrip.

They struggled to the edge of the forest and settled amid brush and boulders. Lucy took the camera out of her pack and peered through the telephoto lens. She scanned the edges of the landing area in close-up. All seemed isolated and calm. The faded orange wind sock at the end of the field hung limp. A small outbuilding with a pole light next to a rusting fuel tank appeared abandoned.

Lucy whispered. "It's hard to believe this place is

crawling with drug traffickers right now, isn't it?"

Hilda shrugged. "Life is full of contradictions and surprises, *sí?*"

"How long do you think 'til sunset?" Lucy asked. She glanced at her watch. Dusk was beginning to color the landscape somber shades of gray and purple.

"I'd say another twenty minutes at the most. If what you heard back in the village was correct, it will happen very soon."

Lucy watched the sky. Her hands trembled as she held her camera. Damn, she had to control her uneasiness. She took another drink of water, then closed her eyes and tried to get centered.

Finally, they heard it—the low drone of a small aircraft. Lucy positioned her camera to survey the field again. A flash of silvery white broke through the haze at the far end of the runway. As the engine's drone grew louder, the quiet jungle came alive like a hive of ants that had just been disrupted.

"I can't believe all this activity," Lucy whispered.

Hilda crouched close by. She rocked back and forth on her haunches.

The Cessna flew over the airstrip, circled once, then came in fast. Dirt and crumbling asphalt sprayed as the wheels touched down. The landing was bouncy and ungraceful. Lucy's heartbeat accelerated. She had seen this plane and this kind of landing before.

A dark, bearded man emerged from the forest and motioned the plane forward. It taxied to a stop. A door swung open. Gary Mercer emerged from the pilot's seat.

Lucy gasped. "What the hell?" A piercing ache began to pound in her skull where his camera had left its mark.

Gary fucking Mercer was working for Alvarez?

"You know this pilot?" Hilda asked. She continued to nervously rock back and forth.

"Unfortunately, yes." *He murdered my uncle.* "When we get back, I've got to get my hands on de Anza's radio." Lucy's eyes were glued to her video camera's viewfinder. "Gotta get this news to my colleagues. A lot of bad things are starting to make sense."

As Lucy burned up the memory card recording images, Mercer directed the on-loading of heroin bricks in transparent garbage bags sealed with duct tape. A dozen men dashed back and forth from the underbrush to the plane, hauling the parcels.

Lucy maxed out the card. She quickly removed it from the camera and dropped it in the side pocket of her cargo pants, amid old tissues and a stiff piece of gum that had gone through the washing machine. In the blink of an eye she reloaded again. Hilda's attention was down the field where a man had tripped and was frantically scooping up stray bricks of product that had broken through a larger bag. Mercer cursed and paced while checking his watch. The workers picked up the pace.

In less than ten minutes, the plane was stuffed like a Thanksgiving turkey.

"Millions of bucks in street value in the belly of that bird." Lucy said.

Hilda nodded agreement. She stopped rocking. Her full, bronze lips were set in a hard line.

As the plane turned and taxied back down the runway, the men returned to the forest. They disappeared as quickly as they had arrived. Would they be lurking along the trail as she and Hilda returned to the village? The two women couldn't let their guard down. She took a deep, shaky breath.

Moments later, the sound of the engine was a fleeting memory, as if the whole scene had been merely a dream. At least Hilda had seen it, too, and it had been recorded digitally. It wasn't just a chimera. Carefully, Lucy placed the camera back into her pack.

All was quiet again, and for an instant, the rays of the setting sun broke through the clouds. Insects resumed buzzing and birds called again. Hilda sat against a boulder and stared into the darkening forest. Lucy reached for her hand and helped her up from the ground. "You're a brave, generous woman, Hilda, and an amazing guide. You've helped me immensely. I'm so grateful."

"Thank you, *señorita*." The woman's affect was flat as the runway. The bubbly, passionate woman seemed robotic.

"Let's get the hell out of here. Soon we'll be back at the schoolhouse drinking margaritas, *sí?*" Lucy felt vaguely giddy at having captured everything she was after.

Hilda glanced nervously about. "We have to get closer to the main trail before it gets too dark. My sense of direction fades with the light," she said.

"Lead the way." Lucy zipped up her pack and retreated with the schoolteacher down the narrow, winding pathway toward Pitacallpa.

When they came to the main trail, they paused for several minutes and listened closely, soaking up the ambience to make sure it was safe to go forward. Lucy heard and sensed only the usual evening sounds. As they made their way toward the village, she felt energized and optimistic. Although Michael would initially be upset with her for taking off into the backcountry with Hilda, the photos she'd got would be worth it all. She'd bring Mercer down if it was the last thing she did.

The two women walked quickly in the diminishing light.

Then, the scene at the airfield replayed.

In a blink of the eye, the tranquil jungle came alive with movement. Armed men, several of whom Lucy recognized as drug runners from the airfield, flooded the path in front and behind them.

Then, Gregorio appeared just ahead. His legs were wrapped in bandages and his face was sweaty and gray.

"Gregorio! What are you doing here?" Lucy called out, completely shocked at seeing him. She turned to the men, enraged. "How could you do this to him? He's sick. Get him back to the clinic, immediately."

They grabbed her by the arms. She struggled to shake them off but was way overpowered.

Ignoring her, Gregorio and the others carried on a calm conversation. Hilda joined them. She pointed to Lucy's backpack. The men restraining her ripped the pack from her shoulders and tore into it.

"What the hell is going on?" Lucy moved closer to Hilda. She stepped away.

At that moment, in her gut, Lucy knew exactly what was happening but she refused to let it register. The desperate fingers of her mind grabbed onto denial.

The dark, bearded man she'd seen directing men at the airstrip twisted Lucy's arms behind her. It felt as if her elbows were dislocating. Another guy, small and jittery, pulled a revolver and aimed it at her head.

Lucy couldn't process the shift that was taking place. "Hilda? Gregorio?"

A third man—they were almost indistinguishable in the gloom—popped open the bottom of her camera and wrenched out the memory chip. Lucy's heart sank, but she remembered the card that still remained in her pocket. It contained the most damning evidence, including images of Mercer.

The asshole threw the camera high into the air and blasted it to smithereens with his assault rifle. Birds squawked. Lucy winced. The others laughed and cheered as if the bastard had done something heroic.

"Gregorio, what in God's name is happening?" Lucy choked.

He didn't answer.

"Why are you just standing there like you're one of . . . of these criminals?" Lucy could barely make out Gregorio's face in the dimness.

"I'm afraid this is it, Lucy." His voice was shaky.

"What are you talking about? Tell them we work for de Anza." And then abject horror seized her. The reality of the betrayal refused to be denied any longer.

"Not you and Hilda?"

"I'm sorry, Lucy. We work for de Anza, but we work for Alvarez, too. We have no choice."

After a moment of speechless devastation, terror flared into fury. "You're sorry? Like hell, you're sorry! What a fool I've been!"

"You were never a fool, Lucia, only human."

"I trusted you! Cared about you!" she cried.

Gregorio's eyes were black pools of nothingness.

She lunged for him, but the men pounced and pushed her brutally to the ground. Something cutting and unyielding twisted around her wrists. She felt like a calf in a steer-roping contest. Her arms were tied in an excruciating position. Tears began to drip down her cheeks.

Gregorio ordered the men to back off. Lucy struggled to her feet. He tried to help her up.

"Don't touch me!" she screamed. "Just tell me why. Goddamn it, Gregorio—why?"

Lucy heard a sob rise from his throat.

"Stop your damn self-pitying whimpering and talk to me!" she said.

He drew himself up straight.

"Because Father Juan Jesus de Anza saved me. He took me in as a boy and gave me a life. Without him, I would be nothing."

"No, Gregorio, you're something, something special, with or without de Anza. You don't owe him your goddamned soul!"

The men grabbed her and slapped a piece of silver duct tape over her mouth. As they propelled her roughly down the trail, Lucy took one last look over her shoulder at Gregorio and Hilda. They became faint shadows on the path behind her—ghosts, vaporous specters that vanished into the sneering night.

Lucy didn't turn around to look back again. She couldn't look forward either because she knew, without a doubt, what she would see there was going to be horrendous.

CHAPTER 49

The next morning in the convent's small kitchenette, Michael Burleson heated a pan of Ramona's leek and potato soup for breakfast. Feeling exceptionally tense, he left the soup to simmer and walked down the hall to Lucy's room. He'd check it out one more time—perhaps he had missed something.

Lucy's belongings appeared to be undisturbed. She hadn't brought much with her on the expedition—a couple of T-shirts, basic toiletries, and underwear. Socks she'd washed out were still damp on the windowsill. Her video camera and daypack, however, were gone. She'd taken off after something, but what and where? It must have been important because Lucy was well aware of the dangers in the surrounding area.

Then Burleson spotted a note that had fallen behind her pillow and wedged against the wall.

MB-

Went to an airstrip to check out a shipment of chocolate. Will see you when you get back. Don't worry, have a guide I trust.

L.

Burleson's heart began to hammer. Gregorio couldn't be her guide to the airstrip—he was barely well enough to stand. Michael had stopped at the clinic before he returned to the convent and the patient been discharged. They said he was back in his room, resting under Ramona's care.

Michael jogged down to Gregorio's room and tapped on the door. No response. Slowly, he pushed it open. Cold panic took his breath away. Everything was gone.

✳

Lucy endured the ordeal stumbling in utter darkness. The men knocked her down, groped her, hauled her back up, and pushed her ahead. She tripped and stumbled. Her revulsion at being held prisoner was magnified by the frustration of being blindfolded. As a photographer, she was an intensely visual person—it was the way she learned and took in the world. She felt cut off at the knees and tried desperately to make her other senses work for her. Before she could get her bearings, she was shoved into a vehicle with others, likely in the cargo hold of a truck.

Packed in tight, Lucy heard only male voices and smelled their humid testosterone-laced presence. Were the other passengers, prisoners, or guards? Were they blindfolded as well? As least some of their mouths were not taped shut—she could hear whimpering and whispered curses. How the hell was she going to escape this nightmare? She was swept by an overwhelming sense of impotence. Just the reaction Mercer was probably hoping for.

When the vehicle finally stopped, Lucy's head spun. Every facet of her life felt completely out of control. What disastrous thing would happen next? What form would the abuse take? Would they riddle her senseless with bullets, or would she slip away in a slow orgy of pain and humiliation?

Stop it, get a grip.

Succumbing to terror wouldn't help. She had to exert power over her own thoughts. And her thoughts would focus on hope and escape, not on the pantheon of dread that could paralyze her with fear and despair. The *mental attitude,* she told herself, was everything.

Rudely propelled from behind, Lucy tumbled out of the vehicle and almost fell onto her face. Someone grabbed her arm and steadied her. She uttered a whisper of thanks to the unseen person, feeling oddly touched by the small act of kindness. She heard chains clink and drag across gravel as they were herded along. Even in the darkness it was becoming clear that she was part of a group of prisoners.

They were led into a building. The space echoed. The air was muggy and stunk of unwashed bodies. Catcalls and suggestive whistles resonated as Lucy passed. Hands grabbed her ass, her breasts.

It's nothing. They are nothing.

The captives were ordered down onto the floor. Lucy sat and tried to make herself as small as possible.

After much discussion among men who seemed to

be the officials in charge, Lucy heard groups of prisoners depart. Periodically, a door slammed shut as people were banished into unknown recesses of what seemed to be a prison. The reek of degradation permeated everything. A deep shudder wrenched her body.

Lucy sensed that she was among the final detainees to be processed. The noise in the room had diminished considerably. Pulled to her feet by hot, sweaty hands, the tape was ripped from her mouth. She tasted blood on her lips.

A man with a high-pitched voice instructed her to state her name for the record. She heard low snickering from somewhere nearby, but no one touched her.

Soon, Lucy was marched down a long hallway. A door whined open, metal protesting against metal. She was pushed inside a room. The door slammed behind her, followed by the ominous *clink* of a lock engaging. Steely panic cut through her chest. Where the hell was she? A cell? From chatter and ridicule, the human sounds changed to hopeless cries and moans. The air smelled stultifying and faintly sulfuric. She visualized the hot, rancid maw of a dragon.

Control your thoughts, Lucia. Focus on escape, freedom.

Cautiously, she moved forward. After a mere two steps, she bumped into a barrier. It was constructed of coarse-cut wood slats. With her hands still secured behind her, Lucy turned back against what seemed to be a wall, and moved lightly, exploring the varied surfaces with the tips of her fingers. She repeated her reconnaissance, sensing and feeling. Her prison was a narrow closet-like space about four feet across and maybe seven feet long. Three walls were wood, and one was cement block, likely an outside wall. She hadn't tripped over any bodies. She was alone—*thankfully, alone!* At least for now.

Near the metal the door, Lucy's shirt was caught by a sharp protrusion—perhaps a nail or splinter of wood. Her morale bounded upward. She bent down and snagged the cloth of her blindfold and managed to pull it off. Torn strips of an old black T-shirt fell to the floor. Her vision was back, but the pleasure was short-lived.

Dark bloody stains pooled around a drain in the middle of a filthy cement floor. Maggots squirmed in a pile of feces and vomit in the corner of the cell. She had stepped in it. Lucy gagged and clenched her jaw tight.

She scanned for possibilities. Murky light from the hall filtered through a small, barred opening in the door. But there was another dim source of illumination in the cell. High above was an air vent. It was a wood-framed rectangular opening covered with a rusted metal grating set in the cinder blocks near the top of the high outside wall. Faint light from a pole lamp filtered in. The vent was small, but if she could knock out its wood frame, maybe she could squeeze through. But how would she get up there?

The vent became her obsession.

❊

Burleson knew he had to get word out to Scanlon alerting him to the badly deteriorating status of their situation in Pitacallpa. Lucy had disappeared, so had Gregorio. If he himself became the next victim, any possibility of their being rescued would be hopeless.

He walked through de Anza's wrought iron garden gate and knocked on the door. "Juan Jesus, you there? *¿Padre?*"

He dreaded coming face to face with a man in whose presence he felt increasingly uncomfortable. Burleson was, however, desperate to get his hands on the priest's shortwave radio. He'd never been beyond the living room door to the rear of the house, but he knew that the radio was kept in one of the back rooms. He guessed there was a study and a bedroom. De Anza always entertained his guests around the large round table that separated the living room from his small, galley kitchen. It was unclear if his supposed wife, Rosa, actually lived with him. Michael had begun to doubt it.

He opened the door and walked into the house as he had many times before. All was quiet. De Anza's living room was starkly white with a single crucifix on the wall. Furnished with simple, locally made furniture, he had a bookcase full of volumes. All was very monastic.

"Juan Jesus? *¿Padre?*"

Michael hesitated for a moment, and then moved quickly down the dim hallway to the rear of the house. He wanted to use the radio without the priest hovering, and this was his opportunity. His SAT phone battery charger had mysteriously disappeared. He had a few minutes of charge left on the phone, if that. He was conserving it for an utter emergency. The radio was his best option.

At the end of the hall, the door open on the left revealed a small bathroom. To his right, he could see into the study. It was filled with books, writing materials, and a single desk with a worn leather chair. No radio.

The door to the only other room was shut. If de

Anza was resting, Michael would apologize for the interruption, but every second he waited to get a call for help out of Pitacallpa could be a nail in Lucy's coffin—in all of their coffins.

When Michael pushed the door open, his breath came in a short gasp. The scene before him was bizarre. Blood red walls were covered with gilded crucifixes of every size and shape. One appeared to be sculpted of pure gold. It had to be a museum piece. Looked like a treasure straight out of the Vatican. The opulence of this room compared to the simplicity of the rest of the dwelling was staggering.

The large, intricately carved bed held a luxurious spread of rich velvet the color of claret, finely threaded with gold filaments. The drapery at the shrouded window had been crafted from the same fabric. On a stand in the corner sat a high-end digital camera and a monitor. The shortwave radio crackled quietly on a rosewood table at the foot of the bed.

Michael sat down on a throne-like chair of inlaid wood with dark green velvet cushions and prepared to transmit. He'd used a shortwave radio many times during his career as a war reporter. He ran through the process of contacting a last-minute connection in Tingo Tia the governor had given him. Waiting for a response, he was distracted by photographs in gold frames. Images of de Anza with various notable men included a famous Mexican government leader notorious for human rights violations. They hung on a wall opposite the crucifixes and were lined up like celebrity photos at a deli in Hollywood.

An embossed leather album sat askew next to the

shortwave. Cautiously, he opened the book. On the first page was a black-and-white print of the former priest and several naked, prepubescent boys, with skinny legs, big feet, and sad eyes. De Anza's arms were around one of them. The boy looked strangely familiar . . . then Michael recognized him. His heart sank.

Gregorio.

"Holy shit," he breathed.

Was Gregorio involved in this, too? Was he a victim, or a perpetrator? Was there even a difference? Quickly, he flipped through pages that featured de Anza and his children, then slammed the album shut. Opening the desk drawer, he was further horrified as explicit magazines and photos of young boys made it clear who de Anza was.

As he closed the drawer, voices sounded nearby. One belonged to the *padre*. He slipped from the bedroom, rushed back down the hall, and planted himself on a chair near the dining table in the living room. He grabbed a newspaper as de Anza walked through the door.

"Michael, an unexpected pleasure," the *padre* said, his smile forced. "I know why you're here but I don't have any news about your two colleagues. Captain Carbajal and his officers, as well as the military in the region, are on the highest alert. We will find them, my friend. In fact, Captain Carbajal is coming by himself to give me a status report within the hour."

"I need to get a message to my embassy and to a friend in the U.S. right away. We need transport out of Tingo Tia. I've been waiting for you so I could use your radio. My SAT phone battery has vanished."

"Ah, how unfortunate. Give me the contact

information and I will take care of it for you. Could take a while to get through."

Michael nodded and stood. He pulled his connection's business card from his pocket and handed it over. "I'm going to pack our gear. I'll touch base with you later." He knew de Anza would never let him near that radio now.

"I'm sorry you've decided to leave us so soon. Can't I convince you to continue your work here?"

"Things are too volatile. Another time, my friend," Michael said, not feeling friendly at all.

De Anza patted Burleson's shoulder in dismissal.

As Michael left the house he was hit hard by a realization. There was only one person who could help him find Lucy and Gregorio. Was Captain Carbajal the kind of man who would sell his own mother down the river for the right price? Michael would somehow have to come up with that right price.

Burleson shut the door to his room and leaned against it. With the miniscule bit of time remaining on the SAT phone's charge he called Scanlon twice but couldn't get through. Thirty seconds wasted. Perspiration beaded on Michael's forehead. With Bea Middleton in the hospital and Truckee in a coma, there was only one other person he trusted to help. He dialed the KLAK-TV number that was still on recall.

"Vargas!" he shouted into the voicemail, then lowered his voice. "Ernie—this is Michael Burleson in Pitacallpa—a hundred or so miles northeast of Tingo Tia in Guerrero. I'm almost out of juice. We have no coms. Lucy and another crew member disappeared last night. We stumbled on a major heroin production and distribution center. The shit is hitting the fan. If I can find Lucy and my other guy, I'll meet you at the Fiesta del Rio hotel in twenty-four hours. Make it happen. And call Scanlon and tell him his CIA people were murdered."

The phone cut out, reconnected for an instant, then died. Michael threw it against the wall and watched it shatter.

CHAPTER 50

The main street of Pitacallpa ran like a river as the rains of *El Niño* poured down again. The knock on Burleson's small apartment door sounded faint against the rumble of thunder.

"Come in," Michael said. He pulled clothes, gear, and notebooks from open drawers and piled it all in the middle of the floor with his duffle bag.

Captain Ramon Carbajal entered. Rain dripped from his dark navy slicker. He blinked water from his eyes.

"Señor Burleson, I have come to discuss our arrangements for transporting you to Tingo Tia tomorrow."

"Ah, yes," Michael said, "our arrangements." He could hear the threatening tone in his own voice.

He motioned for the policeman to sit down at the small dining table. The captain unbuttoned his wet coat, hung it over one of the yellow chairs and planted himself across from Burleson.

Carbajal's lips curled in a frown beneath his pencil-thin mustache. "Señor Burleson, esteemed American journalist, is there something—"

Burleson cut the man's fawning short. "All right, Carbajal, what do you want for them?"

The captain coughed and cleared his throat several times.

"I, uh . . . what do you mean?"

"You know damn well what I mean. I don't have time for bullshit. How much do you want for Vega and Hidalgo?"

The captain fidgeted in his seat.

Burleson knew it was not the Mexican way to be so direct, so hurried, but there was no time to spare on niceties, especially with this slime bag.

Carbajal took a deep breath and studied a speck on his shirtsleeve. Then he smiled and said, "I want one million U.S. dollars."

"A million dollars?" Now it was time for Michael to cough a few times.

"*Sí, sí,* a mill, and I'll show you where she is at."

"She's alive? And Gregorio?"

"*Sí,* she alive but not for long. She at a very unpleasant place. And you'll never find her without me. Your *hermano,* Hidalgo, he is dead."

With clenched fists, his head like a pressure cooker about to explode, Michael moved ominously toward the smarmy Carbajal. "A million dollars? Impossible."

His mind spun with financial calculations. He thought of the money he'd squandered over the years.

He still had alimony, child support, and two college tuitions to pay. A half mill would wipe him out, but he could do it. He gritted his teeth. "A half million is my offer."

The police captain's eyes widened, his fingers ran up and down the smooth, black leather of his holster.

"It's not enough, *señor*. I think it's . . . what do you say . . . too risky business. There is nothing my people hate more than one who is not loyal. The punishment is torture and death. I am afraid I cannot help unless it is worth my while."

"It is all I fucking have."

"But you a big star on TV."

"I'm a news reporter with a former wife and two children, whom I still support. I haven't worked in a year. Five hundred thousand dollars. Take it or leave it, Captain. That's my offer." Michael crossed his arms and waited, praying that the gods of greed would shine their faces on Carbajal.

The captain paused and seemed to think about the options. "I could kill you right now and this would all be over."

"Yes, you could. You'd be broke and Pitacallpa would be crawling with international media coverage by tomorrow morning. If you kill me, how long do you think your secrets down here would last?"

Carbajal stood and pressed his fingers against the cool handle of his gun, then he released it. Grinding his teeth, his glare was murderous. "All right, *señor* Burleson, I accept your offer. When you give me the money?"

Carbajal scowled and whined as they discussed how

the transaction would be made. Then the PAGA officer rose and turned toward the door, a sly look of satisfaction on his face.

"Don't go too far. We're leaving tonight."

He stopped in his tracks. "We leave tomorrow. The weather is too bad."

"No, we leave tonight." Burleson stood, towering over the diminutive captain. "Tomorrow may be too late. A half million U.S. dollars, Carbajal. Now or never."

Grabbing his slicker, the captain nodded and stomped out of the room and down the hallway. Burleson went to the window and watched him exit the convent and speed away in an old Land Rover.

Hidalgo was dead and the jungle and hills had swallowed up Lucy with amazing effectiveness. He had only the greed and ambition of an unreliable minor official to show him the way.

Michael looked at the crucifix hanging over his bed and wished he believed.

✳

The debilitating heat and humidity of the day was in full force. Lucy's cell reeked of human excrement and God only knew what else. She hadn't seen a guard since the early morning when they finally untied her still numb hands and arms. Her fingers felt like wooden sticks.

No one had returned to collect her bowl of half-eaten mystery gruel. Pacing up and down the small room, she was tormented by clouds of merciless flies.

The morning had been silent, the encampment seemed to be abandoned, but now Lucy could hear the men returning. Rustling, talking, laughing—the sounds sent a fresh wave of anxiety coursing through her veins. What plans did they have for her tonight?

The pressure in her chest began to build. Lucy felt her very cells, down to the molecules, begin to agitate, to hum with a low, irritating buzz. Then the molecules began to spin, like tops, accelerating until their screaming whine filled her head. Panic closed her throat and twisted her face. Lucy paced in her claustrophobic confinement and tried to calm her raging electrons. She gulped air like a fish flopping on a dock.

With a rusty, grating sound, the door to her cell was unbolted and two guards, teenagers with big guns, ordered her to follow them. It was such a disgusting tragedy that children were being used in these deadly games. But these two had probably left childhood far behind.

They led her into a large room with a big overhead fan and screens on the windows. A shortwave radio atop an ancient Steelcase desk sounded like it was clearing its throat. At the other end, an older group of soldiers in grimy uniforms drank beer and played cards.

Lucy tried not to hyperventilate, tried to calm her desperate breathing. Then Gary Mercer walked through the door.

Fake Rubio followed a few steps behind Mercer. For a shocked instant, Lucy felt herself begin to dissolve, then willed herself back into composure. She would not give them the satisfaction of seeing her break.

What the hell was Mercer's role here? More than a pilot for hire, he appeared to be the man in charge. Lucy tried not to cringe as he walked a slow circle around her, staring hard, taking measure. His eyes were filled with hatred; his right hand was wrapped in thick bandages. Finally, he settled against the edge of the desk.

"You don't look too good, *señorita* Vega, hot-shot camera bitch. You should have stayed out of it, Lucille, because it's going to cost you big time."

She remained mute.

Mercer, awkwardly, lit a cigarette with his good hand. "Nothing to say for yourself? Never thought I'd see the day."

Lucy's eyes went to fake Rubio, the weasel. "I guess he's not going to pay for my car repairs," she said, nodding toward the imposter photog. He snickered and ambled toward the doorway where a group of guards passed around a bottle of Mezcal.

"Yeah, he's not too good behind the wheel."

"Or the camera," Lucy said.

"But I'm fucking fine behind anything you got, bitch. And I'm a helluva driver—planes, monster trucks. I blasted the shit out of your uncle's nice car before I sent him over the edge. He got too close, like you."

The oxygen drained from Lucy's lungs and she fought for breath. Now she knew the truth she'd long suspected. Mercer murdered her uncle. Her overwhelming anxiety began to morph into something steely and hard.

Mercer took a long drag from his cigarette then blew lazy smoke rings. "Comfortable with your accommodations?" he continued.

"You should list this place on Airbnb." Lucy would not appear intimidated. He fed on fear, lapped it up, lived for it. Let him choke on it.

Mercer laughed, but she could hear something else. Her disdain bothered him. She knew who he was behind the bravado—a fucked-up, sociopathic, parent-killer with insane ambition and a drug habit that consumed him.

"You're disgusting, Gary." Her voice held the slap of a butcher knife slicing through flesh.

The sneer left his face. "Perhaps, but I'm alive, and rich—and you—you're not long for this world, Lucille."

Lucy forced herself to remain calm. She felt light-headed, almost high. "If I'm going to die, will you answer me a question?" She wanted to hear him admit what else he was responsible for.

"I'm capable of occasional acts of charity. Ask away." Mercer took another long suck on his cigarette. The tip pulsed white-orange.

"Did you, Alvarez, and Dynamic Chemical, orchestrate the livestock poisoning?"

Mercer sighed. "I can't believe you don't know this already, but all right. I gave you more credit than you deserve. The Mexicans . . . what should I call them . . . the organized crime cartel. You understand what I'm talking about—right, Lucille?"

"Yes, Gary." He knew she hated being called Lucille.

"Well, they'd been bringing up lots of nasty business to SoCal for years, until George Scanlon got way too serious and threw key players in the slammer, including Carlos Alvarez, a very main man and General Alvarez's brother to boot. Our people tried to negotiate for reduced sentences or extraditions, but George, he just laughed in their faces. Bad mistake. That routine pissed off some very mean and powerful people. Know what I mean, Lu?"

He paused and began walking around, circling her

again. Like a wolf slowly closing in on its prey.

She wanted to murder him, painfully.

"Luis Alvarez is a really bad sonofabitch who runs our organization," Mercer continued. "He loved Coppola's movie, *The Godfather*. Got off on the scene where the guy wakes up and finds the head of his favorite racehorse under the sheets with him. The asshole loved that horse. Remember that?"

Lucy nodded, recalling the grisly image.

"The general was looking for that kind of revenge. Know what I mean? So what does Scanlon love most? What does he love most, Lucille? And don't say his fucking family."

She'd play the game. Scanlon adored being governor. "His political career and the state of California."

"Right the fuck on! The ruins of his career were handed to him on a bloody plate of dead cows." Mercer chuckled. "Californians will be running to their doctors for cancer checks for decades. The asshole actually thought he could take a run for the presidency. All went down as sweet as can be. Looks like a Scanlon fuck-up, the media focuses on him, and everybody leaves us alone. Was excellent."

"Scanlon knows it was payback?"

"Of course. Alvarez'll be running California in no time. Or the water system is next. And don't think he can't do it."

Lucy gulped. Could Alvarez actually manage an undertaking that insane? Would they try to use Dynamic Chemical again?

"What about Carly Montgomery—an accident?" she asked.

"You're being stupid again." Mercer threw the butt of his cigarette onto the floor and crushed it.

"Why Carly? She's a young mother with two babies."

"She was helping you. That's a no-no. She and her sniveling husband are off to Singapore, by the way." Mercer laughed. "And that asshole Ray Truckee, and your old friend Bea Middleton—we worked them over good. And your cameraman, I mean my cameraman—ain't too good with the lens, but he's one hell of a firebug. Took out that whole neighborhood."

Lucy cringed. "The apartment fire. Children died, innocents!"

"Shit happens. And nobody's innocent."

His lack of conscience bore into Lucy's brain like an electric drill. She had to get the hell away from him.

Mercer paused as one of his cronies handed him a cold beer. He guzzled it in several long gulps then was handed another which he consumed as quickly. Desperately thirsty, Lucy licked her lips. He ignored her and continued to enjoy recounting his exploits.

"After the shock-and-awe toxic disaster, Scanlon realized that he was fucked. He knew what happened but had shit for proof. As you know, we're very good at accidents. Alvarez and I are real artists."

Lucy shook her head in dismay. "So when all else failed, Scanlon recruited Burleson, one of his closest friends, to come down here and do a documentary on de Anza and the Mixtec Trail Chocolate Company."

"Yep, Lucille. Burleson had a previous commitment from Scanlon and PBS for a project on economic development, so it was perfect timing. Smelled good on the surface. The governor just hoped that Mr. Media

Star would stumble onto what was really happening and dig up some shit to spread around. He thinks Burleson's too high profile for us to mess with." Mercer lit another cigarette. "Scanlon's a fox. He knew the Alvarez boys had been using U.S. aid money for years to fund this operation. He just couldn't catch the motherfuckers."

"What about Father de Anza?"

"Juan Jesus was doing very well with his end of it. Chocolate. Fuck. And Burleson—Scanlon's CIA stooge. But that's over." Mercer shot her a smug look. "By the way, how did you get this job, Lucille? Burleson must have wanted a piece of your ass the minute he saw it climbing into the chopper that day. One of my watchers said he saw you two fucking like bunnies the other night."

"Shut up, Mercer." Lucy flushed with fury.

"Watch your mouth, bitch." His eyes narrowed. "Meanwhile, I hear your stud has already packed up and moved out."

Lucy felt like the rug had been pulled out from under her. How could he leave her behind? But Mercer was probably lying, playing with her head. She had to believe that. The thought of Michael deserting her was too devastating. He would find her, but would it be in time?

She looked at Gary Mercer standing before her, hands on his hips, legs apart as if he were Peter Pan crowing for the Lost Boys. The big man. So pathetic.

"Bea shoot your hand off, Gar?" Lucy said, nodding at the bandage. "Won't be picking up a camera any time soon, huh? That girl's a helluva shot, but a click to the right and she would have got you between the eyes. Too bad she missed."

He slapped her hard and she fell backwards against a

chair. She struggled to her feet. Blood ran from her ear. Nausea wrenched her belly.

"It's such a shame," Lucy said quietly. "You had a great career, people who respected you, and you traded it in—for this? Gary, you are a certifiable fool."

Mercer smashed Lucy again across the face with all he had. She fell to the floor with a loud crack. For an instant, the room was completely silent. She struggled to her feet, fireworks exploding in her brain. Her vision was a blur.

"I was never the fool, bitch. I'm not the one who's going to die." Mercer was steaming. "This little chat is over. Vicente," he said to a teenaged guard, "she gets it just like the others. But help yourself first."

Lucy noted a fleeting look of surprise and anxiety cross the kid's face. Then quickly, he lowered a curtain of indifference and stepped forward. Vicente made a move to assist Lucy but one drop-dead glance from Mercer stopped him in his tracks.

"I think the boy's a fucking virgin. Pop your cherry, *chico*." Captain Cero growled as he entered the room with a big plate of tamales. "Juice her up good for me."

"I'm not a virg—" the boy began, struggling to assert his manhood in front of his laughing comrades.

"Fucking that flat-chested baby 'ho you hang with don't count."

The boy's face darkened.

"So you love the little white silk *puta*." Several in the room snickered. Cero continued, "She OD'd this morning. Baby's gone."

Vicente's head snapped backwards as if he'd been punched. Cero put his plate down and ambled over to

Lucy. He grabbed her by the hair, pulled her up, and began to lick her face. Lucy gasped at his stench. Pieces of half-chewed food stuck to her skin. "I'm gonna suck your everything, bitch, before I cut it up and put it in a burrito."

He shoved her against the wall then returned to his plate of greasy food. "The boy needs a drink." Cero gestured toward Vicente then grabbed a half-full bottle of tequila from a nearby table. He filled up a dirty shot glass.

Vicente hesitated, his face was a stony mask.

"Drink the fuck up, lover boy," Cero snarled. He pushed the liquor to the edge of the table. Vicente picked up the glass, studied the clear liquid for an instant, then downed it fast. He gritted his teeth and scowled at the big PAGA captain. The men in the room cheered. Cero poured another glassful and nodded at Vicente. This time the boy didn't hesitate. The tequila went down with enthusiasm.

Lucy struggled to remain standing. Lights still popped in her head from Mercer's blows. "Other people have information and it'll come out. Killing me won't stop it, Gary."

"But it'll sure make me feel better," Mercer said. He glanced at his big gold watch. "Time to go now, Lucille. Take her, Vicente. Big Captain Cero will be waiting in line. A man of interesting tastes. I think you should have let me push you out of that Huey a month ago. Would have been a much easier way to go."

"And I was just thinking I should've let you jump off that ledge in Hollywood."

Mercer's face went purple with rage.

CHAPTER 51

The young guard stood in the doorway. The whole situation was so sick that Lucy almost wanted to laugh. As the others urged him into her dark, closet-like cell, he chewed hard on his lip, eyes wide, nervous as a cat. He stunk of alcohol. Closing the door behind him, he began talking fast and furiously in a gruff combination of English and Spanish. She had a vague idea of what he said, but clearly knew what he wanted. He looked childish and vulnerable in the dimness. Maybe he was a virgin after all. She had to tap into any shred of innocence that remained in the boy.

"Vicente," Lucy held up both hands to interrupt his onslaught of words. "How old are you? Fifteen? You could be my son. Does your mother know you're raping women? Is this the boy she raised?"

He blanched and swallowed hard, but puffed up his

narrow chest. "I spent two years in San Diego and I know English. And I am not a boy. I am a man, and you are not my mother." His voice was slightly slurred.

He dropped his pants, revealing a grownup-sized hard-on.

"You're making a mistake and you're going to regret it," Lucy said. "God punishes those who transgress against Him. You'll go to hell, Vicente. You'll be like Mercer and Cero with nothing to show for their lives but shit. You want to be like them? God expects you to do the righteous thing."

She knew he didn't want to rape her. The fear in his eyes, the confusion—he was still on the fence. Not completely over to the dark side.

Yet.

The "Kyrie, eleison" she had sung as a child at Mass with her mother came into her mind. Maybe strange, random thoughts encroached on the psyches of people on the verge of madness. Maybe she was there.

Lucy sang a few bars of the prayer that begged for God's mercy. The boy's hand touched the crucifix that hung around his neck. His erection wilted.

"You're a Catholic." She gestured at the necklace. "It's difficult to be a good Christian and a good rapist and drug dealer all at the same time, isn't it?" Lucy crossed herself.

Vicente chewed at his lip again. The soft down of an adolescent mustache caught the faint light. His fingers tightened around the crucifix.

"I heard Cero teasing you about your girlfriend. She loves you, trusts you? What's her name?"

"Annalisa." His voice was soft and remorseful.

Lucy kept her tone firm. "Mercer and Cero don't understand love. They murdered her and felt nothing."

He nodded. Swiped at a tear and pretended to scratch his nose. "She was beautiful. Alvarez made her a white silk girl, used her, and threw her away."

A white silk girl? Lucy recalled Bea telling her about serial murders of young girls wearing white silk back in Los Angeles. Was Alvarez responsible for that, too? Lucy's fury flared hot.

Her eyes searched those of the young guard. "Mother of God, Vicente, don't fall into darkness. Make the wrong choice and you'll slide down the path to hell so fast you'll never be able to stop."

Vicente hesitated, his shadowy face contorted with uncertainty. "They sent me in here, I must . . . or they will humiliate me, beat me." His voice slurred again—he was drunk as shit.

"Maybe we can fix that, Vicente." Lucy sensed an opportunity she might never have again. "Give me ten minutes alone afterward, and I'll make sure they think we're doing it, right now. You won't have to betray Annalisa. They won't make fun of you. I'll make the right noises, scream, struggle. No one will know the difference, except us, and God."

"Why you want ten minutes?" His eyes narrowed.

To break out of this hellhole.

"To pray," she clasped her hands together in supplication, "for all of us."

The boy shifted nervously from foot to foot. He nodded agreement then shuffled to the corner of the room and threw up.

They went through with the charade. Vicente shouted

abuses. Lucy screamed and cried, then channeled Meg Ryan's fake orgasm scene in the crowded deli in the movie *Harry Meets Sally*. But this time it wasn't funny.

When it was over, Vicente stood quietly in the darkness. The vomiting seemed to have sobered him up a bit. Was he going to change his mind about her time alone?

"We have a deal," Lucy said, voice stern.

"*Sí*." He took a deep breath, left the cell and locked the door behind him.

Lucy smoothly lifted a penknife from his belt on his way out.

Thunder rumbled, deep and lonely in the distance. The storm would make good cover. If Vicente kept his word, she'd have those critical few minutes. This would be her only chance.

Lucy laser-focused on the cell's grated opening high up near the ceiling. Her hands were still numb from being tied but they provided the needed balance. Knife between her teeth, she inched herself up, legs splayed, one foot on each wall, across the four-foot space in her closet from Hades. An image of she and her brother climbing up their bedroom doorjambs when they were children flitted through her mind.

She finally reached the top of her cell, exhausted. Black patches and sparking light mottled Lucy's vision but her plan demanded full concentration. She could do it, just knock out the frame.

Time was ticking. Big Cero would be at the door in minutes.

Lucy's legs shook as she straddled the cell walls. She gripped the knife and hacked at the rotting wood that held the metal grating. A rusted fingernail file stuck out from the top of the frame. Someone else had given the same idea a try. And failed.

Lucy worked desperately. Dripping with perspiration, she wiped the back of her hand across her eyes. Her sweat shone pink with blood.

The wood finally splintered. One corner turned to sawdust after several stabs. Termites ran for cover. The frame began to dislodge. Rain splattering on the metal roof masked the sound as she pushed and sawed. A lightning bolt, then the count: *one one-hundred, two one-hundred*. Thunder boomed. *Push!*

All at once, the frame gave way and the vent popped out, falling to the ground outside. Lucy's balance wavered; her foot slipped precariously down the wall. She caught herself at the last second before crashing to the floor. Her heart almost exploded in her chest as she crept back upward again.

Splinters had gouged deep beneath her nails. Sweat was slippery on her palms and her bloody hands were fast losing strength. A cool breeze blew into the hole where the vent had been. Lightning split the sky. Lucy spotted a second building across the clearing, illuminated by a pale bulb dangling over the front door. Two men loaded what looked like dead bodies into the back of an ancient pickup. The rain poured down in dark curtains as the men jumped into the truck. Headlights turned on and the truck drove away. Lucy guessed they were heading to the road out of camp.

The sound of voices coming down the hall toward her door made her freeze. Her body quivered with anxiety and again threatened her balance.

Now or never.

The voices moved on.

Lucy squeezed her shoulders through the vent and then dangled precariously by her waist, half in and half out. Kicking her legs frantically, she was stuck. She kicked harder and pushed with her hands for all she was worth. Then at last her body plunged through the opening and tumbled onto the ground with a thud. A sharp stab seared her knee and the air was knocked from her lungs.

She lay still for a moment, panting, gasping to fill her lungs. Another bolt of lightning lit up the clearing. The area now looked abandoned. Everyone was probably inside getting loaded, gearing up to torture people to death.

The grisly images sent Lucy scrambling to her feet and into the forest. How long would it be before she was discovered missing?

She stampeded through the undergrowth, possessed. Her knee screamed as she ran and her breath came in shallow gasps that felt like she was breathing in glass. Another small clearing materialized. Lucy dashed toward the far side but caught her foot on something that sent her flying. Face down in the mud, she turned over to pull herself up and saw the thing that had tripped her.

It was not a root or a rock but a small, child-sized hand sticking up through the dirt. Frozen in a gesture of desperation, it appeared locked in rigor mortis. A white silk girl? Vicente's Annalisa?

Lucy scrambled to her feet and ran as hard as her damaged leg would allow. Dogs barked in the distance but they wouldn't catch her scent in this horrible storm.

She stumbled through the darkness in what she hoped was the direction of the road.

The rain came down in violent torrents, concealing her escape. *El Niño* had come to rescue her. Or drown her. Into the jungle she ran, searching for the way out. Finally, she found it.

For what felt like miles, she pushed herself through the dripping undergrowth at the road's edge, until her body shook uncontrollably. Her mind dissolved into a confused tangle of pain and horrifying impressions. Then, there was only blackness.

✳

Vicente fingered the stock of his assault rifle, eyes blank, barely listening to the guards gathered alongside him in the prison office.

"She's a nice looking *chinga*," said a tall slender man with soulful brown eyes.

"Ah, she's a cunt," Cero snarled. "They all are." He alternately sucked on a harsh-smelling cigarette and wolfed down the remains of his dinner. "So, what's gonna be your pleasure, Dalmacio?" he asked his spaghetti-thin *compadre*.

"I dunno," he responded. "I hate it when they cry. Reminds me of my mother when my old man used to beat the shit out of her."

"Holy Christ, you're such a goddamned turd with women. But you have no trouble getting men to spill their guts; I'll say that for you."

The Captain laughed and let out a string of shrill farts. Vicente rolled his eyes.

The other guards groaned and tittered, but Cero

seemed oblivious. He looked them over and shook his head. "First action you assholes have seen here in a while, and you're sitting around scratching your balls, except for young Vicente here."

He grinned at the boy, who had just returned from Lucy's cell. Vicente forced a smile, the taste of sour vomit still on his lips.

The big man tossed greasy leftovers to two bony, squabbling gray cats that prowled through the dimly illuminated guard office. The shortwave intermittently buzzed with garbled chatter.

"Come on, you sniveling bastards. We got some good-looking ass right here. And tonight it'll be free. Let's bring her in, give her some goodies, make her entertain us. She's dead meat anyhow. We just have to watch it with the face. Mercer says it has to be recognizable." Cero's enthusiasm was unrelenting. Someone turned the radio to a pop station. "Gonna get me pussy tonight." He sang the words over and over to a salsa beat.

Vicente struggled with a wave of nausea as the PAGA captain danced around the room. Cero's stupendously large rear end shivered and shook. Slowly, the subdued group began to catch his infectious spirit. They turned up the radio that had almost been muted by the storm and passed around a coke pipe.

"Get her, Vicente—now!" Captain Cero commanded. The others cheered.

The young guard glanced at his watch. Eleven minutes had passed, more prayer time than she'd bargained for. Slowly, he walked down the hall to Lucy's cell. When he opened the door, he was sure he'd entered the wrong room. Pulling a flashlight from his jacket pocket, he searched the tiny chamber and couldn't believe his eyes. It was empty.

When he noticed the vent gaping open high above his head, the boy was struck by a mixture of relief and horror. Would they blame him? Would they catch her? Uncooperative prisoners didn't beg for their lives—they begged for their deaths. This time would be no exception.

CHAPTER 52

Although the road was the usual disaster during the rain, the old four-wheel *Policía de Agricultura* Land Rover 90 plodded steadily onward. Michael Burleson and Carbajal barely acknowledged each other. Their mutual contempt hung in the air like humidity. Only the intermittent squawking of the police radio provided any relief. Carbajal, a man whom Burleson knew liked to talk, was the first to break the silence.

"I wonder when *Padre* de Anza will figure out you're gone. You won't get out of here alive." His fingers tapped annoyingly on the steering wheel.

"You'd better hope I do," Burleson said, his voice barely audible, "or you'll never get your hands on that money."

Carbajal scowled, his face ghoulish in the green light of the instrument panel. His thin mustache looked like it had been drawn above his lip with a Sharpie pen.

A call came in on the radio. Carbajal pressed the receive button. The message was fast and staticky.

"What is it?" Burleson asked. "Escaped?"

The officer glanced over at his passenger; a nasty snarl curled the edges of his mouth. "This woman of yours, she's gone."

"What?" Burleson choked on the tepid coffee he was drinking from a thermos.

"They underestimated her. The contest is now, who will find her first—you, or them."

"If you're bullshitting me, Carbajal—"

"I'm not. It's what the dispatcher said! And I still get my money. I brought you here!"

Burleson rubbed his eyes hard—*time to wake the fuck up.* "How long before we're in range of the prison?"

Carbajal sulked behind the wheel. "I'd say five miles. This road's the only way in or out."

"When did she escape? They say what time?" Burleson glanced at his watch.

Carbajal shrugged.

"What time?" Burleson grabbed the PAGA officer by his scrawny neck. The vehicle swerved.

"Okay, okay. Early in the night, like nine or ten."

"She could've made it this far. We'll go slowly and look for her."

Carbajal grimaced.

They stowed the Land Rover's canvas top. Michael sat on the back of the front seat for the best view. As the drizzly gray dawn began to brighten, he peered deep into the woods, looking, listening—his senses heightened by anxiety.

"Damn. I wonder how far she got." He scrubbed at the bristles on his cheek.

Carbajal glanced at Burleson and smiled. "Depends what kind of condition she was in."

Michael's hands clenched into fists. He hopped out of the Rover and walked along the road, peering intently into the encroaching jungle. Although the day was still cool, perspiration beaded on his face.

Carbajal, humming an annoying *Narcocorrida* tune, followed just behind Burleson in the PAGA vehicle.

✴

Lucy was aware of the change in light despite her closed eyelids. Day had come; she had survived the night. Her body felt deathly cold and unmoving as concrete. As she lay on the ground, her mind drifted apart from her physical self. It looked down as a removed observer. Her eyes opened, or rather, one eye opened; the other had swollen shut.

Pale, chill mist blanketed the forest floor. Botanical forms of deepest emerald materialized like liquid stalactites dripping their condensation onto her skin. She shivered violently and her teeth clacked together like castanets.

Remembering the videotape on treating hypothermia from her Red Cross first aid course, she guessed she was well on her way. Blue-cold extremities, listlessness, confusion, sometimes euphoria, then loss of consciousness and death. It was doubtless a better way to go than what the bastards had planned for her at the prison.

Time to press onward. Tottering precariously as she

stood, Lucy was shocked as she inspected her hands and legs. Her knee was the size of a cantaloupe, and her fingers were raw with splinters. Biting flies began to collect on her wounds.

Walking like the Tin Man after a rainstorm without his oil can, she knew that she would have a tough fight through the undergrowth in this condition. But her only hope was to stay concealed in the forest and follow the edge of the road out of this hellhole. Surely, Mercer and Lt. Cero's posse was out looking for her. If they caught her, they weren't going to take her alive. She'd kill herself first rather than give them the satisfaction of torturing her to death.

How would she do it? She pulled out Vicente's knife, which was tucked in her pocket, and also fingered the memory card. It was still there, wrapped in a soaking wet tissue. Lucy smiled. She'd destroy Mercer yet.

Dizzy and weak, fighting fits of violent trembling, Lucy withdrew into the deeper part of the forest. Nearer the road, the undergrowth was thick with young plants competing for sunlight provided by the clearing. Farther from the roadway, the light was soft. The forest floor was less choked with vegetation and more easily navigable.

Exhausted after hours of walking through the night, Lucy came to a wide stream which was partially dammed into a deep pond. Lusty frogs croaked at her approach. The water was stirred up and silty from the storm. In the pond, huge water lilies bloomed with creamy, white flowers the size of magnolias. Some of the lily pads were as large as saucer sleds. How she yearned to curl atop one of their warm, air-mattressy surfaces and sleep forever.

Downstream, where she had been only minutes before, Lucy became aware of several male voices moving in her direction. Holding back a cry, she ducked behind a large boulder at the stream's edge and sank into cold water to just above her swollen knee. Lucy shivered and touched her pocket. Would a wet memory card still work? Everything was drenched.

The men—it sounded like two of them—had stopped next to the steam, about twenty feet from her hiding place. The metallic sounds of guns clattered against the rocks; they were sitting down. The two discussed soccer teams . . . and food. Food! They were eating. Perhaps they would leave some scraps behind—a bread crust, anything.

Again, Lucy began to shudder. Her teeth chattered, making her jaw throb in pain. She pressed hard against the smooth rock and hoped the men were sufficiently preoccupied so as not to notice the slight agitation in the atmosphere that her movement caused.

After what seemed like an endless pause, the men continued their football discussion. Lucy had visions of them setting up camp for the week. But at last, they got up, left the area, and moved farther into the forest to stalk their prey. Had they only known how close they had been to finding it.

With hesitant motions, she rounded the boulder and emerged from the water. The skin on her legs felt tingly, like minnows nibbling at her skin. She looked down and pulled up her pant legs. Biting her lip to keep from screaming, she gagged at the sight. Hundreds of slimy black leeches stuck to her skin.

Battling hysteria, she peeled off the worm-like

creatures and hurled them into the forest. Bloody pink circles oozed where their sucker mouths had attached to her skin. Her legs looked like she'd broken out with a strain of virulent pox. *Ring around the rosy*—her mind went to the nursery rhyme about the plague. Tears of frustration streamed down her face.

She limped over to where the men had been eating and found a half-eaten tortilla. Her jaw was locked so tight she could barely open her mouth to eat it. Mercer had a helluva right hook. She ripped the tortilla into tiny pieces and nibbled it down like a baby bird.

The sustenance, though small, was heartening. Lucy continued her slog through the dusky interior of the forest with the barest infusion of new energy. Her thoughts went to Burleson. The short time they had spent together seemed like much more. Had the closeness been an illusion? Probably. Where was he now? On a plane back to L.A.? She wanted to believe that he would find a way to rescue her from this death march, but it was too much to hope for. She was on her own.

The day was deeply overcast, the gloom was depressing; Lucy craved light and decided to head for the road. The closer she got to the brightness the more elated she became. After fighting through heavy undergrowth, Lucy stood in the middle of the muddy rutted excuse for a road. Her shivering was constant but she was feeling more reckless and carefree by the minute.

Fingering the knife in her pocket, it felt like a talisman in her hand, instilling confidence and daring. Feeling powerful with it in her grasp, she decided to walk along the side of the roadway instead of subjecting her battered body to the rigors of the forest. If she heard a vehicle approaching, she'd duck into the bushes. She smiled to herself and stumbled along like a sleepwalker, lost in some pleasant hazy fantasy, oblivious to the rest of the world. The well-being stage of hypothermia was setting in.

✳

When Michael first saw the movement at the edge of the road, he thought it was an animal who'd heard them approaching and bolted away. But something felt different. Could it be her? Or was this just desperate, wishful thinking? He jumped onto the vehicle's running board.

"Ahead, step on it," he ordered Carbajal. "Right up there!"

The police officer had seen it, too, and sped up. It was definitely Lucy.

Burleson leaped from the Rover and took off into the vegetation. With his whole being, he could feel her presence. He wanted to shout her name but knew calling any kind of attention to her could bring disaster.

She moved in an awkward, disoriented way, and he gained on her easily.

"Lucy," he said as loud as he dared. "Lucy, I'm here! Lucy, stop!"

She ignored his plea and managed to stay just out of his grasp until she slipped and fell forward onto her stomach. Burleson saw the flash of a knife gripped in her fingers. She slashed at her own outstretched wrist. Red beads emerged from the lacerated skin.

"Jesus, no—Lucy, stop!" As she began to slice across the vein, Michael caught her arm in a hold she couldn't throw off.

"You won't take me alive," she screamed.

He pressed his hand over her mouth. "Lucy, drop the goddamn blade and be quiet! I've got you."

Her body went limp and she began to sob. "Am I dreaming? Are you here?"

"I'm really here. You're not dreaming. Maybe hallucinating a little bit, though."

"You're a helluva fine hallucination." Her arms found his neck and she pulled him close.

He held her wet, cold body and stroked her hair until she settled down, then carefully helped her stand. His eyes registered complete shock at her appearance. Putting his arm around her waist for support, he guided her back to the PAGA vehicle.

As they drew near to the edge of the road, Lucy froze. Burleson was momentarily taken aback by the abject terror on her swollen face.

"He'll kill us both!" Lucy gaped at Captain Carbajal. He lounged against the side of the vehicle, weapon in hand. She tried to run but her legs buckled.

"Lucy, he's on our side, for now." Burleson lowered his voice. "Well, not actually on our side. I bribed the hell out of him."

Lucy was unconvinced. She tried to flee but was too spent to resist. Burleson carried her to the vehicle and laid her down on the back seat. He covered her icy body with both a blanket and a tarp. Her hand slid from her side into her pocket. She pulled out the memory card and handed it to Michael. Carbajal had moved across the road and was relieving himself.

"What's this?"

"Has everything we need to put these assholes away, or at least give it one helluva try."

Michael took the card and put it in his shirt pocket. Carbajal zipped his pants as he returned to the vehicle.

"You're almost home free," Burleson said to him. "When we get to Tingo Tia I'll call my banker and he'll release the money. It'll be at the *Banco de México* branch as we discussed. Now, get us the hell out of here."

Carbajal slipped onto the driver's seat and eyed Lucy in his rearview mirror. He glowered with disdain at the filthy, broken woman. "For this, you risked your . . . our lives?"

Michael cringed at the man's cruel sarcasm but refused to get caught up in it. He turned and looked at the shivering, fragile person tucked beneath the old plastic tarp. Her skin was pallid and her lips were almost white, but she was alive.

"Michael," Lucy called, her voice raspy.

He turned, leaned toward her, and rested his hand gently on her cheek. Her jaw was swollen and bruised like a bad peach.

"Gregorio. . . do you know . . . ?" she began. Coughing caught her short.

Michael took her hand. "I know. He's dead, Lucy. Carbajal heard it from good sources."

"Dead?" She tried to sit up. "Hell, he is." Her voice became stronger and then faded away again. She grimaced and slumped back down onto the seat. "He and Hilda set me up. He's the traitor who turned me over to these . . . monsters."

"What? You sure?" A mere day ago Burleson would have been incredulous at her accusation, but after seeing the photos of Gregorio and de Anza, it was beginning to make sense.

"It's true," Lucy said. "Ask your man here about Gregorio Hidalgo."

Michael turned his intense, questioning eyes in the policeman's direction.

Carbajal shrugged his shoulders. He looked vaguely like a guilty dog that had just chewed up his master's best shoes and secretly had no regrets.

"The girl is correct," he admitted with an edge of smugness. "You'll never prove it, though. We've taken care of everything."

"Just shut your mouth and drive," Michael interrupted. He looked ready to strangle the sonofabitch.

A disgruntled Carbajal turned the vehicle around and headed back toward the main road to Tingo Tia. Although they made good time on the muddy, washboard road, they were soon aware of a vehicle on their tail.

Alvarez's men had found them.

CHAPTER 53

Lucy watched Burleson peer down the road behind them. "Ah, shit. Looks like a PAGA Jeep, maybe a quarter mile off, gaining fast." He turned to Carbajal. "Floor it, man."

The Sergeant glanced over his shoulder and let out an expletive. He gassed it, but after a short attempt at flight, he changed his mind. "We can't outrun these motherfuckers."

He swerved onto a right-hand fork in the road and slowed to a stop.

Michael glared at him incredulously. "Why the hell're you stopping?"

"Shut up and let me handle this." Carbajal waved cordially to the oncoming police car, his smile forced.

Lucy hauled herself up in the back seat. Neck stiff, she turned to see a speeding vehicle tracking them like a heat-seeking missile. "God, no," she whispered to herself. Her icy body went even colder. Another few degrees and she'd shut down completely.

"*Buenos días, mis amigos,*" Carbajal called.

The driver of the racing vehicle slammed on the brakes, skidded around the parked Rover and finally stopped at a ninety-degree angle across the narrow roadway, blocking any escape.

Carbajal stood up in his seat and leaned cheerfully over the old Land Rover's windshield. "Some pretty impressive driving there, Captain Cero," he said with a big smile.

Cero frowned, eyes furious. The Jeep's rear doors swung open disgorging several gunned-up flunkies. Mercer was in the Jeep's passenger seat, manning the radio and communicating vigorously with some unknown listener.

"What? You think we were trying to get away from you or something?" Carbajal's pencil-line mustache quivered like the needle on a seismograph. Although the AK-47 he'd pulled from beneath his seat appeared relaxed in his hand, the man's fingers tapped nervously near the trigger. "I have them both," Carbajal declared like he'd won the lottery. "The girl's here. I got them!"

"What the hell," Michael gasped.

Carbajal pointed the firearm at him. His fingers now tapped double-time even closer to the trigger.

"We're real glad to hear you captured the fugitives," Mercer said, his voice cynical. He ostentatiously cocked a .357 Magnum and rested it on the dashboard. "We also overheard your brother-in-law saying you got a cool half mill to get these two out of here under our noses."

"My brother-in-law? He's full of shit, always talking nonsense," Carbajal said, his voice strident.

Lucy could see sweat dampening the back of his khaki shirt.

"Then why are you heading toward Tingo Tia, not Pitacallpa?" Mercer asked.

Captain Carbajal made a sudden move. Bad decision. His head exploded off his body. Crimson liquid and bits of flesh, bone, and brains sprayed over the hood and windshield. Pink mist covered Lucy's arms. She could taste his blood on her lips.

Lucy grabbed the headless policeman's automatic as his dead body collapsed on top of her. She clawed out from beneath him. Michael kicked open the passenger door and crouched behind it, firing on full auto. Bullets flew through the air with cat-like hisses. A line of ragged circles tore into the back of the seat next to Lucy's shoulder.

Everything happened in a blur. The PAGA guard riding shotgun dropped sideways and collapsed on the road. Michael strafed Captain Cero's vehicle with round after round until he obliterated its gas tank.

A spark flared. Lucy aimed Carbajal's gun and emptied it at the growing spray of gasoline. There was a millisecond of stillness when everybody knew what was going to happen.

Mercer leaped from the car but Cero was too slow. An explosion rocked the forest. A fireball billowed upward like a roman candle. The concussion hurled Mercer, flaming, into the brush. Shrapnel landed in the front seat of Carbajal's Rover. Birds squawked and flew from the trees.

Cero managed to wrench his car door open and fell screaming into the road. His desperate movements fanned the flames. He began to incinerate into a hulking black cinder. Michael pushed what was left of Carbajal out onto the sizzling mud next to the writhing lieutenant, then grabbed a .357 and another assault rifle from a dead guard near the Jeep.

He jumped back into the Land Rover. Lucy crawled, wincing, into the blood-splattered front seat. Burleson scrubbed blood and tissue from the cracked windshield with his hand so he could see ahead. The Rover's fender held fine as it shoved the Jeep out of the road and onto the spongy shoulder. Burleson pressed the pedal to the metal and rocketed toward Tingo Tia.

Lucy struggled to stay awake as they barreled along. Just before they came to the crossroads into town, where the surface turned from mud to crumbling blacktop, Michael abruptly pulled over.

"What . . . why are we stopping?" Lucy said, eyes wide with alarm.

"We've got to take care of you before we go any farther," Michael said in a no-nonsense voice.

"I'm fine."

"Uh-huh, and de Anza is the Pope. Michael went to the rear of the vehicle and grabbed the first aid kit. It was riddled with a string of bullet holes but was otherwise useable. Returning to the front seat, he brought a fresh solar blanket in a plastic bag and antiseptic.

"First, let's get you out of those wet clothes."

Lucy untied her boots and peeled off her socks with palsied hands. This small effort sent her into another fit of trembling. She was fast losing control of her arms and legs.

Taking off his long-sleeved cotton shirt and wrapping her in it, Michael gathered Lucy into his arms and nestled her tight against his chest. She tried to feel his warmth, but it was as though they were separated by a piece of cold glass.

"Babe, your skin is absolutely freezing. You're definitely hypothermic. Don't want you to go into shock. You need some sustained heat." He struggled with knobs on the vehicle's dash but nothing worked. The heater switch fell off in his hands.

Lucy's tongue felt thick as she tried to talk. "I feel paralyzed," she stuttered. "This body belongs to someone else . . . like an old person who's dying."

"No, it belongs to a gorgeous young woman who is living, and is going to continue living so I can make love to her again."

"So you rescued me just to get laid?"

"Ah, you're getting to know me too well."

Lucy smiled. Michael offered her water from his canteen and crackers to eat, covered her in the solar blanket, and cleaned off her face with the antiseptic.

"Lucy, I like you," Michael said, tucking wild strands of hair behind her ears. "I mean, I really like you a lot."

The words warmed her, almost as much as the solar blanket. "I like you, too. Possibly a lot, but I'm not fully committing to that."

"Let's keep the c-word out of the discussion." Michael peered back down the road. It was still empty. He stepped on the accelerator and they were off again. "If we make it to Tingo Tia, we're going to have to lay low until we can find a way out," Michael said, now all business.

"Mercer was on the radio blabbing away just before the car blew up," Lucy said.

"Yeah, I saw him. Every cop in the Upper Guerrero valley has gotta know we're out here."

Lucy chewed at her thumbnail. Even her saliva was cold. "You think he's dead?"

Burleson glanced over at her. "Mercer? The asshole couldn't have survived that inferno."

"I wish I could believe that. He's like the undead." She picked up the .357 Magnum that sat on the floor between the seats and looked it over carefully. "I think I accidentally dropped the other one out the window. Sorry. The metal was really hot."

"Not as hot as Gary Mercer," Burleson said, then glanced over at Lucy and nodded toward the big revolver. "Can you use that thing? You were pretty damn good with that AK, young lady."

Lucy smiled. "I was raised around guns. I don't like them, but I've fired one of these before. Tough recoil. If I can only get my fingers to work."

She laid the weapon across her lap and covered it with the solar blanket. The food and dry shirt had revived her a bit. Still, everything seemed to take such effort. Slumping against the door as they bumped their way toward Tingo Tia, Lucy somehow knew Mercer was still on their trail. Maybe she'd have a chance to put him down with his own gun. She closed her eyes and flexed her hands over and over.

✻

Several miles outside of town, Michael raced around a

bend, hell on wheels, and careened into a full-on police roadblock. He slammed on the brakes to avoid crashing into the barricades where a group of deathly serious-looking local cops aimed rifles at his head.

When he started to turn the Land Rover around, a PAGA convoy materialized from the jungle and blocked the road behind him.

Lucy didn't have to be introduced to recognize Luis Alvarez. In military garb with golden epaulets glistening, he emerged from a shiny, clean Range Rover. It was a pricey new one, not the 1980s Banana Republic antique Land Rover Michael was driving.

Gregorio Hidalgo moved close behind Alvarez. Another four thugs disgorged from their fancy vehicle. Gregorio didn't meet Lucy's eyes as he passed by, but his handgun was trained on her. She covered her mouth to try and suppress a sob of grief. He had betrayed her once, and now he would do it again.

"So, Mr. Burleson, it is a pleasure to meet you at last," the cartel boss said in a patronizing voice. In his blue, white, and gold uniform, he looked like he'd just stepped from a Ralph Lauren photo shoot. "General Luis Alvarez, chief of the *Policía de Agricultura de Guerrero Alta,* at your service." He saluted.

"And chairman of the board of Dynamic Chemical Company," Lucy said, "among other things." The .357 was warm under the silver thermal blanket.

He sneered and gave her a curt nod. "All part of my many diversified business activities. *señorita* Vega, is it?"

She didn't respond.

Gregorio and half a dozen police officers surrounded

Lucy and Burleson, weapons
drawn, ready to blast.

"Enough with the introductions, Alvarez. I have urgent business in Tingo Tia," Michael said.

"I'm sure you do. And you're planning to drive there in what looks like one of *my* police cars?" Alvarez walked slowly around the Jeep, eyeing its contents, particularly Lucy.

Her exhaustion suddenly faded, her senses became as sensitive as a raw wound.

"And where is the legitimate driver of this vehicle?" the general demanded.

"Sergeant Carbajal is with another group of your men who were, supposedly, looking for two of my missing crew members," Michael said. He nodded toward Lucy and Gregorio.

"You stole my sergeant's vehicle?"

"I borrowed it. He was in no shape to drive."

Alvarez shared a skeptical frown with a nearby officer. Then he looked toward Gregorio. Lucy noticed the general's face momentarily flicker with confusion when Gregorio's eyes met his. Just as quickly, Alvarez's condescending self-assurance dropped back into place. He lit up a cigar and ambled toward the Land Rover.

Stopping next to the driver's seat, he leaned against the door toward Michael. When Alvarez realized that the vehicle was covered with a sticky film of coagulated body liquids, he stood back and scowled with disgust. His impeccable uniform had been defiled. He made a show of bushing off the contamination, to no avail.

Then he turned the smarmy charm back on like the flick of a light switch. "Perhaps we might be able to work something out and get you to Tingo Tia, Mr. Burleson. We must, however, insist that your passenger remain with us."

Burleson's eyes narrowed. He glanced at Lucy then returned his attention to the cartel boss. "Is it now a crime for a woman to be kidnapped, molested, and tortured by the police? I would think you're the ones to be arrested."

"Watch yourself, Mr. Burleson." Alvarez's face hardened. His arrogance turned to deadly menace. "Or neither one of you will make it to Tingo Tia. Officer Leon, take *señorita* Vega into custody."

The burly, pock-faced Leon reached for Lucy.

"No!" When Gregorio realized he had shouted, he lowered his voice and visibly struggled to keep it calm. "No, this is not the woman you are looking for."

Alvarez stared at him as if he had lost his mind. "This must be her. Mercer radioed that it was her."

"He was mistaken." Flushed and trembling, Gregorio's eyes burned brightly. Slowly, he moved the focus of his rifle from Michael and Lucy to Alvarez. The officers looked around at each other with uncertainty. Lucy could sense what they were asking themselves. *Was it her, or wasn't it her? What the hell was Gregorio Hidalgo trying to pull?*

"Take her, you idiot," Alvarez growled to Officer Leon. The general's Adam's apple pulsed up and down, his jaw clenched and unclenched.

Lucy's heart hammered, her fingers crept toward the revolver on her lap. No one was going to take her—not Gregorio, not Mercer, and definitely not Alvarez.

"It has all come together, right here and now,"

Gregorio said. He turned to face Alvarez directly. Despite his nervous appearance, Gregorio's voice was steely and smooth. "Yours is the face in my nightmares. You tortured and murdered my father."

The general went as pale as his favorite white silk. His hand hovered close to his pistol but he still had the cigar between his fingers.

"Go!" Gregorio screamed to Michael. "Now!"

The jungle reverberated with Gregorio's electrifying wail. At the same time, he turned his gun toward Alvarez, the general took aim back at Gregorio. Lucy had the Mag in her hands before either could fire. The general's eyes skittered toward her, mocking, taunting. Then the realization appeared to hit him like the bullet that pierced his chest. *The fucking girl got me.* Alvarez dropped where he stood.

"You piece of shit!" Lucy screamed. Spots of exploding light flashed before her eyes as weapons discharged. Their already cracked windshield shattered. Bullets zoomed by her head and lodged in the door.

The shooting was chaotic. Burleson hit the gas and tore out, smashing through the roadblock. Several of the policemen tried to leap out of the way and rolled off the hood. One man's machine gun discharged on impact. Michael groaned as he floored the accelerator.

As Lucy turned to look at the bedlam behind them, Gregorio was thrown against the PAGA vehicle by a series of blasts that turned his light T-shirt a ghastly crimson. An agonized groan ripped from her throat as the cops pulverized him.

Alvarez, and several others lay splashed across the road in bleeding heaps.

In the end, Hidalgo had sacrificed his life for her. Had he redeemed his soul? "Gregorio," Lucy whispered to no one, "he never had a chance."

CHAPTER 54

On the outskirts of Tingo Tia in their heisted PAGA vehicle, Michael and Lucy sped by a family packed into a dusty truck and a young boy leading a scraggly herd of goats. No cops.

"We should slow down so we don't call attention to ourselves." Lucy struggled to keep her eyes open. Every pore in her body begged to float away into oblivion.

Michael took his foot off the gas. "I think the hotel's only a mile or so away."

Lucy hoped Michael's old *amigo,* the ancient bellboy Tito, would cooperate if they needed him. She began to give in to the smallest edge of relief—until flashing red lights pulsated in the passenger side mirror, vivid even behind her closed eyelids.

"Shit, cops're on our ass. Must've found the trail of dead PAGA guys in our wake." Michael punched the accelerator again.

Sirens whined, and vehicles slid in behind the two fugitives in a growing procession. A shot of adrenaline crackled through Lucy's veins and slapped her back to full awareness.

Michael took a hard right and narrowly missed a pack of feral dogs dining on roadkill. Lucy watched them scatter then immediately regather around the bloody carcass. He careened through back alleys of a commercial industrial section of Tingo Tia. The streets were lined with old warehouses and long-abandoned *tiendas*. They hit a patch of washboard road and the vehicle vibrated like a dentist's drill.

"Hang on, sweetheart." Michael fishtailed their ride into another narrow lane.

"Gotta ditch this car. Makes us too much of a target," Lucy said.

They abandoned the vehicle in a garbage-strewn lot between two businesses several blocks from the hotel. As a police cruiser zoomed by, they ducked behind a row of trash cans and a rusted refrigerator until the sound of sirens receded.

Struggling alongside Michael, Lucy clutched her weapon and forced herself to keep up. She gritted her teeth at every step. In place of a knee, she had grown a giant purple football. Finally, they spotted the hotel with its hot pink neon sign that alternatively pulsed out "Fiesta" and "del Rio." Burleson took a deep breath and picked her up in his arms. He sprinted across the street into a thicket of oleander adjacent to the front parking area.

As she reached her arm around his neck to hold on

tight, Lucy saw the wide, dark stain on Michael's back. She touched his sticky, blood-soaked shirt.

"You've been hit! Jeez, Michael, put me down."

"It's okay." Gently, he set Lucy on her feet, gripped her hand, and tugged her along. She did her best not to drag behind but her leg was cement. They hid in the shadows, panting, as another police car passed by and vanished along a side street. Lucy's heart hammered like an AK-47 firing on full automatic.

A bizarrely familiar voice called from a gray van parked roughly fifteen feet away from the hotel entrance. "Michael! Lucy!" The sign on the side door said *Vargas & Vega Tortillas*.

Lucy smiled.

Michael frowned. "What the—"

"It's us!" Bea shouted. "Me and Brent the intern."

"Please stop calling me 'Brent the intern,'" Brent the intern said.

Bea called out to them again. "Over here. Run for it before they're back."

Lucy could make out Brent's dim form as the side door to the vehicle rolled open. "I'm hallucinating again," she gasped.

"I think it's for real." Michael grabbed her hand.

The sounds of police sirens grew louder by the second. Lucy and Michael staggered over and tumbled into the back seat of the van. The door rolled shut just as several cop cars and a PAGA truck pulled into the parking lot.

"Stay down," Brent said.

Bea pulled out of the lot, gravel flying. Her eyes darted between the road and the rearview mirror.

"Thank God we found you."

Lucy struggled to sit up. "You guys are angels from heaven—I've never been happier to see anybody. And my God, Bea, I thought you were practically dead."

"Me too. I'm lucky to be alive, but Truck, bless his big ginger-haired soul, may not make it. There are no words to describe how damn furious I am." She gave the steering wheel a hard slap. "Couldn't sit in bed watching Oprah reruns for another damn second. I've got holes in these gorgeous Michelle Obama shoulders that no makeup's going to cover. And nobody messes with my friends and family—nobody."

"And her Bea-ness grabbed me to help because I am such a good intern," Brent said. "And I signed that damned 'other tasks as required' clause." He jacked a clip into his rifle.

Bea glanced over at Brent and flashed him a quick smile.

"That, and because I read your résumé before we hired you, yes I did. Special Ops-Afghanistan. You've done this shit before. I figured if anybody could get to you guys, it would be us—special forces and one pissed off mama."

"But how in the world did you know we'd be at the hotel?" Lucy asked.

"Michael got a message to Ernie," Brent said. His eyes never left the side mirror. "More on that later. Gotta concentrate on getting to the goddamn airport."

"Don't think those creeps saw you guys jump in." Bea down-shifted. The manual transmission lurched in protest as they labored up a steep hill. "But they're going to figure it out real fast."

When they reached the crest, she ground the gears and shifted again, flooring it past the little *El Fresca* restaurant. Lucy saw the teenage boy who had served her a week earlier wipe off a picnic table in front.

"I wish you'd let me drive," Brent said. "If you slow down, they won't suspect—"

The rear window was hit by an explosion and shattered into a million fragments. Lucy and Michael were pelted with stinging glass shards.

"Too late for stealth." Bea glanced at her driver's side mirror. "Shit. There's a motorcycle on our ass."

Lucy turned to see a motorcyclist pull up alongside the van and leap off his speeding bike onto their back bumper. Just as he managed to rip open the rear door, Bea hit a deep rut. The van swerved wildly. The motorcycle cop was thrown into the oncoming police cars. Lucy heard the man scream.

"Might have cracked an axle on that one," Bea shouted.

"You'd make a hell of an ambulance driver." Lucy winced at every bump in the road.

"Shit, they're gaining on us." Brent rolled down the passenger side window and pushed his body out so he was riding on the window ledge, automatic rifle in hand.

Michael rolled down his window and did the same on the opposite side next to Lucy. He blasted out the clip in no time. The gunfire temporarily slowed down their tail.

"Think this heap can hit warp speed?" Lucy shoved her revolver toward Michael. "Got seven shots left."

"Hell with warp speed," Brent said. "Let's just hope the guts don't fall out of this piece of crap before we get to the plane."

Bea careened toward the airport's chain link back entrance. The gate twisted off its hinges as the van ripped through and sped onto the tarmac.

"That our transpo?" Michael nodded at a Cessna ahead. It was bigger than Mercer's.

"Yeah, baby," Bea said, "Eight-seat turbo prop. Borrowed it from the DEA. Should be ready and raring to go."

The van screeched to a halt next to the aircraft. Flashing lights hurtled through the mangled airport gate in pursuit.

Laying down fire with the big revolver, Michael leaped out with the .357 and covered Bea, Brent, and Lucy as they dashed for the plane. Lucy saw him shoot through the windshield of a cruiser about to overtake them. She gasped as a round hit the driver. The vehicle swerved, crashed into another oncoming squad car, then stopped, dead.

Bea and Brent hoisted Lucy into the aircraft. The engines whined as she struggled through the door. Michael's gun spit out its last piece of lead as police black-and-whites raced closer. Bullets pinged across the hood of the van. Brent leaped back beside him and emptied his last clip at the storm of vehicles.

Lucy felt the bird begin to taxi down the runway without Brent or Michael onboard and was seized with panic. She looked out the window and saw the two men grab the moving wing, pull themselves up, and clamber into the cabin. Lucy shuddered with relief.

"Kick it, Diego," Brent yelled.

A voice over a scratchy loudspeaker on the tarmac

ordered them to surrender or face being blown out the sky.

"Fuck you!" Bea yelled back.

Brent grabbed the door handle and pulled it shut.

"You tell 'em, Beebs," Lucy croaked. Her throat burned and she felt delirious.

The plane peeled down the runway pursued relentlessly by strobing red and white lights. The sound of machine guns, like jackhammers, rose just above the whine of the engine.

"Oh shit!" Bea cried.

Lucy gasped. A maintenance truck pulled in front of them. "We're gonna crash!"

A warped face melted like candle wax, sneered at her through the side window of the vehicle. Her heart almost stopped. Lucy blinked and he was gone. Her imagination was working overtime. Even in death, the specter of Mercer was pursuing her. No. She would not let that happen.

The plane lifted off over the roof of the truck; its wheels skimming the top. Brent mopped at the sweat that streamed down his face. The empty AK smoked in his hand and filled the craft with the stench of burned gunpowder.

Lucy leaned her forehead against the cool window as the tiny airport receded into the distance. Soon it became simply two rows of fading blue runway lights and a knot of flashing police cars.

CHAPTER 55

The chaos at the airstrip waned, but Lucy's head still spun. She sat on a stained leather seat patched with silver gaffer's tape, her bad leg extended onto the armrest across the narrow aisle in the eight-passenger plane. She wore a warm pair of Bea's sweatpants and gray sweat socks out of Brent's duffle. An ice pack was wrapped around her knee, and she held another to her swollen jaw. The two women sat together. Burleson was in front of them.

In the tiny cockpit, Brent schmoozed with the pilot about Trump and American policies on the Korean Peninsula. Michael fell asleep seconds after Bea cleaned and bandaged his arm and shoulder. One bullet seemed to have passed through, the other was still lodged just below his bicep.

Bea nodded toward Brent. "He's really depressed.

He was supposed to finish his degree in June."

"What happened?" Lucy asked.

"Got a letter last week. He's being redeployed to the Middle East on February first."

"What?" Lucy said, incredulous. "He thought his military days were done."

"Stop-loss has been initiated again. They need people and don't have enough recruits with experience."

"He put in his time. It's not right to force him back in," Lucy said, agitated. She rubbed her forehead.

"Absolutely true, but it is what it is. And that one," Bea nodded toward Burleson, "I don't like the way he's looking. He's feverish and the skin around the wound is hot and red, as in possible blood poisoning. As beat up as you are, honey, he's doing worse."

Lucy peeked over the seat to where Michael sat, slumped against the window. He was still dozing. "How long before we're back in the States?" She glanced at Bea's wristwatch.

"This ain't no Dreamliner, darlin'. I'd say three more hours. We're landing at a private strip out by the Salton Sea south of Palm Springs."

Lucy grabbed Bea's hand as they hit a pocket of rugged air over the Sierra Madre del Sur.

"Gonna be bumpy for a while," Brent called back. "Hang tight."

"Let me get you some of that airplane-ride Xanax," Bea said to Lucy. "Diego's first aid kit is stocked better than a Rite Aid pharmacy."

Lucy couldn't suppress a smile but her bruised lips protested. "You know what? I'm not freaked by the turbulence. At least not right now."

"What happened?" Bea asked. "Twenty-something years of panic attacks at the thought of flying, and now you sit there looking very Zen."

"I'll be Zen when we're all home." Lucy removed the ice pack from her jaw and dropped it onto the seat tray in front of her. "Been about six hours since Michael was shot. I think we should put down in Guadalajara and get him to a doctor."

"Diego will throw us out minus parachutes before he lets that happen," Bea said. The plane lurched again; the storage bin rattled like a tin can with shotgun pellets inside. "He plans to refuel in the desert south of the Salton Sea in Imperial County, get rid of us, and then fly on to undisclosed locales." She lowered her voice. "I think he's a gunrunner."

Lucy scrunched her brows together. "I thought you said he was DEA."

Bea shrugged. "Brent found him on the dark web. Says his name is Diego Ernesto Aguilera, hence, DEA." She winked at Lucy.

Lucy hiked herself up to check out the pilot. "Nobody's who they seem to be out here." DEA had dark scruffy hair tied in an off-center man bun and didn't look like he believed in any kind of hygiene. She dropped back into her seat. In front of her, Michael still slept. She reached forward and touched his arm to sense his warmth. He was still alive.

"Just a few more hours, baby," Bea said. "When we get in range, Brent will radio ahead. An ambulance is going to meet us at the airstrip to take y'all to Palm Desert Hospital. Beyond that, we paid this guy a lot of money and promised not to ask any questions." Bea squeezed Lucy's hand.

"What if Michael doesn't make it?" Lucy asked quietly. "This kind of thing can turn into sepsis. It's like a death sentence."

"Brent gave him penicillin tabs," Bea said. "Michael's a tough guy, kiddo. Probably been through worse. Your hottie's going to be okay." She fidgeted in her seat as if trying to find a comfortable position without any luck. "Luce?"

"Yeah?"

Her voice dropped to a whisper. "He as good in bed as I thought he might be?"

"You have no idea." Lucy closed her eyes, remembering. She couldn't believe she'd allowed herself to have such intense feelings for this man. She cursed her vulnerability, but what the hell? They could all be dead tomorrow.

"Details?"

Lucy shook her head. "*Nada.*"

"I can hear you," Michael said from the front seat.

"Go back to sleep," Bea said, smiling. "Stay out of the girl talk."

Brent abandoned the pilot and joined the group. He moved into the seat across the aisle from Michael and turned toward the women. "Can I ask you about what happened down there, Lucy?"

She gazed out the window. The sun eased below the horizon as they bounced down the tops of stormy cumulus clouds. The atmosphere felt sad and dark. "A lot of people died," Lucy said. "We're so lucky to be here. God bless you both." She swiped at a stray tear. "Luis Alvarez is dead, along with one of Michael's crew members, and three supposed CIA agents sent by Scanlon's people. Even more very bad guys were either shot or burned to death in a Jeep explosion. Last I saw of Mercer, he was a ball of fire—hair, clothes, everything. Collapsed into a ditch next to the road. Eventually, he stopped screaming." Her imagination had conjured up an image of him in the maintenance truck back at the airport. She was seized by a violent shiver. Where else would his horrible face materialize?

Bea nodded. "Can't say I'm not glad he was torched. Hopefully, it was a slow, painful death."

"Evidently, you'd blown his fingers off. His right hand was wrapped in a bandage when I saw him at the prison." Lucy gingerly touched her damaged jaw. "He could still deliver a helluva wallop."

Bea said. "Too bad I missed his ugly face."

As Lucy looked over at Bea and Brent, her heart swelled with gratitude. "Break out some of that tequila I saw up front, will 'ya?"

"Hey, Diego," Bea called. "Can we commandeer a bit of your good stuff? The bottle with the worm?"

"*Sí, señora,*" he said. "Pour me a shot, too."

"No way. We're paying you to get us home alive." Bea reached for the bottle.

He glanced over his shoulder and flashed a gold-toothed smile at Bea. "A nasty woman, as they say." He adjusted his headset and began singing "La Vida Loca" in a decent tenor voice.

Brent joined Lucy and Bea for a drink. He splashed booze into plastic cups and they clinked their glasses together in tribute. They were all alive. Michael had zoned out again and Lucy was glad he was resting. The tequila made the rounds a couple more times before she felt ready to talk about the experience.

Lucy took a final hit of tequila then spent the next few minutes sharing the gist of the story. "When I snagged the kid's knife, I had a chance at freedom in my hands. I didn't feel like that child in a car accident—impaled in a tree, a helpless victim with my family dead on the road around me. When I broke out of that prison, something that has weighed me down for as long as I can remember, lifted."

Bea stared at Lucy in silence, then finally said, "maybe that's why flying in a plane isn't so terrifying anymore. You feel more in control of your life again."

"Could be. Who knows if the feeling will last." She tried not to be cynical, but life had a way of shaking up even the strongest foundation.

Turbulence shook the Cessna again.

Michael woke. "Lucy?"

She maneuvered out of her seat, hobbled next to him and perched on the armrest. His skin was pale, his breathing labored. Lucy tried to tamp down her anxiety. She helped him drink most of a bottle of water, then kissed his forehead and stroked his damp hair.

He looked up at her, eyes glazed. "A lot to do when we get back to town. We have enough evidence to help the feds put a serious dent in the cartel. It'll spring right back up like Hydra, but maybe it'll slow them down and save a few lives in the short run."

Lucy nodded. The tequila was giving her a warm, welcome sense of optimism. "And you," she said to Burleson, "you're gonna need to take some serious time to heal. I was thinking"—she took a deep breath—"since 'm moving into the main house at my uncle's . . . I mean *my* ranch, maybe you'd like to stay in my former digs over the barn until you get back on your feet. Haven't been there since the night I got called out to cover my uncle's car crash." Lucy sighed. "It's got a beautiful view."

Michael wove his fingers through hers.

Lucy straightened her posture and smiled a Mona Lisa smile. "I have skills in physical therapy that have yet to be revealed," she said. "Could be very helpful to your recovery. And yoga too. Lots of downward dog and *Namaste*."

"I will definitely need all the therapy you can provide, nurse Vega." Michael smiled back at her. "And it could be a long recovery."

"We'll see what kind of a patient you turn out to be." She rested her hand gently on Michael's blood-caked shoulder and gazed out as the Coachella Valley desert unfolded below. Groves of date palms were green islands against the chalky landscape.

Mercer's melted face flashed through Lucy's mind. Her chest tightened. She forced a deep breath to release the tension. The sonofabitch was dead. No way would she let his specter haunt her. It was over.

✳

"You okay, girlfriend?" Bea asked Lucy as they stood at Truckee's side in his hospital room.

"Good as I'm gonna get, all things considered." Lucy balanced on aluminum crutches and watched the ventilator breathe for her friend. The wheezing noise broke her heart. Truckee seemed to have shrunken in the mere ten days since she'd seen him last.

Bea said, "I spoke with his wife this morning. She's upbeat and the kids are all really pulling together to help around the house and take care of each other. They're a strong family. They send their love."

Lucy nodded and swiped at a tear. "I texted with Carly, too, by the way. First impressions of Singapore are good. She wants to work for an English-language news site. She can do that from home. She's in a rehab facility there for a month. Likes it." Guilt still crushed her at thoughts of Carly's dire injuries, the Montgomery family, and their flight out of the country.

A nurse hustled by with a bag of saline for Truckee's I.V. Lucy and Bea moved aside so she had room to work. Drawings and photos from his kids were taped to the wall. Vases of flowers, candy, and cards were crowded onto his bedside table.

A fortyish Indian doctor with a goatee and a full head of shiny, dark hair followed the nurse.

Bea's eyes lit up. "Dr. Kapoor!" She rushed up to give the man a big hug, then turned to Lucy. "He took out my bullet!"

Lucy shook his hand and thanked him for his hard work on her friends.

"So, Bea, you're looking good. How's the shoulder?" he asked.

"All's feeling fine, unlike my friend, Truckee."

Kapoor raised his eyebrows and grinned. Another nurse, a slim young man with curly brown hair, scurried into the room to check the patient's vitals.

"I'm happy to say," the doctor said, "our man Truckee took an important turn for the better yesterday. Brain swelling is way down and his EKG's much improved. We're bringing him out of the medically-induced coma and off the respirator this afternoon."Lucy and Bea both hugged the doctor and each other. They pressed close to Truckee's bedside and planted light kisses mixed with tears on his forehead. Dr. Kapoor and the nurses were reassuring and smiling as the two women left the hospital room and ambled slowly down the hall toward the elevator, spirits raised.

"So much stuff's been happening here, I can hardly keep up." Lucy paused to adjust her crutches and grimaced as she shifted her weight. "You got promoted to evening news director while I was away? Pretty cool there, sister."

Bea smiled. "It's the job I've always dreamed about, but somehow I don't trust it'll be mine for long."

"Why not?" Lucy asked. "You planning some bad behavior again?"

Bea chuckled and filled Lucy in on all the upheaval taking place at KLAK-TV News with the impending ownership and management changes. "Everything's moving fast now. The potential shake-up could be seismic."

Lucy nodded, stopped in the hallway and repositioned her crutches. "I hate these things." She tottered along next to Bea until they reached the elevator. "So what's Maxwell's take on all this?"

"He may have an opportunity with the PBS station in Chicago," Bea said, "and Ernie's baby is finally sleeping through the night. At least some of the time. You're going to be putting your documentary together on the U.S.'s role in the Guerrero drug culture and feds from both

9 781942 856221

About the Author

Sue Hinkin is a former college administrator, television news photographer, and NBC-TV art department staffer. With a B.A. from St. Olaf College, she completed graduate work at the University of Michigan and was a Cinematography Fellow at the American Film Institute. She lives with her family in Denver.

sides of the border will be crawling all over Pitacallpa and Tingo Tia hunting down those cartel assholes." She hit Lucy with a sidelong, appraising look. "You coming back to work any time soon?"

Lucy watched the numbers descend on the elevator floor screen. "I think I'll take those weeks of vacation days you and Max have been nagging me about. Focus on getting my head straight, then, we'll see."

"In the meantime, I assume, you'll shack up with your hot, blue-eyed boy in the mountains over the Pacific, drink wine, make mad love, and tend the sweet little farm animals."

"The way you just put it sounds like a helluva fine plan to me," Lucy said.

Bea grinned.

The elevator door opened. Lucy left the crutches leaning against the wall and hobbled into the lift.